NITSCHKE

66

NITSCHKE

EDWARD GRUVER

TAYLOR TRADE PUBLISHING

Lanham • New York • Dallas • Boulder • Toronto • Oxford

First Taylor Trade Publishing edition 2002
First paperback edition 2004

This Taylor Trade Publishing paperback edition of *Nitschke* is an original publication. It is published by arrangement with the author.

Published by Taylor Trade Publishing
An imprint of The Rowman & Littlefield Publishing Group, Inc.
4501 Forbes Boulevard, Suite 200
Lanham, Maryland 20706

Distributed by National Book Network

A previous edition of this book was catalogued by the Library of Congress as follows:

Gruver, Ed, 1960–
Nitschke / Edward Gruver.
p. cm.
Includes index.
1. Nitschke, Ray, 1936– 2. Football players—United States—Biography. I. Title.
GV939.N57 G78 2002
796.332'092—B21 2002001547

ISBN: 1-58979-127-4 (pbk. : alk. paper)

The paper used in this publication meets the minimum requirements of American National Standard for Information Sciences—Permanence of Paper for Printed Library Materials, ANSI/NISO Z39.48–1992.
Manufactured in the United States of America.

For Kathie and Patrice,
two of the best sisters a brother could have

CONTENTS

INTRODUCTION

THE VOICE, with its distinctive tires-crunching-over-gravel tone, was instantly recognizable on the other end of the phone.

"Hey, how's it goin', man?" Ray Nitschke asked. "How ya doin'?"

October 1995, and a long-distance phone call had been placed to the Oneida, Wisconsin, home of the Green Bay Packers' Hall of Fame middle linebacker to talk about his career. Nearly a quarter century had passed since the aging warrior had last worn the green-and-gold, a quarter century since he had last patrolled the field for the Packers during the Green Bay glory years, a time so special and romantic in the memory of those who were there that Packer guard Jerry Kramer likens it to Camelot.

Nitschke, Vince Lombardi, Bart Starr, Jim Taylor, Willie Davis, Willie Wood—they were the faces of victory in America's fastest growing sport during the sixties, and they created a national following by dominating their decade like no NFL team before or since. Lombardi led the Packers on a heady run of excellence—five league championships in seven years, an unprecedented and still unmatched three straight NFL titles from 1965 to 1967, victories in the first two Super Bowls over the rival American Football League.

Amid the sit-ins and drop-outs of the psychedelic sixties, the Packers were throwbacks to an earlier era. They embodied the Spartan qualities of teamwork and self-sacrifice, and their success inspired a generation of fans. Future actor Tommy Lee Jones idolized Kramer; the singer Meat Loaf wanted to be Fuzzy Thurston, Kramer's partner at pulling guard.

Nitschke understood the adulation. In an era of social and political turbulence, when riots were engulfing cities like Newark and Detroit, the town team from Green Bay stood as a symbol of excellence. At a time when U.S. troops were bogged down in the jungles of Vietnam, the Lombardi Packers were sweeping to victory with the power and precision of Patton's Third Army.

"The Lombardi teams wanted to get into the big games," said Nitschke, his gruff voice still carrying the growl that marked this lion in winter. "We had a great record in post-season games. We lost the first, but never lost another."

Not counting the meaningless "Playoff Bowl" held in Miami every year following the NFL championship game, the Packers won nine straight post-season games from 1961 to 1967. They became pro football's "Team of the Decade," the measuring stick for the dynasties that followed—Pittsburgh in the '70s, San Francisco in the '80s, Dallas in the '90s.

What set the Packers apart? To Nitschke, the answer was clear. Green Bay had an advantage no other team could claim at that time: a hard-driving force in a camel-hair coat who pushed them through practice and prowled the sidelines on game days.

"Lombardi represented preparation and hard work," Nitschke said. "Every game was important to him. So when we got to the real important games, we were ready to go, man. Every game was a championship, and that made it easier when we got to the big games because we weren't awed by it, we weren't nervous about it. We were more relaxed than the opponents, and in those years, we always played to our experience. That's how we handled it. That's what you work all season for, to get into the playoff games, and you don't want to blow it."

The Packers lost their first championship under Lombardi in 1960, then never lost another stakes game the next seven years. Their post-season games, played on ice-glazed fields under steel-gray skies, burn in the memory. They carried the NFL banner in the first two Super Bowls against the rival American League following the '66 and '67 seasons, and reinforced the notion of NFL supremacy by outscoring Kansas City and Oakland by a combined 68–24.

Green Bay's no-nonsense, no-frills style perfectly suited an era when pro football was still more of a game than a business, when players covered themselves with equal parts mud and glory.

"It was another day to go to work, man," Nitschke said. "One of the great things about football is that you don't cancel the games because of weather. It shows a little about yourself and about the character of yourself.

"Everybody can play in 50-degree weather, but can you play in 100-degree weather? Can you play in a windchill of 50 below? It's a test, a test of your character and your team's character, and you have to make adjustments. It's like life, you know. Things don't always go your way, and you have to make the right adjustments."

Nitschke's life was all about making the right adjustments. His father died when he was three; his mother when he was thirteen. Adopted and raised by his older brothers, Nitschke's teenage years in the urban cauldron of Chicago were undisciplined to say the least. He knocked downed slugs of whiskey and neighborhood toughs with equal vigor. His overriding redeeming quality was his ability on the playing field. He excelled in baseball, and in a high school state tournament hit what was estimated to be a 560-foot home run. He was offered a $3,000 signing bonus by the St. Louis Browns, but his first love was football. An all-star quarterback at Proviso East High in Maywood, Illinois, Nitschke was persuaded by both his older brother, Robert, and his high school football coach, Andy Puplis, a former Notre Dame back, to accept a football scholarship to the University of Illinois. Converted to fullback, Nitschke averaged 6.5 yards per carry and closed out his varsity career by rushing for 170 yards against Northwestern.

Though he had hoped to play for his hometown Chicago Bears, he was taken by the Packers in the third round of the 1958 NFL draft; a pick made possible because of a trade Green Bay had engineered with the New York Giants. Nitschke had to literally take out a map to find out where Green Bay was, and once he arrived in camp was converted to linebacker. It was an idea that suited him fine, since he always reasoned that on the football field, it was better to give than receive.

"I like contact," he said at the time. "It brings out the meanness in me."

Nitschke rode the bench his rookie year, and the Packers won just one game under head coach Ray "Scooter" McLean. In 1959, Green Bay hired Lombardi as its head coach and general manager.

Lombardi was the ultimate disciplinarian, and Nitschke, frustrated by his lack of playing time, remained the ultimate undisciplined player.

"Just call me the judge," he would shout when Lombardi was nearby, "'cause I'm always on the bench."

Lombardi's response was less than understanding.

"Hey, Nitschke."

"Yeah?"

"Shaddup."

"It was hard to miss Ray," Lombardi's son, Vince Jr., recalled. "He had that raspy voice, and he was always yelling and screaming."

Privately, the Packer coaching staff worried that Nitschke's wild ways might end in tragedy. Lombardi confided to friends that he thought Nitschke "might kill somebody" and threatened to trade his troubled middle linebacker in 1960.

"Raymond was headed for bad trouble," halfback Paul Hornung remembered. "His drinking was out of control."

Under the guidance of Lombardi and defensive coordinator Phil Bengston, Nitschke was molded from a player who tried too hard and was overly aggressive into one who combined punishing hits with perceptive reads. As the Packers drove to their first Western Conference title under Lombardi in 1960, Nitschke began splitting time in the starting lineup with Tom Bettis. In 1961, Nitschke played a pivotal role in Green Bay's 37–0 win over the New York Giants in the NFL title game. One year later, in a game that was more grudge match than rematch, Nitschke recovered two fumbles and forced an interception as the Packers beat the Giants 16–7 amid cyclonic winds and sub-zero temperatures at Yankee Stadium. Nitschke was named the game's Most Valuable Player, a fitting tribute to a man whose fierce play perfectly suited one of the most brutal defensive struggles in league championship history.

Nitschke's rising stature on the field was due in large part to his stability at home. His 1961 marriage to Jackie Forchette proved to be a major turning point in his life. To Jackie, he was always "Raymond," and friends recalled how just the sound of her voice lit a spark in her husband's hard-as-flint face. The couple eventually adopted three children—John, Richard, and Amy—and Nitschke's transformation from barroom brawler to doting dad was underway.

"It was the greatest thing I've ever seen," Hornung said. "He adopted three kids, became a model citizen, and just did a fantastic job turning his life around. I loved Raymond for that."

Stability in his personal life led to tremendous strides in his professional life. Aimed by Bengston and triggered by Lombardi, Nitschke combined the best elements of his forerunners—the strategy of Joe Schmidt, the strength of Bill George, the sideline-to-sideline pursuit of Sam Huff—and by the mid-sixties had become the best ever at his position. From 1964 through '66, Nitschke was named the league's top middle linebacker by two of the leading wire services at the time, the Associated Press and United Press International. He covered the field with a crablike scurry; a powerful, pitiless presence with an appetite for the ball or the man with it. Over the course of his 15-year career, he buried ballcarriers and blanketed receivers with equal fervor, and established himself as a premier ballhawk with 25 interceptions and 20 fumble recoveries.

With his huge shoulders and padded arms, his skinny calves and the big number 66 on his jersey, Nitschke became one of the ornaments of the modern NFL.

"I always thought his number was 99," wide receiver Tommy McDonald said. "When I was looking up after he had knocked me upside down, his 66 always looked like 99."

Nitschke's big-game battles with future Hall of Famers were legendary. He hand-fought Philadelphia center Chuck Bednarik in the 1960 NFL title game, engaged in mental gymnastics with New York quarterback Y.A. Tittle in '61 and '62, and shadowed Cleveland fullback Jim Brown over a field slick with icy mud in '65.

"To me, Ray Nitschke was the perfect definition of the word 'presence,'" said Steve Sabol, the president of NFL Films and an astute historian of the game. "When he was on the field, it was almost like there was an odor about him. You could smell it, you could feel it."

The sixties were a decade dominated by defense, by great gangs of four in Minnesota, Los Angeles, and Dallas, and by the middle men who lurked behind them. From the Purple Gang, Fearsome Foursome, and Doomsday Defense to Nitschke, Dick Butkus, and Willie Lanier, the NFL had never seen such a collection of defensive dominators. At the top of that impressive list in the eyes of the fans stood Nitschke and Butkus. They were warriors both, physical enforcers bonded by their past as Illinois natives and former Illini, by the Packers–Bears rivalry, by their ferocious play at middle linebacker.

"There was a mutual respect between us," Butkus remembered . "I liked his desire. Green Bay had some great players on defense, but at that time, the middle linebacker position was *the* impact position on the field. I think we played the game with the same intensity, the same desire."

Nitschke brought that intensity and desire to bear in the biggest games. When Green Bay met the Kansas City Chiefs of the rival American Football League in January 1967 in the first Super Bowl, the Age of Aquarius was in full swing. Anguish clashed with achievement, tradition with upheaval. Some saw that first AFL–NFL showdown as a reflection of the times, the Establishment versus the Rebels. Whatever, Nitschke became the first of the Super Bowl tough guys, and set a trend for future enforcers when he unnerved the Chiefs before what was officially billed as the AFL–NFL World Championship Game. The AFL to that time had never produced a middle man as violent and perceptive as Nitschke, and the Chiefs were wary of what to expect. "We had heard the stories about Ray's past," Kansas City guard Ed Budde recalled. "He was a wild man."

Nitschke lived up to his billing, helping Green Bay to a 35–10 victory that gave the cocky upstarts their comeuppance, at least for the time being. One year later, Nitschke provided the fire amid the ice as Green Bay made its historic run for a record third straight NFL championship. The Packers were nearing the end of their magnificent run; injuries and exhaustion were everyday companions. Power backs Taylor and Hornung were gone from the team, and many of their aging stars, including Nitschke and Starr, played virtually every game of their 23-game season hurt and heavily taped.

The marathon that was the '67 season provided the Packers with pro football's ultimate challenge, and through it all, there was Nitschke.

Nitschke, shouting at officials in the pewter-gray twilight of the Western Conference playoff against the favored Los Angeles Rams, imploring them, begging them, to let L.A.'s offense have a first down. "Give it to 'em," he snarled at the refs. "We're not ready to leave the field yet."

Nitschke, ignoring his frost-bitten feet one week later in the final, frozen moments of the epic Ice Bowl and exhorting Green Bay's offense from the sideline. "Don't let me down," he screamed, pumping his padded right fist in the brittle air. "Don't let me down!"

Nitschke, flipping Oakland fullback Hewritt Dixon heels-over-helmet to short-circuit a Raiders sweep two weeks later in Super Bowl II in the sun-drenched Miami Orange Bowl. A hit so explosive that Packers' public relations director Lee Remmel said it left the 220-pound Dixon trembling like a tuning fork. "Dixon wasn't a factor the rest of the day," Remmel said. Super Bowl II became one of the great games of Nitschke's career. Fighting off the blocks of Oakland center Jim Otto and guards Gene Upshaw and Wayne Hawkins, he made nine tackles that day. Five of those stops were solo, and of those, four came within three yards of the line of scrimmage, a defining stat for a middle linebacker.

The Packers' 33–14 win over Oakland marked the end of the Green Bay glory years. Lombardi stepped down as head coach the following February and died of cancer in 1970. One by one, Packer veterans retired or were traded. By 1972, the 36-year-old Nitschke remained one of the last links to the legendary Packer teams of the sixties. Few knew, as Packer trainer Domenic Gentile later revealed, that Nitschke had played his entire career on one good leg. His left leg had been injured so often in high school and college that the muscles had atrophied and never fully regenerated, leaving it 50 percent smaller than the right.

Nitschke retired after the '72 season, then built a life after football that saw him do many things but make a career of none. From 1975 to 1987, he appeared in 138 national television commercials, including the first Miller Lite Beer spot. He was a pitchman for Oldsmobile; did public relations work for Clairmont, a trucking firm; and worked as a good-will front man for a major Wisconsin dairy. Though he appeared an unlikely thespian, Nitschke was cast in two feature movies. In 1968, he played a character known only as "One" in *Head*, a movie featuring the TV rock group, the Monkees. In 1974, he was cast in the movie *The Longest Yard*, portraying a prison guard named Bogdanski.

That was the public Nitschke. Privately, he supported his wife's involvement with The Bridge, Inc., an organization dedicated to helping recovering alcoholics and their families, and he and Jackie were long-time co-chairpersons of the Cerebral Palsy Telethon. He became a born-again Christian in 1995, ending a long-time grudge he had held against God for the perceived injustice of losing his parents at such an early age. When he first joined the Packers, he alternated between jersey numbers 33 and 72. He was eventually given 66, and in later years Jackie would tell him that the change had occurred for a reason.

"You wore number 66, and there are 66 books in the Bible," she would tell him. "For some reason Raymond, you got that number."

In time, Nitschke traded Sunday morning tee times for time in prayer at the Bayside Christian Fellowship Church, and Amy remembered him having very strong views on abortion, and how much he was opposed to it.

"Dad was such a family man," she said. "Anything that dealt with children, he felt very strongly about. All three of us children were adopted, and he always felt there were better options out there than abortion."

Through time spent in church or with the children, in charitable causes or on the cruise trips they took every year, Ray and Jackie maintained a close partnership. When she died of cancer in July 1996, he was devastated.

"He was kind of lost after Mom died," his son Richard said. "He just kind of let himself go. Not physically, but mentally and emotionally."

Over the next two years Nitschke spent increasing time with Amy and his newborn granddaughter, Jacqueline Rae. He was traveling with them to visit friends in Venice, Florida, on Sunday, March 8, 1998, when he began suffering chest pains at around 12:30 P.M. He was rushed to nearby Venice Hospital, but at 1:30 P.M., the man who had been a heartbeat for so many causes was pronounced dead.

In death, Raymond Ernest Nitschke left a legacy that was both lasting and puzzling.

If, as Charles Dickens wrote in 1859, every human creature is constituted to be that profound secret to every other, then Nitschke presented the ultimate in profound contradiction. Off the field, he was the modern, urbane man—bespectacled and given to conservative business suits. Quiet and intelligent, he reposed in thoughtful, articulate conversation. He embraced friends and family in bearhugs that have become legend and were warmly remembered by his oldest son, John, at his father's service.

"Who here has ever been hugged by my dad?" John asked the assemblage that packed Bayside Christian Fellowship Church in Green Bay to pay their final respects. Seeing the high number of raised hands, John smiled. "Pretty neat, huh?"

Reverend Arni Jacobson, the pastor at Nitschke's church, remembered the most famous member of his flock as a pied piper of sorts, a Santa Claus with an ever-present cigar. Nitschke took seriously his obligations as an ambassador for pro football and role model for those looking to turn their lives around, and he took so much time in carefully signing autographs—"Ray Nitschke #66"—that during his playing days teammates kidded him, but always from a distance. "Hey Ray, what are you doing?" they would yell from the team bus. "Running for office?"

Nitschke always had a warm and ready smile for the children who approached him, but he loved to startle adults by suddenly taking on his grim football persona.

"Whaddya want?" he would say roughly, fixing the approaching person with a game-day stare that Sabol said was more than frightening. "He made Freddie from *Nightmare on Elm Street* look like a Muppet," Sabol said. Nitschke would quickly calm the trembling fan by throwing an arm around his shoulder and sharing small talk.

"He had some sort of unspoken relationship with the fans," former teammate Boyd Dowler said. "In the sixties we would play 30, 35 exhibition basketball games in and around Green Bay during the winter months. We would go into the locker room after the game and get showered up and he would say, 'C'mon let's go out and there and sign autographs,' and we would get out there and sit at the scorer's table. For the most part, we wanted to get out of there, but he would hang around and talk to the fans until the last person was gone. While the rest of us were somewhat detached, you know, out doing our own thing, Ray communicated a little better with the dyed-in-the-wool, hard-core Packer people. And they related to him a little more than they did to the rest of us."

Nitschke maintained a home in Oneida just outside of Green Bay, and never tried to shield himself from the public. The address—410 Peppermint Court—was well-known to Packer fans. His two-story brick house sat just 2.6 miles from the western city limits of Green Bay, and those seeking autographs or a few moments reliving the glory days would follow Highway 54 to Riverside Drive and then look for the house that sat on a slope facing east amid a collection of young trees, sumac, and other assorted brush.

Driving to his home was one way to contact the Packer legend. Simply picking up the phone was another. When Al Pahl was hired as the editor of *Ray Nitschke's Packer Report* in February 1986, he looked to get in touch with the Packer legend and introduce himself.

"I come to Green Bay, get out the phone book, and Ray Nitschke is in the *gaddamn* white pages," said Pahl, his midwestern accent still tinged with astonishment at that fact some 15 years later. "That just amazed me."

Nitschke maintained his connection with the Packers through his *Packer Report*, a publication he helped start in 1970, and by being a regular at Green Bay games, where team photographer Vern Biever remembered him heading down to the sideline to spur the team on.

"He was very much into the game even when he retired," Biever said.

"He'd be on the sidelines telling a player, 'Hey, you're not doing this properly,' or 'You should be doing this.'"

Amy witnessed the transformation her father underwent every time he entered Lambeau Field. Four season tickets were held in his name for every home game, and for years his seats were always the same—Section 16 on the Packers' side of the field, in-between the 35- and 40-yard lines in the north end of the field. The last decade of life, his seats were switched to Section 21 behind the opposing team's bench, near the 40–yard line on the south side of the field.

Regardless, just walking into Lambeau Field on game day stirred his inner passion.

"I know that he missed it really terribly," Amy said. "You could see it. Walking into Lambeau Field, he would almost become a different person."

It was a transformation reminiscent of his playing days. Game days in Green Bay would see Nitschke remove his front teeth, place them on the top shelf of his locker, and replace them with a gummy mouthpiece that gave his mouth a cruel, downward curve. Smears of eye black were substituted for his dark-rimmed glasses, yards of pads and tape took the place of his business suits. The carefully constructed autographs he handed out to fans were replaced by scrawled messages inside the knee pads of his gold football pants: *Beat Chicago*, he would write, or whatever team the Packers were playing that day. He covered his balding head with a battle-scarred green-and-gold helmet, and it was said at the time that when he peered at opponents through the bars of his full-cage facemask, he wore the look of a lifer peering through the prison bars of a padded cell.

"He was ugly with his facemask and no teeth," former Atlanta middle linebacker Tommy Nobis remembered, and ex-Dallas center Dave Manders said seeing Nitschke up close was a surreal experience.

"Probably one of the most ugliest and frightening sights was Ray Nitschke lined up in front of you," Manders said. "No teeth, sweating hard, breathing hard, talking a lot of rough B.S. And he didn't have any teeth to keep the saliva in his mouth. Just a real weird picture."

Minnesota quarterback Fran Tarkenton said once that Nitschke played with a gleam in his eye that no other defensive player of his era had. Pittsburgh Steelers halfback Preston Pearson remembered the gleam, remembered a 1970 game in Three Rivers Stadium when he took the ball from Terry Bradshaw on a sweep and out of the corner of his eye caught a heart-sinking glimpse of Nitschke closing in.

"I saw this monster only a moment before he hit," Pearson said. Nitschke exploded into the right side of Pearson's helmet, and the Steeler back's first thought was that a bomb had gone off inside his head. It was the kind of hit, Pearson said, that could break a man's back. As he was going down with Nitschke on top of him, Pearson saw the "gleam" that Tarkenton had talked about. Nitschke had a wild look in his eyes, Pearson said, and even more incredibly, seemed to be foaming at the mouth.

The devastating hit left Pearson stretched out on the snow-covered Tartan Turf. The next thing he was aware of was a Steeler trainer waving smelling salts under his nose and shouting, "You okay?" In 14 years of playing professional football, 14 years of playing with and against Joe Greene, Jack Lambert, Lanier, and Butkus, Pearson said the hit by Nitschke was the hardest he had ever endured.

Others backed up Pearson's testimony. Hall of Fame running back Bobby Mitchell recalled getting leveled by Nitschke, recalled what he described as the "tremendous force" of a body blow.

"Ray had tremendous strength," Mitchell said, "and he tried to make sure you felt his force."

Bears running back Ronnie Bull felt Nitschke's force as a rookie playing in Lambeau Field for the first time. The date was September 30, 1962, but to Bull, it remains as vivid nearly 40 years later as if it had happened yesterday.

"I was running around right end, and just as I planted my foot to cut upfield it was like a two-ton truck hit me," Bull said. "I got up looking for the truck, and there was Nitschke, smiling at me. It was a blind-side hit, and he caught me flush. It was the hardest I've ever been hit."

Three years later, Bull had another encounter with Nitschke, but this time it was memorable because of a hit Nitschke *didn't* deliver. "We're playing up in Green Bay again," Bull said, "and Willie Wood intercepts a pass. He's going across the middle and I'm chasing him, and just before I get there, the whistle blows. Somebody grabs me on my shoulder and I turn around and it's Nitschke. With his helmet on and no teeth, he's uglier than sin. And he just kind of smiles at me and says, 'Saved by the whistle.' I was so flabbergasted all I could say was, 'Yessir.' "

At a time when the Temptations scored a Motown hit with *Get Ready 'Cause Here I Come*, Nitschke was scoring direct hits on NFL ballcarriers and announcing each one. He would hunch over center before the snap, call out the offensive formation, call out the defensive signal, and then call out a running back or offensive lineman.

"Hey you," he would shout, pointing a threatening finger. "Yeah, you. I'm gonna git you."

When Nitschke and Bobby Mitchell were teammates at the University of Illinois, Nitschke always called Mitchell by his middle name, Cornelius. When the two played against each other in the NFL, Nitschke punctuated his tackles against Mitchell by announcing his presence.

"Cornelius!" he would shout. "Here I am, Cornelius!"

Nitschke's distinctive voice emanated across NFL battlefields for parts of three decades. He chattered constantly, in the locker room, on the practice field, on game days.

"Ray was our holler guy," recalled Willie Davis, Green Bay's Hall of Fame defensive end during the Lombardi years. "He would do a lot of talking and make a lot of noise, but he would also be the first to create an impression on a running back or a receiver with one of those Ray Nitschke kind of hits, where you could pick up that sound any place in the stadium."

One such hit occurred late in the third quarter of the epic Ice Bowl, when Nitschke pursued a Dallas sweep down the line and met halfback Dan Reeves at the line of scrimmage. The violent collision of pads caused a crackling sound that is clearly audible on the videotape of the game.

Bald and toothless, and with all the sympathy of a bill collector, Nitschke sacked quarterbacks and smacked running backs. He exuded an aura few others could match. When the Vikings opened their 1962 regular season on September 16 in Lambeau Field, rookie Mick Tingelhoff was starting his first NFL game at center. Spinning out of the huddle to lead the Vikings offense to the line of scrimmage on their first play, Tingelhoff immediately became aware of the man opposite him.

"He looked pretty bad," Tingelhoff said. "He didn't have his teeth in, and he was out there yelling and hollering. I didn't know what the hell was going on."

Nitschke's teammates sometimes felt the same confusion. When defensive tackle Mike McCoy played his first preseason game with Green Bay in 1970, Nitschke stood behind him, shouting instructions.

"Hey rookie! Watch the pass! Watch the run! Watch the draw!"

The ball was snapped, the offense ran a draw play, and the runner hacked out a few yards. After the players unpiled, Nitschke walked up to McCoy.

"I told you what they were going to do," he told the startled rookie.

"He liked to talk a little bull," Kramer said. "He had that distinctive voice—'Hey, man, let's go, let's do it, man.' But when I think of Raymond, I think of him more as a person than a player. His journey through life showed so much improvement. He had a rough childhood and he took it out on everyone. But he went from being half an ass to being a tremendous person, a beautiful, loving, giving person."

Bart Starr, whose career in Green Bay paralleled Nitschke's, remembered Nitschke's loud and sometimes abrasive personality, but he remembered the softer side of the man as well.

"On the field, Ray was one tough hombre," Starr said. "But off the field, as we walked from the practice field, he might be the first one on the team to help an elderly lady across the street. Just a marvelous personality. Couldn't be any tougher on the field; off the field, a perfect gentleman."

Indeed. There were two Ray Nitschkes. The man who belonged to the Green Bay Packers, and the man who belonged to Green Bay and the rest of the country.

This is the story of both of them.

ONE

THE WORLD Raymond Ernest Nitschke was born into on December 29, 1936, offered a dichotomy of peace at home in the United States, instability abroad.

President Franklin Roosevelt had carried the November election in record fashion, winning every state but Maine and Vermont in a landslide victory over Republican Party candidate Alf Landon. Overseas, Edward VIII became king of England but abdicated his throne after the British government opposed his marriage to Mrs. Wallis Warfield Simpson. While FDR opened the Inter-American Conference in Buenos Aires, where Latin American nations consulted with the U.S. for "mutual safety," Hitler and Mussolini signed the Rome-Berlin axis. Italy annexed Ethiopia, and Germany occupied the Rhineland. Rightist uprisings against Spain's government began in Morocco and spread to Spain, and successful coups toppled governments in Greece and Nicaragua.

News from the old country was of particular interest to Robert and Anna Nitschke. He was of German ancestry; she was Danish. Both were solidly built; Robert was half a foot taller, with a thick shock of curly, light brown hair parted neatly on the left and combed over. He was given to wearing white open-neck shirts, dark cuffed slacks, and patent leather shoes. He favored a white fedora, and his rolled-up sleeves revealed thick forearms. He had broad shoulders and large hands, and the same wide mouth and sharp features that marked the Nitschke family. Anna was thickly built, with a round face and short, dark hair parted on the right and reaching to the tops of her shoulders.

In 1936, Robert and Anna's home was the top floor of a duplex in Elmwood Park, Illinois, a working-class suburb on the fringe of Chicago. Visitors to Elmwood Park today are drawn to Conti Circle, which has become ground zero for providing improved public facilities. But where the renovated library and civic center and recently added family aquatic center now stand, Conti Circle once featured a grand French fountain as the centerpiece of a tree-lined walkway. The community park was dedicated to the community in 1927 by real estate developer John Mills, with the stipulation it remain a place for passive recreation. At the time, Conti Circle was an open, grass-covered area of five acres. Neighborhood boys played baseball there, and on occasion dropped soap bars swiped from home into the fountain waters. The soap would drain into the pipes and come up out of the fountain as foam. The sight of the fountain spouting bubbles became something of a tradition in Elmwood Park, as did the sight of perpetrators who had lingered long enough to watch being chased away by police. Elmwood Park remained a wide-open area until 1973, when the Mills' last surviving heirs responded to the overtures made by town officials to lift the restrictive ban on the use of the park area surrounding the fountain. Conti Circle's development since then has transformed Elmwood Park from its appearance during the thirties, when Robert and Anna Nitschke, like the rest of America, were trying to cope with raising a family amid the Great Depression.

By 1936, the couple had two children—Robert Jr., age eight, and Richard, four. Four days after Christmas that year, the Nitschkes welcomed a third son, Raymond.

Life in Elmwood Park was not easy for the Nitschkes. The nation was still enduring hard times, and bread lines and soup kitchens were not far removed from the memory. Robert Nitschke carved out a living for his family with the Chicago Surface Lines, and while their life was no-frills, the Nitschkes never complained. How could they, Ray asked years later, when he and his brothers always had clean clothes and full stomachs?

In 1940, fate dealt a body blow to the Nitschke family. Robert Sr. was returning home from a union meeting when a trolley collided with his car. He was killed in the accident, and Anna was left to raise three growing sons on her own. With her husband deceased, Anna went to work for a relative, Pete Rasmussen. To the Nitschke kids, he was Uncle Pete, the owner of Pete's Place. Located on the corner of Grand Avenue near the railroad tracks in River Grove, Pete's Place was a tavern typical of the neighborhoods of Elmwood Park. The food was home-cooked, there was always a card game in the back room, and the same people showed up every Friday and Saturday night. The clientele was mixed, factory workers mingling with white-collar types, but they were all on a first-name basis.

"It was kind of a hard place to live because it was right near the railroad tracks," remembered Jan Smid, who grew up in nearby River Grove and was a long-time friend of the Nitschke brothers. "It wasn't the slums, but it was mediocre housing. It was a small town, and everybody knew everybody from the three or four towns around us."

Chuck Heyward, a friend of Richard Nitschke's who also lived in Elmwood Park, remembered the Nitschke's home as a "fixer-upper," located in a very poor section of Elmwood Park. Anna worked two jobs to support the family, yet despite his mother's absence from home, Ray grew extremely close to her. She was his life, and he recognized how hard she worked for her children. On most days, her only relaxation came after she had finished her shift as a waitress at Pete's Place. Taking a seat at the bar, she would relax with a beer before heading home. Years later, Ray remembered that as the only fun she seemed to have.

Anna's work ethic undoubtedly made an impression on her children. When he was old enough, Ray worked alongside his mother in Pete's Place, peeling potatoes and doing odd jobs. Times being what they were, he literally was paid in pennies for his work. But it was spending money, and he picked up a few extra coins from his grandmother. Anna worked long hours at the tavern, but by the time Ray was six, the family was struggling so much financially his oldest brother Robert, who was getting ready to start high school, went to work for the railroad to earn extra money for the family. He was just 14, but at six feet tall was big for his age. With his mother away at work, Robert often took on the role of family disciplinarian. He knew how to administer justice, but he also knew when to back off. On one occasion, Robert was disciplining Ray with the belt, and the thought crossed Ray's mind that if Robert hit him one more time, he was going to have an injured kid brother. Robert must have known it too, because he quickly ended the punishment.

Of the three brothers, Richard was the quietest. Because they were the same age, Smid hung out most with Richard. To Smid, Richard was more easy going than Robert, but when he told Ray "no" on occasion, Ray would listen. While friends would call the brothers "Bob" or "Rich" or "Ray," the brothers always called themselves by their full names. It was always "Robert," "Richard," and "Raymond."

While Robert and Richard had quickly grown to an impressive physical size, Ray was smaller and thinner. He was enrolled in Elmwood Park grade school, then transferred to Elm School. He had his father's facial features—the wide mouth, the prominent nose—and his thick shock of sandy hair was close-cropped on the sides with bangs hanging just above his eyebrows. A school photo shows him wearing a dark button-down sweater, horizontal-striped shirt and jeans cuffed at the ankles. His large, scuffed shoes protrude from the bottom of the desk.

"Ray was a tag-a-long," Smid said. "A skinny, scrawny, snot-nosed kid."

Little Ray was skinny but aggressive. He hung around the nearest playgrounds, playing football, basketball, and baseball with Richard and some of the older, bigger kids in the neighborhood. Since Robert was working and didn't have time for sports, Ray spent much of his free time with Richard. The two competed with one another constantly, and because Richard was older and bigger, he usually beat Ray at whatever game they were playing. The losses bothered Ray but didn't discourage him; he still competed hard with Richard, still tried to outdo him in football, basketball, and baseball, still worked hard to be better than Richard was.

Heyward, who went through grammar school and high school with Richard, remembered joining with kids their age from the neighborhood to play sandlot tackle football games in an empty lot on Fullerton Avenue and 78th Street in Elmwood Park. "Ray would come over and ask to play," Heyward recalled, "and we told him to run off because he was too small. He was very slim, didn't weigh much."

Ray's determination eventually become a trademark of his Hall of Fame career. Just as he grew used to taking on kids who outweighed him by 50 pounds in playground scuffles, Ray grew used to taking on linemen who outweighed him by the same amount during his NFL career. Just as he competed hard with Richard and was never satisfied with second place, Ray competed hard to become the starting middle linebacker in Green Bay and was never satisfied with being second-string.

By the time he was 13, Ray followed Richard's path to Proviso High School in Maywood. Elmwood Park didn't have a high school, so students graduating eighth grade had a choice of choosing between several high schools in the area. Richard had gone to Maywood, located some five miles from Elmwood Park, and played football there, and Ray decided to do the same. He was 13, just starting high school, when his mother was admitted to the hospital. Ray was stunned. For 10 years she'd had two jobs and had taken on the dual role of mother and father to her boys. Yet she had never taken time off for illness, never gone to the doctor. She was still young, just 41 at the time, and because of her youth and vigor, Robert, Richard, and Ray believed their mother would spend a few days in the hospital and then return home.

Later, the boys would find out that their mother had been bleeding internally but hadn't gone to the doctor. Anna had always been self-sufficient, and any time she had been sick, she had taken care of herself rather than seek medical treatment. A week after her admission to the hospital, Anna died of a blood clot. Her death devastated her sons. Robert was 21, Richard 17, and Ray 13, and when their mother passed, Ray said later it was as if the world had come crashing down on their shoulders. They were orphans, and at Anna's funeral, Ray overheard his aunts and uncles discussing which of the boys they would take in. "I'll take one," Ray heard one person say, "if you'll take another of the boys."

Robert and Richard, however, decided there would be no dividing up of the Nitschke boys. Together they would raise Ray, who was just starting his freshman year.

"Bob was a father figure," recalled Smid. "Their mom raised them, and then Bob took over when their mother passed. He was of age, and he took it upon himself to raise them and keep the house and family together."

Ray entered high school confused and angry over his mother's passing. He wondered why he had been orphaned, what he had done to deserve such a fate. "Why did she have to die?" he asked himself. She was the one who had given him all his love, the one he loved so much in return. He seethed at the loss of his mother, and without the discipline of his parents to help him deal with his anger, channeled his rage into street fights. He weighed barely 100 pounds as a freshman but grew up, as he said later, "belting the other boys in the neighborhood and getting belted back." He signed up for a Boy Scout troop, got into a fight at the first meeting, and was told to never come back.

By his own admission, Ray became a loner; he was against everyone and everything. He didn't seem to have any friends and didn't seem to want any either. All he knew is that every other kid in the neighborhood had a mother, and his had passed away. He spent hours after school and on weekends away from everyone else. He would take his football out to the park and kick it, chase it down by himself, and kick it again. He played basketball alone too. When winter storms covered the Chicago courts with snow, Ray would carry his shovel to the playground, clear the courts, and shoot baskets alone.

Ray used his shovel in other ways as well, earning spare change in the winter by clearing snow-filled sidewalks. Because his neighbors shoveled their own walks, he would head over to River Forest, an upper-class neighborhood where residents would pay to have their driveways and walks cleared. During the Christmas holiday he would go door to door in River Forest, singing carols until residents paid him to stop. In the summer, he returned to River Forest to mow lawns and picked up pocket change as a caddie at a local golf course. He found the pastoral settings of River Forest pleasing. His world in Elmwood Park was strictly steel and mortar—neighborhoods, schoolyards, playgrounds, city streets. Neither Robert nor Richard owned a car, so Ray rarely did any traveling. To him, anything ten miles outside the city limits could be classified as "the country." Since he had been kicked out of the Scouts, Ray was never able to take part in camping trips. Golf offered scenery he could appreciate, a chance to explore nature. Caddie Day offered something else, an opportunity to actually play the course. Nitschke, who owned an awkward but strong swing, developed a love for the game that remained with him the rest of his life.

When he wasn't caddying, he was delivering papers for the *Chicago Tribune*. The job was solitary, and Ray liked it. He would rise at 5:30 every morning, roll the papers up tight, and then send them spiraling toward porches. He saw every paper as a football and every delivery as a long bomb. His errant heaves shattered porch lights and windows, and early risers could mark his route by the sound of breaking glass and an irate customer's screech. In time, Ray lost so much money paying for broken property he could no longer afford to be a paper boy.

Sports provided Ray an outlet for his aggression and role models for him to follow. He had no one to look up to in the business world, so he turned his attention to the athletes making the headlines on the sports pages. He collected baseball and football cards and studied them with such intent he could rattle off player's statistics from memory. He knew, for instance, that when Chicago Bears fullback Bronko Nagurski retired in 1943, he had gained 4,013 yards rushing in a nine-year NFL career. Ray followed Chicago Bears football and Chicago Cubs baseball and since Wrigley Field served as the home field for both teams and was just a short bus ride from his home, he made the trip on several occasions to see firsthand the heroes he followed on the radio and in newsprint.

Ray attended his first Bears game at Wrigley Field in 1949. The Bears that season were a team in transition, much different than the '43 championship team that had captured his attention as a seven-year-old. Head coach George Halas had sold a young quarterback named Bobby Layne to the New York Bulldogs, and when veteran Sid Luckman contracted a thyroid condition that sidelined him for much of the season, Halas turned control of the Bears offense over to Johnny Lujack, a second-year pro out of Notre Dame. Lujack led the NFL in touchdown passes, completions, and yards, and he set an NFL record when he beat the Bears' crosstown rivals, the Chicago Cardinals, by throwing for 468 yards in a 52–21 win. Halas's "Monsters of the Midway" were a colorful team, renowned for their rough physical play. Linebacker Ed Sprinkle, nicknamed "The Claw" for his clothesline hits, symbolized the Bears' style. Ray grew enamored of the team's fierce, no-frills play, and dreamed about playing in the NFL for Halas and the Bears.

Ray had little ambition outside of sports and went to school only because he knew he had to. Classmates thought he came from a tough but loving home, yet since there was usually no one to go home to after school, Ray would head to his aunt's house or go off by himself. He walked alone, thinking about where his life was heading and what he was going to do. He was still small, but as he entered Proviso High he was determined to prove he was as good as anyone else, even the boys with mothers. He would prove it the only way he knew how: by being a better athlete than they were.

Proviso was, and is, a sprawling school district with a large student body. It draws students from a dozen different communities, and while the school has since been divided into Proviso East and West, in Ray's time it was one school with student attendance numbering more than four thousand. Located just ten miles west of Chicago, Proviso serves students from Maywood, Melrose Park, Broadview, and Forest Park. The school, a brown-brick building constructed in 1910, is situated on First Avenue in Maywood and over the years has undergone renovations in the form of two additions. The Proviso East/West split occurred on July 1, 1958, and Proviso West was founded in Hillside. The school's motto of "Peace, Pride, and Power" has long encouraged Proviso students to promote peace in their school community and the world; pride in their school, staff, and in the success of the students; and the tenet that knowledge is power.

Because of the large number of students in 1951, Proviso fielded three freshman football teams. Ray played on the C team, the least talented of the three. He was an underdeveloped 13-year-old, competing against boys aged 14 and 15. He became a fullback, and while the sight of a 100-pounder carrying a ball that seemed almost as big as he was didn't scare too many defenders, Ray never backed down from an altercation, on or off the field.

The void in his life continued to grow. He pushed himself to go to school and thought privately about running away from home. Robert and Richard were working, and while Ray loved them both, he saw them as being not much more than boys themselves. He went to school mainly to get away from his home life, but his lack of interest caused his grades to suffer. He needed a C average to stay eligible for sports, but with his mind occupied by his mother's death, he failed two subjects. When he returned to Proviso High for his sophomore season, he was told he was academically ineligible to participate. Since sports was one of the primary reasons why he was still going to school, Ray was jolted into improving his grades. He raised them enough to become eligible again his junior year, but for the rest of his life he regretted letting his grades slide and losing his eligibility during his sophomore season.

The year away from sports saw Ray change not just academically but physically as well. He had large feet and hands, as well as a sizable desire to be at the center of action for every sport he played. He wanted to control every game he played in, so he tried out for quarterback in football, center in basketball, pitcher in baseball. His oversized hands helped him excel in all three sports. The summer before his junior season Ray was throwing a football around the field when Proviso's varsity football coach, Andy Puplis, caught a glimpse of him while driving by. Ray uncorked a pass that Puplis later said flew "a country mile." That fall, Ray became the starting quarterback on the Proviso varsity.

Ted Leber, a sophomore at Proviso when Nitschke was a junior, saw the dramatic change in Nitschke from his sophomore to junior seasons.

"He was a 5-foot-9 guy, and over the summer, he became a 6-foot giant," Leber said. "Was he a tough guy? Sure. I'm sure there were times when people were ticked off at him because he was mean. And he didn't care. If somebody wanted a poke in the nose, he'd poke them in the nose. If somebody challenged him, he stood up to them. Ray was one bad sucker."

Heyward saw the change in Ray too after returning to Elmwood Park from the University of Louisville, where he was a teammate of a young, crewcut quarterback named John Unitas. "I had played football at Proviso and at the beginning of Ray's junior year I had come back to work out with the team before going to Louisville," Heyward said. "We had a drill where one back would post and the guy behind carrying the football would stiff-arm him, spin, and pull away. I posted for Ray one time and he practically knocked me over. Ray had grown up and was a lot stronger."

Jack Meihlan shared a study hall with Ray at Proviso, and the two would head off to the school's training room to work out together. Meihlan was an Illinois state wrestling champion but, at 127 pounds, was much smaller than the hulking Nitschke.

"He was supposed to be giving me a massage to loosen me up, and he'd be bouncing me around the wrestling mats," Meihlan said. "He would literally lift me off the mats and pound on me. I'd ask him, 'What the hell, Ray?' He was known to be kind of a rough kid, and he did have a temper. He clobbered one of the P.E. teachers at the school once."

Of all the authority figures at Proviso, Ray most admired Puplis. A former All-America quarterback at Notre Dame, Puplis inspired his rough-hewn quarterback with his gentlemanly ways. To a 15-year-old who had been lacking a father figure in his life since the age of three, Puplis provided a role model that later influenced Ray in his own future dealings with children.

"Andy Puplis was very soft-spoken," Meihlan remembered. "But he was a great leader and a fine educator. He was also a helluva football technician. We had some hellish football teams in the fifties."

Tony Fiovani was a freshman quarterback the year Nitschke was a senior. To Fiovani, Puplis was a coach that the younger players in the program were eager to play for.

"A lot of the assistant coaches at Proviso were from Maywood, so they already had their teams picked beforehand," Fiovani said. "And a lot of the kids they picked were Maywood kids. So you had a lot of guys playing out of position on the lower levels. But once we got to the varsity, Puplis would tell us, 'I'm going to keep my eye on you.' He was very fair, just a phenomenal guy. I just couldn't wait to get to practice. All the kids in the neighborhood wanted to play for him.

"He was real quiet, real mild-mannered, but a real good technician. He spent a lot of time with his quarterbacks, and he made athletes out of them.

I had him for study hall, and he would teach me how to read defenses, what to look for.

"Puplis made successes out of people because of his work as a coach and an educator. He probably saved Ray's life. Ray didn't have a father figure and Puplis filled that role. A lot of the success Ray had in his formative years was due to Andy."

Puplis showed Ray not only how to handle himself on the field but off the field as well. Nitschke was still feeling sorry for himself, still feeling resentful of others. He disliked those peers who seemed to have it all—a great family life, a new car, new clothes, plenty of money. Ray had none of those luxuries, and just to level the playing field, would level the egos of the rich kids whenever he could. If one of them did 10 pushups, Ray would do 15. If one of them ran a mile, Ray pushed himself a mile-and-a-quarter. He had an inner hunger to prove himself equal, and he knew the only place he could do it was in sports. He learned at an early age that nothing comes easy, but he found out that if a person is willing to give that extra effort, they can succeed. Whenever he became discouraged, whenever he felt like quitting, Ray gave himself a pep talk. "Uh-uh," he would say, "I'm not going to give up." That hunger to prove himself, to push himself to be better than the next guy, was an advantage he carried through the rest of his career.

"When Ray was a young person growing up, he had a fair amount of rage," said Al Pahl, who as editor of *Ray Nitschke's Packer Report* from 1986–95 became close to Ray. "His father had been taken from him at an early age and he literally was mad at God for a great number of years. Football was a way for Ray to channel that rage, even though I'm sure it was an unconscious thing. A kid at 15 years old doesn't make a conscious decision, 'Well, I better play football so I don't get my ass in a sling.' But it was football that kept his ass out of the sling."

Ray funneled his aggressive nature into football, prompting Puplis to call him the meanest kid he had ever coached. Puplis loved Ray's aggression on the field, but he sat him down on several occasions to talk about the virtues of controlling his temper to avoid being thrown out of games. It was fine to be aggressive on the field, Puplis told him, but if a player didn't harness his aggression he hurt not only himself but the team as well. Always eager to be where the action was, Ray made a lot of tackles on defense from his safety position but made a lot of mistakes as well. He often left his assigned position early, and smart quarterbacks would take advantage by floating passes over Nitschke's head to the receiver he was supposed to be covering.

"Ray played safety like a linebacker," Fiovani remembered.

Nitschke took the talks with Puplis to heart and realized that playing aggressively, playing "mean" as he put it, was fine since to him "mean" meant playing hard and never giving up. But he remained an abrasive, belligerent type, even to teammates.

"I had been a manager of the freshman and sophomore football teams," Leber said, "and at some point in my sophomore year I said, 'I can play as good as these third-stringers.' So I went out for football, and I was going through a drill where the quarterback puts the ball in your stomach. And Ray put that ball in my stomach and I collapsed. He did it on purpose because I was the smallest guy on the field and he didn't think I belonged there. And that was just Ray. He was a gentleman in later years, but then he was a mean S.O.B."

Leber carries a constant reminder of Ray's hard play just below his right knee, a quarter-inch scar courtesy of Nitschke's cleats. "I played safety against the varsity and he just ran right over me," Leber said. "I have this permanent scar because I tried and just couldn't stop him. I remember his mean streak in various forms. He picked up one of our first-string guards and threw him into a locker. I looked into the locker after the guy got up and it was halfway bent. Ray was a strong, tough guy."

Nitschke carried his aggressive style to the basketball court, playing that winter under Proviso varsity coach Joe Hartley. Hartley also coached the freshman C football team and remembered Ray as a skinny fullback from two years earlier. When he saw him on the basketball court, he took one look at Nitschke's oversized feet and thought he must be wearing his older brother's sneakers. But when Hartley looked closer at Ray's hands, he called assistant coach Ray Rice over.

"This kid's feet are for real," Hartley told Rice. "Take a look at the size of those hands."

Smid, who later played the line for the University of Illinois and has large hands, said Nitschke's hands were so large they engulfed everyone else's. "We'd shake hands," Smid said, "and I would look down and say, 'Where the hell is my hand?' "

In later years, Green Bay Hall of Fame cornerback Herb Adderley would express the same amazement at the size of Nitschke's bearlike paws. "He had huge hands," remembered Adderley, who played alongside Nitschke from 1961 to 1969. "Great hands. He didn't drop many balls that came his way. He and (tight end) Ron Kramer had the best hands on the team. I never saw Ron Kramer drop a pass in practice or during a game and Nitschke, very seldom would he have a chance for an interception and not get it."

Ray's growth spurt continued, and when he returned to play football his senior season, he added another 20 pounds in weight and two inches in height. He was now 6-foot-1, 190 pounds, with tremendous hand and arm strength.

"He got awfully big awfully fast," Meihlan said. "It was kind of strange because he lost his hair too, and he had always had a big head of sandy hair."

Ray's increased size and strength allowed him to throw a football a great distance, and throw it with great force. He once knocked the helmet off his receiver with one of his passes, leaving his teammate temporarily stunned by the impact.

"He threw the ball hard, no question," Leber said. "And there were a lot of times when he threw it too hard to one of the ends and the coaches would say, 'What do you expect? They can't catch that stuff.' "

Proviso had posted a 3–4 record during Ray's junior season in 1952, but the Pirates improved dramatically the following year. With Nitschke starting at quarterback, Proviso cruised to victories in its first four games of the season. Week Five saw Proviso trailing New Trier High, 29–18, as the fourth quarter approached its midway point. Nitschke looked up at the stands, saw fans filing toward the exits, and shook his head. He couldn't understand. He looked at the clock, saw there were eight minutes still remaining, and thought, "We're going to win."

Resisting the notion to use his arm strength to throw for deep scores, Ray relied on a short passing game. He finished with 153 passing yards in the fourth quarter alone and led Proviso to two touchdowns and a 30–29 comeback win. One week later, the Pirates settled for a tie against Highland Park, but with a 6–0–1 record, Proviso entered its final game of the season needing a win over Oak Park to become champions of the Suburban League. At the time, the Suburban League was considered the toughest high school league in Illinois. The championship game against Oak Park reflected the league's balance. Proviso trailed 19–14 in the final quarter, and the visiting Huskies had driven down to the Pirates 7-yard line. With seven minutes remaining, an Oak Park score would have clinched the victory. But the drive stalled on the 1, leaving Nitschke the option of engineering a 99-yard drive to the title-winning score or losing the championship. It was the kind of scenario Ray had been dreaming about for years, ever since his childhood days when he and his mother would go to the games to watch Proviso play Oak Park. Sitting in the stands with his mother, Ray was amazed at the physical size and talent of the high school boys, and he would dream of one day being one of them, being a Pirate and playing the Huskies.

Now the opportunity was his, and he looked to make the most of it. With a sell-out crowd of more than 7,000 fans rocking Proviso's home field, Nitschke dropped back from his own 1-yard line and fired an 11-yard completion to Pete Fiorito. Nitschke drove the Pirates to the Oak Park 1, thanks in large part to Fred Keys, who made several spectacular catches to keep the drive alive. With 1:03 remaining, Nitschke turned and handed off to Fiorito, who plunged in over right tackle for the game-winning score. Ray closed out his senior season with 50 completions in 99 attempts. He threw for 750 yards and nine touchdowns, rushed for an additional 213 yards, and averaged nearly five yards per carry. He had been named "Prep Player of the Week" during the regular season, and when his name appeared in the *Chicago American* newspaper, Ray clipped the article and showed it around Pete's Place. *Scholastic Coach* magazine tabbed Nitschke and Fiorito as honorable mention selections to their 1953 All-America high school football team.

Following the football season, Ray played center for Proviso's varsity basketball team. Hartley called Nitschke his "tiger," but had to suspend him for one game when Nitschke lost his temper and told the coach to go screw himself. He was reinstated because he was a good athlete and the team needed him.

"He wasn't that tall, maybe 6-1 as a senior," Leber said, "but he was tough under the boards. He got into position and he got his shots and got his rebounds and he hustled up and down the court."

Nitschke admitted later that while he wasn't the smoothest center who ever played, he did have good elbows. He took every game as a challenge to prove himself, and he would get angry with Hartley if the coach chose someone other than him to guard the other team's best frontcourt player.

"Ray was a competitor," Leber said. "Every inch of the way."

As a team, Proviso was solid but unspectacular, and the highlight of the season came in a game against Oak Park. With both teams using stall tactics, Proviso led at halftime, 6–2. Both teams loosened up in the second half, and the Pirates walked off with a 41–30 victory. Albert Lee Stange, who started at the guard position and overshadowed Nitschke both athletically and socially, was the star of the team. Stange, who went by his middle name Lee, ranked sixth in the conference in scoring and was named all-conference. He later went on to pitch 10 years in the major leagues and compiled a 62–61 record with four American League teams.

Nitschke's personal highlight came in a game against St. Edwards, when he scored a school-record 36 points. That mark remained a school record for 17 years, until Dave Roberts surpassed it during the 1970–1971 season. At season's end Nitschke was passed over for all-conference honors but did gain an honorable mention selection.

"Ray could shoot a basketball," remembered Boyd Dowler, a teammate of Nitschke's in Green Bay from 1959 to 1969. "We used to play exhibition games during the off-season in Green Bay and he could really shoot. He had real good hands, and a lot of athletic ability."

In the spring, the Proviso baseball team advanced to the state championship game against Bloomington. Nitschke had earned a reputation as a strong-armed pitcher; Leber thought Nitschke's fastball was the most explosive he had ever caught at the high school level.

"He was a great pitcher," said Leber, a catcher on the Proviso team. "He had the fastest ball I ever caught. And every time he threw it, it hurt."

The state championship game was played at Tom Conners in Peoria, and while Nitschke didn't pitch, he batted third and started in leftfield. He contributed to the Pirates' win with a massive home run over the centerfield fence. The Proviso school newspaper, *The Pageant*, described the ball as having traveled "a stated distance of 700 feet." Actually, the distance was later estimated at 560 feet, but it was a tremendous blow nonetheless. Nitschke batted .500 in the state tournament and his baseball skills impressed major league scouts. The *Chicago Tribune* named him to the paper's Second Team All-State squad, and the St. Louis Browns offered him a professional contract and $3,000 signing bonus. The money was tempting to Ray, as was the idea of someday playing major league baseball. He'd always enjoyed the game and found it easier to play than football. But he saw baseball as a game for individualists. Football, he thought, required more teamwork and was more physical, two intangibles that appealed to him.

Until he reached his senior year in high school, Nitschke hadn't given much thought to what he wanted to do after graduation. He didn't think seriously about college, simply because no one he was close to had ever continued their education beyond high school. To people with blue-collar backgrounds like the Nitschkes, college was for the rich kids who lived in River Forest, the kids whose driveways he used to shovel and whose lawns he used to mow. Since college didn't appear to be an option, Ray never prepared himself academically while in high school. He didn't take prep courses, merely went through the motions in classes like math and composition. When he found a course he liked, as in history, he usually did well in it.

"When I was tutoring him in math he was not bright, but he didn't study either," Leber said. "He showed himself to be a competitor and an outstanding performer, and I think everybody thought he could be a great ballplayer of some sort. But we all thought that he would flunk out because he was that kind of guy."

Meihlan agreed, and he recalled that the talk among Nitschke's classmates at Proviso was about "how the hell he was going to get through it because he had so many problems with school work."

Ray considered the baseball offer from the Browns and also thought about joining the military or going to work in a factory or with a construction crew. They were jobs, he thought, that didn't require a lot of schooling.

When he first got to Proviso, Ray had been mistrustful of his teachers. If he had problems in their course and the teacher would try to help him, he would wonder to himself why were they trying to help him. "Why should they bother with me?" he thought. He had been trying to just get through high school, to keep his grades up just so he could remain eligible to play sports. His outlook on college changed, however, when he began receiving offers for football scholarships to major universities. With the baseball offer from the St. Louis Browns still on the table, and with scholarship offers from football coming from various universities and colleges, Ray had a decision to make. Once again, Puplis provided direction.

"Go to college, Ray," Puplis said. "Get an education. Make something of yourself. Take advantage of your God-given ability."

The $3,000 baseball offer from the Browns was hard for Nitschke to turn down; to him, it seemed like all the money in the world. If he didn't take the money now, Ray thought, he might never see that much money in a lump sum the rest of his life. His respect for Puplis was so strong, however, that if his coach told him to go to college, it must be the right thing to do.

Nitschke turned down the Browns' offer, then turned his focus on deciding which college he should attend. Since he had only maintained a C average at Proviso, some schools weren't interested in him. Ray visited several universities, including the University of Miami, but his desire to play for a Big Ten school and in the Rose Bowl influenced his decision to accept a scholarship to play football at the University of Illinois. In high school, he had written an English theme paper about the Rose Bowl. As he pondered his future, the Fighting Illini featured a great player in J. C. Caroline, and the fact that Puplis had sent other Proviso players to Illinois and that the Illini coach was Ray Eliot were a positive factor in Ray's mind. Nitschke had met Eliot at an all-state football dinner hosted in the Executive Mansion in Springfield by Governor William G. Stratton. Eliot quickly became one of Nitschke's mentors, much like Puplis had been.

When he committed to Illinois, Nitschke believed firmly he was about to fulfill a long-time dream. With him at quarterback, he thought, the Illini would win the Big Ten, qualify for the Rose Bowl, and then win that game as well.

The Rose Bowl was still the number one bowl game at the time, and Nitschke wanted to be the quarterback who won it. That would be his way of showing everyone at Proviso that Ray Nitschke was as good as anyone, as long as he was playing football.

TWO

FOOTBALL had earned Ray Nitschke a full scholarship to the University of Illinois. But it would take two full years before the blue-collar kid from Elmwood Park would believe he really belonged in college.

By the time he enrolled at Illinois in the fall of 1954, Nitschke was showing signs of social growth. His senior year at Proviso High had seen him excel as a three-sport athlete, and Nitschke started to shed his loner status. His athletic ability allowed him to feel more like an equal, and he began hanging around his peers at the local pizza parlors and drugstores. Once he reached college, however, Nitschke again began feeling out of place. He had grown up on the urban fringe of Chicago, and with the university situated in a rural setting, Nitschke saw himself as a big-city guy among hayseeds. Because he had lived in Elmwood Park, people assumed he was street-wise and tough, and Nitschke not only went along with that stereotype; he tried to live up to it. He started smoking, favoring Chesterfield cigarettes and pipe tobacco, and began drinking regularly. Nitschke and alcohol were a combustible mix, and he didn't handle liquor well. A few beers and Nitschke would begin mouthing off. On several occasions, he went from trading barbs to trading fists.

Nitschke's troubles his first two years in college weren't confined to off-the-field activities. He majored in physical education because it was the field of study that interested him the most, but it didn't take long for him to realize he wasn't prepared academically for his courses. He had never done much homework at Proviso and didn't really know how to study. Classes at the university were larger than they had been in high school, the pace was quicker, and for the most part didn't have the same one-on-one relationship with college professors that he had at Proviso. His status as a scholarship athlete was both help and hindrance. Some of his professors, particularly those in the physical education department, gave Nitschke extra help because they wanted to see him remain eligible to play football. Other teachers, however, denigrated him as a dumb jock, and Nitschke believed they were tougher on the student-athletes than on the regular students. One professor, upon finding out that Nitschke was a football player, made him sit in the back of the classroom by himself.

Nitschke struggled through his courses, and English and botany proved particularly difficult for him to grasp. He had never been good in English, couldn't write very well, and the only thing he knew about botany was that his aunt had cooked similar-looking plants and served them in his Uncle Pete's tavern. The customers at Pete's Place didn't care about the private lives of the greens they were eating, and Nitschke didn't know why he had to study them in botany.

When Chuck Heyward returned to Illinois from Louisville to take a summer job with Coca-Cola, he saw Nitschke hitch-hiking along the road and picked him up. During their ride home Heyward asked how things were going. Football's going okay, Nitschke said, but his grades weren't so good.

Feeling somewhat like a big brother, Heyward offered Nitschke some advice.

"Now, Ray," he said. "You've got to work on those grades because you can't make a living playing football."

Nitschke's academic difficulties were compounded by his lack of available study time. Along with becoming a member of the Illini's 60-man freshman football team, he took a job to earn a little spending money and made $50 each month working in the school's athletic association laundromat. Nitschke found help for his studies from two sources. The Illinois Alumni Association hired a tutor to assist with his studies, and Jan Smid, his roommate, did what he could to speed Nitschke's acclimation to the quicker pace of college life. The captain of the Illini's varsity football team and an All-America guard, Smid was three years older than Ray. They had known each other for years, Smid having grown up in River Grove not far from Nitschke's neighborhood in Elmwood Park, and he had been a friend of Ray's older brother Richard.

To Ray, Smid was like a big brother. And like an older brother, Smid was always trying to ditch Ray. "I always told him to stay the hell away from me," Smid said. "I didn't want him hanging around with me."

Smid saw Nitschke as an outgoing kid and knew he had a reputation for trouble as well. "He was a hell-raiser," Smid said. "When you have the kind of life he did, you're around a different element. But he was a good guy. I never had any problems with him. I'd tell him to shut his face and he'd shut up."

Nitschke credited Smid with helping him smooth his transition from being a well-known star in high school to being just another face in the crowd in college. The transition was less difficult on the football field, where Nitschke started at quarterback for the freshman team and quickly made a name for himself as a physical player who relished contact.

Nitschke wasn't graceful but he was effective, particularly when he broke from the pocket and ran with the ball. One writer observed that Nitschke "didn't run to daylight, he ran to flesh." Nitschke's physical play made him perfect for the special teams, and he was used as a punt returner. In the course of returning one particular punt, Nitschke collided with a large lineman on the opposing team, and the force of their contact reverberated throughout the stadium. Both men recoiled from the blow, but while Nitschke recovered to gain extra yardage, he saw his would-be tackler falling stiff and motionless.

As a quarterback, Nitschke loved to throw the long bomb, and in fellow freshman Bobby Mitchell he found a wide receiver with the speed to outrun defenders and the sure hands to haul in the deep ball. A star running back and wide receiver with the Cleveland Browns and Washington Redskins from 1958 to 1968, Mitchell and Nitschke formed a future Pro Football Hall of Fame combination on the Fighting Illini freshman team. The two practiced together constantly, Nitschke heaving long passes to the end zone and Mitchell hauling them in, and they looked forward to the time they'd become eligible to play varsity and be an All-America quarterback– receiver combination.

"At that time, freshman couldn't play on the varsity team," recalled Mitchell. "I had been seeing this big guy walking around and I thought he was a linebacker or a lineman, but as it turned out he was a freshman quarterback. We talked and all, and when the freshmen practiced against the varsity, Ray and I would tear them up. Ray would throw the ball about 60 yards in the air and I would run under it and catch it. The freshmen were killing the varsity and they didn't know what to do about it.

"So that's how we got started together, and we both made the varsity the next year and we had a good time together. We played together those three varsity years and I got to know him real well. We would ride each other all around the campus. My middle name is Cornelius, and he was the only one on the team who knew it. I'd be walking across the campus and hell, I'd be a quarter of a mile away and I could hear him screaming. *'Cornelius! Cornelius, where ya goin'?'* People would be looking around and I'd say to Ray, 'Shut up, man!' "

A sudden lack of depth in the Illini running game caused head coach Ray Eliot to reshuffle his offense the following season. Joe Gorman, the Illini's starting fullback, was declared ineligible before the first day of practice, and three days later, Gorman's replacement, Don Kraft, was hospitalized with an appendectomy. With his team down to just one fullback in Danny Wile, Eliot went looking for backfield depth. Remembering the running ability Nitschke had displayed as a freshman quarterback and how he enjoyed running the ball, Eliot called Nitschke into his office.

"Which would you rather be," Eliot asked Nitschke, "the second-string quarterback or my first-string fullback?"

Nitschke's heart sank. He knew that as a sophomore he was deep on the quarterback depth chart behind the more experienced Hiles Stout and Em Lindbeck. Yet while Eliot didn't believe Nitschke could beat out either Stout or Lindbeck for the starter's job, Nitschke did believe it.

"Coach," he said, "I'd rather be the first-team quarterback."

Eliot was unmoved. "Ray," the coach said, "as of now, you're not a quarterback on this team. You're a fullback."

Realizing his dream of quarterbacking the Illini in the Rose Bowl was over, Nitschke broke down and cried in Eliot's office. "Cried like a baby," Mitchell remembered. "But when he was moved to fullback and linebacker, that changed his whole career."

Later, Nitschke would see the justification in his coach's decision. It was a decision made in part because Nitschke lacked the touch on his passes to be an accomplished quarterback at the major college level. No one doubted his arm strength, and in later years the Packers would be amazed at how far he could throw the football. Boyd Dowler, who played quarterback at the University of Colorado before being converted to a wide receiver by Green Bay head coach Vince Lombardi, swore Nitschke could throw the ball 70 yards in practice. Green Bay defensive coordinator Phil Bengston knew of Nitschke's days as a high school quarterback and entertained the notion of making his middle linebacker available to Lombardi as an emergency quarterback if the Packers were ever faced with a sudden shortage.

Every Saturday morning during the regular season, some of the Packers would loosen up before their light workout with a long-throw contest. Even on a team loaded with former and current quarterbacks like Dowler, Bart Starr, Zeke Bratkowski, Paul Hornung, and Willie Wood, there was no doubt who would win.

"Ray won it every year," Starr said. "And it was really funny because what we were doing was seeing who would throw for second place. He literally could just hurl the ball into space. It was unbelievable how far he could throw it."

Asked if Nitschke had any "touch" on his short passes, Starr laughed. "Are you kidding? He'd kill you with the shorter passes," he said. "He'd throw the ball right through you, and I think that was his intent."

Eliot had seen Nitschke zipping his passes around the Illinois practice field, had seen Illini receivers struggling to catch the short throws. Tom Haller eventually became the Illini quarterback, and his strength and throwing accuracy are best reflected in the fact that he later became a major league catcher and played 12 years with the San Francisco Giants, Los

Angeles Dodgers, and Detroit Tigers. He was a member of the 1962 Giants team that lost a seven-game World Series to the New York Yankees, batting .286 in 14 at-bats with one home run, three RBI, and four hits.

Eliot knew Nitschke lacked the necessary skills to lead the Illini offense, and he knew that Ray's grades were so low his freshman year he had to go to summer school just to remain eligible for football. Carrying nine credits, the maximum number allowed at Illinois at the time, Nitschke studied harder than he ever had and earned passing grades in both English and botany. Because of his difficulties in the classroom, Illini coaches weren't sure Nitschke was going to be able to remain academically eligible to play as a sophomore.

The other factor in Eliot's mind was that in 1955, the college game was still one of single-platoon football. Free substitution, instituted in 1941, had been eliminated in 1953. Coaches responded to the rules change by reverting to the single-platoon, meaning players started on both offense and defense. On the change of possession, offensive linemen became defensive linemen, receivers played the secondary and running backs became linebackers. Often, the fullback became the middle guard when the offense switched to defense.

Eliot had watched Nitschke closely in practice, had seen how much the 18-year-old sophomore enjoyed the physical contact during scrimmages. To Eliot, Nitschke was a vicious player, and his aggressive attitude was something the coach was looking for in his fullbacks and linebackers.

"Ray was a tough, hard-nosed football player," Smid remembered. "And he got bigger and nastier."

Nitschke might have been more opposed to switching positions had he not respected Eliot as much as he did. Dark-haired, with clear glasses and a wide, bright smile, Eliot was known as "Mr. Ilini." He held the position of head coach at U of I longer than anyone other than the legendary Bob Zuppke and had graduated from Illinois in 1932 as a three-year letter-winner at the tackle position. After coaching at Illinois College in Jacksonville, Eliot returned to the university in 1937 as an assistant under Zuppke. When Zuppke retired in 1942, Eliot took over as head coach. His teams won Big Ten titles in 1946, '51, and '53, and Rose Bowl victories on New Year's Day in '47 and again in '52.

With his gray fedora, light gray blazers, V-neck sweaters, and patterned ties, Eliot was the picture of authority. He gained a reputation as a motivator and toured the country giving speeches at coaching clinics. To players like Nitschke, Eliot was both father figure and football coach, and he inspired his teams with a simple nine-word motto that in time became a mantra:

"Anything you *think* you can do," Eliot would say, "you *can* do."

In later years, Mitchell would see Nitschke socially, see him with his dark-rimmed glasses, receding hairline, and conservative business suits, and be struck by the influence Eliot had on Nitschke. "I couldn't believe how much they looked alike," Mitchell said with some astonishment. "Ray had become Coach Eliot."

Eliot's influence on his players was evident long after they had left the school, Smid said.

"Eliot made me, as far as I'm concerned," he said. "And he probably made Ray too. He was an inspirational person. He'd get you all worked up for a game, and you would be ready to go through a brick wall for the man. Could he get you up for a game? Oh, yeah. And that was something I missed after I got out of school. When I played a post-season game, I'd say 'Where the hell is Ray Eliot?' "

"Eliot was a Knute Rockne type," Tony Fiovani remembered. "He was a rah-rah, a real motivational speaker. He'd get you so fired up you'd want to run through the door for him."

Nitschke benefited from playing under Eliot at Illinois, and then playing under Lombardi in Green Bay. "Lombardi was hell on wheels," Smid said, "and Ray Eliot was like that too. He was the leader, and he kept you focused and got you to play above your head."

In later years, Nitschke would talk with some amazement to Fiovani about the great run of coaching he had received at Proviso and Illinois, and in Green Bay. "Puplis, Eliot, and Lombardi," Nitschke would say to Fiovani. "Can you find anything better?"

Nitschke took Eliot's inspirational words to heart, and they helped carry him through the difficult transition from quarterback to fullback. He hadn't played fullback since his freshman year at Proviso, and he struggled to reacquaint himself with the technical aspects of the position. As a quarterback the past four years, he had played the game in an upright position. Now, he was down in the three-point stance again, the fingers of his right hand digging into the grass and dirt as he positioned himself in the proper stance—weight balanced on the balls of his feet; right arm forming a tripod with his feet; shoulders squared and back parallel to the ground; head up and eyes looking straight ahead and not to the area to he's going to run.

Every running back has his own distinctive style of running, but all good runners have explosion out of their stance and quickness to the hole. Nitschke wasn't exceptionally quick off the snap and lacked the natural feel for running laterally along the line of scrimmage. He had difficulty absorbing the coaching points of his new position, and it would take two years before Nitschke finally felt comfortable again playing fullback.

"Ray was an offensive-minded guy," Mitchell said, "and once he couldn't quarterback he set out to become a great fullback. But he didn't have that kind of speed and elusiveness to be a great runner."

Even though he was no longer a quarterback, playing varsity football in the Big Ten was the realization of a dream Nitschke had held since he first became a fan of the conference as a boy in the mid-forties. Growing up in Illinois, he had watched the Illini on television several times—in 1948, when Illinois made its first appearance on regional TV and dropped a 6–0 decision to Minnesota on October 16; on New Year's Day in '52, when the Illini defeated Stanford 40–7 on NBC, a game made historic by the fact that it was the first national network telecast of any bowl game and the first national telecast of a college game; and again in 1953 and '54, when the Illini were carried regionally by NBC and nationally by ABC, respectively. So Nitschke knew the history of Big Ten football, knew how it had become arguably the most competitive conference in the country.

American football had been born on the eastern college campuses of Princeton and Rutgers, Harvard and Yale, and the game was nurtured by men like Walter Camp and Amos Alonzo Stagg, Pop Warner and Percy Haughton. Architects of the game—their formations, shifts, and special plays—proved key to the sport's strategic evolution. But it was the midwestern schools, Chicago and Illinois, Michigan and Minnesota, that brought college football to what many considered to be its highest level. After Illinois coach Bob Zuppke, in his thick German accent, declared the Big Ten the "anchor of amateur athletics in America" in the mid-twenties, many viewed his words not as an idle boast, but as a statement of fact.

Coached by Camp, Yale had become college football's first dynasty, dominating the game from 1872 to the turn of the century. But in 1901, Fielding Yost became the first midwestern coach to snatch supremacy away from eastern teams. A master of rapid motion on and off the field, he was called "Hurry Up" Yost and his famous "Point-a-Minute" Michigan teams proved a mirror image of the man. With Yost driving his players—"You're not movin' out there," he would shout, "ya think we got all day?"—the Wolverines overwhelmed opponents. At Ann Arbor in 1904, Michigan defeated West Virginia 130–0, prompting a West Virginia newspaper to headline its account of the game with the words, "Horrible Nightmare." In the 1901 Rose Bowl, the inaugural Tournament of Roses game, Michigan was on its way to an overwhelming win when Stanford coach C. M. Fickert requested the game be stopped. "No sirree," Yost replied. "Let's get on with it." With close to eight minutes left and Michigan leading 49–0, the Wolverines team captain finally agreed to end the game when Stanford pleaded exhaustion.

In 1903, Michigan tied with Minnesota 6–6 in a game that became historic for two reasons. In order to stop Yost's "Point-a-Minute" offense, legendary Golden Gophers coach Dr. Harry Williams employed what is recognized as the first four-man defensive backfield in history. Because the forward pass was rarely used at the time, most college teams stacked the line with nine men to stop the run. Once a runner broke the initial line of defense, however, he was usually on his way to a big gain. To combat Wolverine back Willie Heston, a game-breaker and consensus All-America choice, Williams put just seven men on the line and kept four back. The alignment frustrated Yost, whose team had been winning games that season by scores that staggered the imagination—88–0 over Ferris Institute, 79–0 over Beloit, 76–0 over Albion, 65–0 over Ohio Northern, 51–0 over Indiana. When the Minnesota game ended with the Michigan supermen having scored just six points, Yost was in such a rush to get his team out of town he left behind the brown plaster jug used to supply his team with fresh spring water. Spotting the jug on the departed Michigan sideline prompted one Minnesotan to chidingly remark, "Yost loft his 'yug.' " Minnesota's team trainer followed up by sending a note to his opposite at Michigan, telling him the Gophers had the jug and challenging Yost and the Wolverines to try to get it back the next season. The challenge led to the creation of the Little Brown Jug trophy, given annually to the winner of the Minnesota–Michigan game.

Yost and Michigan set the standard for midwestern football, and through the years men like Zuppke, Iowa coach Howard Jones, Northwestern's Pappy Waldorf, and Minnesota's Bernie Bierman built powerhouse teams that competed for national supremacy. Zuppke's 1923 Illinois squad featured a sophomore named Harold Grange, a redhead whose name in the Roaring Twenties would become as synonymous with college football as Babe Ruth's was with baseball, Jack Dempsey's with boxing. Zuppke once said that All-America players were often made "by a long run, a weak defense, and a poet in the press box." But when it came to Grange, who in Zuppke's thick Berlin accent, was pronounced "Grench," the hard-crusted Illini coach acknowledged that has was coaching the greatest player in college history.

"I will never have another 'Grench'," Zuppke said, "but neither will anyone else."

From Ann Arbor came word that Yost and his Michigan men were unimpressed with the Illini superstar. "All Grange can do is run," Yost snapped. At the time, the statement was akin to saying that all Dempsey could do was punch. Grange responded on game day, running for five touchdowns and 402 yards on 21 attempts. He also threw a touchdown pass, showing Yost he could do more than just run, and personally accounted for six touchdowns as Illinois christened its new stadium with a 39–14 win before a jam-packed crowd of 66,609.

Stagg called Grange's performance the "most spectacular single-handed performance ever delivered in a major game," and the magnificent redhead rode it into legend. Everything about Grange captured the imagination of the sporting public. His uniform number, 77, was the most famous in football. He was lyricized by the most influential sportswriter of his time, Grantland Rice, who immortalized Grange as "The Galloping Ghost" and seemed mesmerized by Grange's sweeping end runs out of the single wing:

A streak of fire, a breath of flame,
Eluding all who reach and clutch;
A gray ghost thrown into the game,
That rival hands may never touch;
A rubber bounding, blasting soul
Whose destination is the goal—
Red Grange of Illinois!

Led by Grange the Illini offense, with its single-wing and split time, wide sweeps, and novel trap blocks, became the talk of college football. Zuppke once told football historian H. A. Applequist in 1943 that his contributions to the game also included the spiral pass from center to the backs, the screen pass, forward and backward lateral passes, guards protecting the passer, and the formation of the huddle. His greatest contribution, however, could be found in the football itself. Cutting the design from leather in his own workshop, Zuppke remodeled the rounded, bloated footballs of the time into a more streamlined version to suit the modern passing game.

Ray Eliot had been a guard on Zuppke's Illini teams from 1929 to 1931, and in 1941 served as line coach for his aging mentor. When Zuppke stepped down prior to the '42 season, Eliot took over as Illinois head coach. In 1946, the Illini emerged as one of the nation's most improved teams and finished 8–2 to capture the Big Ten title. Illinois capped the season by defeating a previously unbeaten UCLA team, 45–14, in the Rose Bowl. The Illini captured the Big Ten title in 1951 with a 9–0–1 record, the program's first unbeaten season since 1927, then crushed Stanford 40–7 in the Rose Bowl. In 1953, the season before Nitschke's arrival on campus, Eliot guided the Illinois to a 7–1–1 record and a share of the Big Ten championship. The title was the Illini's eleventh conference crown, and the third for Eliot since 1942.

At the start of the 1955 season, Illinois was picked by various observers to supplant Ohio State as Big Ten champions. Captained by future NFL star J. C. Caroline, the Illini opened the season September 24 at the University of California. Playing behind Wile at fullback, Nitschke came off the bench and proved pivotal in the win. Over the summer, Eliot had added a series of "belly" plays to his T-formation offense. The inside belly play is a hard, quick-hitting play in which the quarterback fakes a handoff to the fullback, influencing the flow of the defense in one direction, then gives a reverse handoff to the halfback, who then runs counter to the flow of the defense. The fullback's fake is key, since he must convince the defense that he is the lead runner on the play. The play is most effective against defensive tackles who read and react to the initial flow of the offense.

Eliot had planed to save his belly series for Ohio State, but decided to open the season with it against California. Pulling on the Illini's bright orange helmet that was *sans* facemask and his number 32 jersey, Nitschke smashed fearlessly into the line time and again, selling the fake so well the belly play broke for several sizable gains. California defensive tackles grew increasingly frustrated chasing Nitschke along the line of scrimmage only to realize too late that he didn't have the ball.

Illinois won its opener 20–13 and Eliot was so impressed with Nitschke's play against California he started him the following week in the Illini's home opener against Iowa State. Dressing in the Illini's home colors—dark blue jersey with orange numerals, bright orange pants—and making his varsity start before a throng of 43,457 fans, Nitschke came out anxious and overeager. He fumbled twice in the early going but, rather than become overcautious as some sophomores might have, Nitschke instead became more determined, displaying the same tenacity that had caused him to compete extra hard against his brothers as a kid, the same tenacity that had caused him to outperform many of his peers at Proviso High. He scored three touchdowns and gained 88 yards on 12 carries to lead the Illini to a 40–0 win. Nitschke's hard play prompted one sportswriter to label him the "Proviso Pounder" in his account of the game. When he returned to classes Monday, Nitschke found he had been transformed almost overnight from a nameless, faceless sophomore into one of the Illini's more recognizable players.

Illinois followed the big win over Iowa State by traveling to Ohio State. The Buckeyes were the defending Big Ten and Rose Bowl champions and had gone through the previous season unbeaten and untied. Despite losing Nitschke to a charley horse suffered in practice the week before the game, Illinois was confident entering the game, believing that a victory over OSU would pave the way for the Illini to win the Big Ten. Ohio State, however, had other ideas. Coached by Woody Hayes and led by All-America halfback Howard "Hopalong" Cassady and guard-linebacker Jim Parker, the Buckeyes were a powerful unit that had won the conference in 1954 with a 9–0 record and beaten USC 20–7 in a rain-drenched Rose Bowl. Cassady was enjoying a Heisman Trophy and Maxwell Award season, and was on his way to final totals of 958 yards rushing and 15 touchdowns. With Cassady providing the breakaway threat in Hayes' "three-yards-and-a-cloud-of-dust" offense and a thunderous crowd of 82,407 providing a deafening roar, Ohio State rolled over Illinois, 27–12.

Still struggling with his charley horse injury, Nitschke sat out the next game as well, a 21–13 win at home over Minnesota, then returned to the lineup for the Illini's road trip to Michigan State. The Spartans were led by quarterback Earl Morrall, a player Nitschke would become more familiar with in the NFL. Morrall had gone to Michigan State on a football and baseball scholarship. But after committing five errors at third base against Wisconsin, he decided football would be his sport of choice. In 1955 Morrall accounted for 1,047 yards of total offense and was in the midst of leading Michigan State to a 9–1 record and a 17–14 win over UCLA in the Rose Bowl. From his linebacker position, Nitschke spent much of the afternoon chasing down Morrall, but the Spartans earned a 21–7 win.

Playing opposite Nitschke that day was Spartans center Dan Currie. Like most college players of that era, Currie played offense and defense, and while his job on offense often saw him taking on Nitschke with blocks, his job on defense was to stop Nitschke's bull-like rushes. Ironically, Currie and Nitschke would later be part of a 1958 Packers draft that included fullback Jimmy Taylor and guard Jerry Kramer and is still considered by many to be the best in franchise history.

"I played against Ray for three years when he was at Illinois," Currie recalled. "The NCAA wanted to give the smaller schools a chance, so they figured it would be a penalty for the big schools to have their players play both ways. So we knew each other quite well before we ever ran into each other at Green Bay."

The loss to Michigan State summed up a season that fell far below the Illini's own expectations. Illinois followed by falling to Purdue 13–0, a game marked by a steady Illinois rain and by Nitschke's own difficulties in dealing with the Boilermakers' huge offensive linemen. The Illini defense featured a six-two alignment—six down linemen and two linebackers. Since there isn't a middle linebacker in the six-two, Nitschke always positioned himself over the opposing team's guard or tackle. Against Purdue, Nitschke was startled when he saw the Boilermaker linemen get down in their three-point stance, pick their heads up, and although he was upright, look him straight in the eye because of their great size. Battered physically by Purdue's huge tackles, Nitschke spent a long day picking himself up off the muddy turf.

"He worked so hard at becoming a fullback that he was just another guy at linebacker," Mitchell said. "You couldn't look at him and say this guy was going to be great. There was no way you could get a read on him in college."

Upset by his performance, Nitschke took his revenge out on Michigan in Week Seven of the regular season. He knocked a Wolverine running back unconscious in the first quarter, and the Illini defense held a Michigan passing game that had produced 289 yards and three scores a week earlier to just three completions in 22 attempts in a 25–6 victory.

Nitschke's development as a linebacker was aided by his work with Chuck Studley, his position coach. A standout guard-linebacker with the Illini's 1951 Rose Bowl team, Studley was a strict disciplinarian with a forceful personality. He would grab players by their shoulder pads, and shout in their faces. To Fiovani, Studley was not unlike Lombardi—and Nitschke responded to his coaching.

"Ray got along real well with Studley," Fiovani said.

Following the home win over the Wolverines, Illinois earned a 17–14 win at Wisconsin in a game carried regionally by CBS, Nitschke's first televised collegiate game. The Illini closed their campaign with a 7–7 tie at Northwestern. The Illini finished with a 3–3–1 record in the Big Ten and a 5–3–1 overall mark, but Nitschke's first year on the varsity had left his coaches impressed with his on-field development.

"He improved steadily as a linebacker," Nitschke's 1956 bio reads in the Illini's press book, "and by the end of the season had convinced coaches of his defensive ability."

Impressed them so much that Eliot began telling NFL scouts about Nitschke.

"Ray Eliot was telling NFL scouts that he had a guy he thought could play pro football," Mitchell said. "They asked about me and he said, 'No, he can't play.' He told them to pass me up, that I wouldn't be any good to them. But he said Ray was the one guy that he had that could go pro. He told them, 'Obviously, Nitschke would have to play defense.' He hadn't seen enough of Ray to say he was going to be a great linebacker. No one could. But Ray took that determination that he had offensively and put it into his head defensively.

"One other thing about him. From day one, you could see he had that leadership in him, and he always wanted to express that. I think that came from being a quarterback in high school. He had that leadership thing in his head. Everybody would say, 'Ray, shut up. You don't know what you're talking about.' And that would bother him because he felt he knew what he was talking about. He'd say something and we'd say 'Ray, shut up,' and he'd go right on talking. When he knew for a fact that the only way he was going to play this game was to play defense, then he worked at it."

Nitschke was known around the campus for his hard play and hard drinking, though he was disciplined enough not to imbibe as much during the football season.

"During the week before the game, I seldom saw him drink," Mitchell said. "He was true to his sport. But on the weekends, when his brothers got together, they went farther than beer. If he did anything during the week it was probably just a beer. I'm proud to say that for him. He didn't have his nose red the week of a game."

The off-season was another story. Nitschke frequented assorted Champaign taverns, and his hangouts included Kamm's Annex and the Tumble Inn. The latter proved notable, since it was at the Tumble Inn that Nitschke met Al Herges, a man who, like Andy Puplis and Ray Eliot, would become a role model for Ray. Herges and his wife, Lorraine, had three children—Nancy, Butch, and Peter. Herges took to the rough-hewn Nitschke, and took him home on Sundays to have dinner with the family and relax and talk. Nitschke saw in Herges a father figure, and Herges saw in Nitschke a young man who really had no home life. Hanging out with the Herges family helped Nitschke get away from the pressures of college life. He appreciated Herges so much Ray gave him the baseball cards he had collected since grade school. Some day, Nitschke told Herges, NFL teams will have player cards like major league baseball teams did.

"You'll see my picture on one of them," Nitschke said.

Herges smiled. "Sure, Ray. Sure I will."

That Nitschke was already thinking ahead to playing pro football was indicative of his intense drive to succeed, to prove himself. Mitchell saw the inner drive that Nitschke had, saw the various sides of the boy who was becoming a man.

"I watched him change," Mitchell said. "At Illinois, he was a pretty violent guy. His brothers would come down and they'd turn out all the other bars. Ray became a very close guy with the chief of police, he was with him so much. Our sophomore year, he and another player on our team, Abe Woodson, got in a fight. The fight spilled outside and all around the building, and we all followed it. Abe was backing up and Ray was coming forward the whole time, and Ray couldn't hit him. Abe would hit him two or three times then duck and run back, and Ray just kept coming. It didn't matter what Abe did, Ray just kept coming. Finally, Abe picked up the top of a big trash can and hit Ray over the head with it. It didn't really hurt him, and even Ray had to laugh. It just showed how tough Ray was. You couldn't hurt him, and Abe just got tired of hitting him.

"Back in those days, with the racial situation the way it was, there were a number of places on campus that I couldn't go. But Ray didn't care where it was, we were together. And if we went into a place and somebody said, 'Get outta here,' Ray said, 'Shut up!' That was a helluva thing, and we knew when we were with Ray nobody was going to bother us. He never talked about race, never cared about it. It didn't bother him. Ray was just one of the guys.

"He kind of grew up without a mom and dad, and he and his brothers had to make it on their own. They fought for what they needed and protected their baby brother, although he grew to be bigger than them. Oh, they were rough guys. When they came to the university, Coach would send word to Ray. 'Now tell them damn brothers to cool it! We got a game this weekend and I want you on the field, not in jail.' He'd get excited when they'd show up. He got in fights, and usually they were pretty quick. He'd hit you once and that would be it."

In later years, Green Bay defensive captain Willie Davis remembered Nitschke as someone who saw past the color of a person's skin, an attribute that was of particular importance in a decade as emotionally charged with racial issues as the sixties were.

"Ray went out of his way to help make the minority players feel at home in Green Bay," Davis said. "Green Bay wasn't as diversified in the early sixties as it would be years later, but Ray was one of those guys that the rookies could go talk to."

The Illini opened the '56 season with a 32–20 win at home over California, then promptly dropped three straight. Included in that skein was a 26–6 defeat at home against Ohio State on October 13. The date was significant for Nitschke, who picked up what would become a future trademark on the opening kickoff. Hustling down the field in his facemask-less helmet, Nitschke caught a Buckeye helmet in the mouth. The collision caused two of his teeth to break off and go flying; the other two were dangling by their roots. A teammate shoved a wad of cotton in Nitschke's mouth to slow the flow of blood, and Ray played on—played the whole 60 minutes while spitting blood all over the field. At game's end, Nitschke headed back to the deserted field and began scouring the scarred field for his missing teeth. "How am I going to look with no teeth?" he thought.

His thoughts were interrupted when someone approached and asked Nitschke what he wanted the missing teeth for.

"I want them because they're mine," he said, growling through blood-caked gums.

Nitschke never did find them, and eventually he replaced the missing teeth with a false plate. In future years, his toothless face terrorized NFL opponents, and on occasion, he would startle unsuspecting Ohio State alums by suddenly yanking his bridgework out upon introduction.

"That's what your school did to me," he would say, then issue a gummy grin.

On October 27, Illinois welcomed top-ranked Michigan State to Champaign. The Spartans were the defending Rose Bowl champs, having beaten UCLA 17–14 on Dave Kaiser's 41-yard field goal with seven seconds remaining. Experts listed the Spartans as 21-point favorites over the Illini, and the first half did little to dispel that lopsided line. Illinois trailed 13–0 at halftime, but Eliot opened up the offense in the third quarter. Rather than be restricted to just blocking for halfback Abe Woodson, Nitschke was given a chance to run the ball, and he responded by ripping off a 38-yard gain. The big play set the stage for a Woodson touchdown, and the Illini rallied to score twice more while shutting the Spartans out.

The upset of the No. 1 team in the country proved to be the last highlight of the season for Illinois. The Illini tied Purdue 7–7 the following week, lost to Michigan 17–7, tied Wisconsin 13–13, and fell to Northwestern 14–13 to finish 1-4-2 in the conference and 2–5–2 overall. Nitschke's numbers were a little more rewarding. He had gained 255 yards on 48 carries and averaged an impressive 5.7 yards per carry. He had also been used as a punter, averaging 32.2 yards per kick.

Defense, however, remained his forte. Viewers who had seen the Illini's two televised games his junior season—against Ohio State and Purdue—didn't have the benefit of slow-motion replays that future generations did, so Nitschke's play at linebacker went largely unnoticed by the fans. Coaches around the conference, however, knew that Nitschke was emerging as one of the top linebackers in the Big Ten. By his senior season, he had grown to almost full maturity, standing 6-foot-3 and weighing 225 pounds. Nitschke was still outweighed by as much as 70 pounds by various Big Ten offensive tackles, but three seasons of varsity football had taught him how to deal with the size disadvantage.

Nitschke learned how to sidestep would-be blockers, how to shed linemen by taking a step or two to either side to avoid full contact. He learned, too, to make ballcarriers remember who it was that was leading the Illini in tackles.

"Each time I tackled somebody, I tried to make sure that when he got up and walked away he'd remember Ray Nitschke," he said later. "And I don't mean socially."

Purdue halfback Len Wilson remembered. After being stopped hard by Nitschke in a Week Six game in Champaign, Wilson told a sportswriter he had never been hit as hard during his career as the hit he had taken from Nitschke.

The 1957 season got off to a difficult start for both Nitschke and the Illini. They opened the season with a 16–6 loss at UCLA, and Nitschke was demoted to second-string fullback for the home opener the next week against Colgate. Jack Delveaux, who later went on to play pro football in the Canadian Football League, was promoted to first-string fullback but was injured in a practice scrimmage the week before the game. Eliot returned Nitschke to the first string, and Ray responded. On his first carry of the game, he burst through the middle of the line for a 32-yard pickup. He followed with an 11-yard touchdown run, the first of his three scores in a 40–0 win.

Illinois lost three of its next four games to quickly fall out of contention in the Big Ten and eventually finished with a 3–4 record in the conference and a 4–7 mark overall. The last game of the season provided Nitschke with a fitting finale to his college career. Before hosting Northwestern on November 23, Nitschke had been talking with Bert Bertine, a sportswriter from the *Champaign–Urbana Courier*. The conversation centered on Nitschke's career, and Ray told Bertine he would be satisfied if he could break off just one long run for a score. In practice that season, Nitschke once rambled 99 yards for a touchdown, and he came close to repeating that against Northwestern. Taking the handoff, Nitschke hit off right tackle, picked up blocks from Dick Nordmeyer and Percy Oliver at the line of scrimmage and a downfield block by Rich Kreitling, then shook a tackle by Nick Andreotti en route to an 84-yard TD. At the time, his run was the second-longest in Illini history behind Buddy Young's 93-yard jaunt against the Great Lakes Naval Station in 1944.

Nitschke capped his afternoon with a three-yard scoring run and finished with a career-high 170 yards gained. His final statistics from his senior season included 514 yards on 79 carries, a 6.5 yards per carry average, and five rushing touchdowns. He also caught a touchdown pass and led the team in punting, averaging 32.7 yards per kick. Nitschke hoped his numbers would earn him a nomination to the All-America team. Along with playing in a Rose Bowl game, being an All-America player was a goal Nitschke had since his childhood days in Elmwood Park, when he spent fall weekends reading Big Ten football stories in the sports pages.

Nitschke took his case to the Illini's public relations director, but was turned down. Because Illinois had a losing record, the university didn't think it had a chance to have two of its seniors named to the All-America team, so it was decided to push for just one: Rod Hansen, a two-way end. Hansen didn't make All-America either, but he did make first-team Big Ten. Nitschke had to settle for being named to the Big Ten's second team, but he did gain solace that Cleveland Browns head coach Paul Brown, considered at the time to be the leading football authority in the country, included Nitschke on his list of college seniors the NFL was most interested in drafting and called Nitschke the best linebacker in college football.

Otto Graham, who had quarterbacked Cleveland to seven league championships before retiring in 1955, agreed with his former coach. Serving as head coach of the College All-Star team that would face the NFL champion Detroit Lions in the annual preseason opener in Chicago's Soldier Field, Graham named Nitschke to his roster. The College All-Star lineup that season offered a who's who of future NFL starters: Nitschke, Currie, Jim Taylor, Jerry Kramer, Gene Hickerson, Bobby Mitchell, Lou Michaels, and Wayne Walker. With Mitchell scoring two touchdowns and the College All-Stars outrushing the NFL champions 179–3, the collegians earned a 35–19 win.

Nitschke also played in the Senior Bowl, an experience made memorable for him because it was the first time the game was broadcast nationally and the first time he was ever paid for playing football. He returned home to await the 1957 NFL draft , the first four rounds of which would be held December 2.

For someone who had grown up in Illinois and followed the on-field exploits of Bronko Nagurski and Sid Luckman, there was only one NFL team Nitschke could see himself playing for, only one team he wanted to run on the field with.

The Chicago Bears.

THREE

ON DECEMBER 2, 1957, representatives of the 12 National Football League teams held the first four rounds of their annual college draft. Players who weren't selected in the first four rounds would have to wait until January 28, 1958, when the NFL would hold rounds five through thirty.

The split draft was relatively new to pro football. Until 1956, the NFL held a one-day draft in mid-January; the actual date fluctuated on a year-to-year basis throughout the early 1950s, ranging from as early as January 17 to as late as January 28. In 1956, league officials decided to split the draft into two rounds and move the first three rounds two months earlier in order to give NFL teams an even start with the Canadian Football League, which was looking to upgrade its talent by signing name players from U.S. colleges and universities.

Like hundreds of other college football players in 1957, Ray Nitschke anxiously awaited news of the NFL draft. He knew he could play in the NFL if given the chance, and he wanted more than anything for that chance to come with his favorite team, the Chicago Bears. As a six-year-old in 1943, Nitschke had followed a Bears team featuring Sid Luckman at quarterback, Bronko Nagurski at fullback, and Bulldog Turner at center. On December 26 of that year, he had cause to celebrate three days prior to his seventh birthday, when Chicago claimed a 41–21 win over Washington in the NFL championship game.

Winning the Western Conference for the fourth straight year, these were the Bears of "Monsters of the Midway" fame. The team was coached by George Halas, whose career as an end, coach, and owner paralleled the rise of the NFL. He was the "Papa Bear," and to Chicago-area youths like Nitschke, Halas was football. Halas had attended the University of Illinois, played in the Rose Bowl in 1919, and been named the game's Most Valuable Player. On September 17, 1920, Halas was in Canton when the NFL held its first organizational meeting. For the next three decades he was instrumental in the league's growth but by 1955 had decided in favor of a younger coach. Long-time assistant Paddy Driscoll, who was just two years younger than the 59-year-old Halas, took over and led the Bears back to the NFL title game. Chicago was embarrassed by the New York Giants 47–7 on an icy field in Yankee Stadium, and when the Bears struggled to a 5–7 finish the following season, Halas returned as head coach.

Nitschke sat through the first two rounds of the '58 draft hoping Halas and the Bears would select him. It was a long shot, since Nitschke had starred at linebacker in college, and Chicago was already strong at that position. NFL teams at that time usually drafted players to shore up a weakness, and with veterans Bill George and Joe Fortunato, the Bears had two linebackers of all-pro caliber. Nitschke knew the Bears were loaded at linebacker and wasn't entirely surprised when Chicago used its first two picks to select West Virginia guard Chuck Howley, who would later become a linebacker for the Dallas Cowboys, and Southern Methodist end Willard Dewveall. Dewveall later created a stir when in 1961 he became the first player to voluntarily move from the NFL to the young American Football League, playing out his option with the Bears and joining the Houston Oilers.

Nitschke was startled, however, when he was selected by the Green Bay Packers in the third round. Green Bay's first two choices had been Michigan State center Dan Currie and Louisiana fullback Jim Taylor. The Packers' first pick in the third round was North Carolina State back Dick Christy, and Green Bay used its second pick of the third round, obtained in a trade with the Giants, to select Nitschke. The pick surprised Ray, since one of the few things he knew about the Packers from following their games against the Bears was that they had two solid linebackers in Bill Forester and Tom Bettis. In the Packers, Nitschke was joining a team that had gone 3–9 the previous season and finished last in the Western Conference.

Coached by former Marquette boss Lisle Blackbourn, Green Bay was quietly assembling the nucleus of a great team. Quarterback Bart Starr and offensive tackles Forrest Gregg and Bob Skoronski were products of the 1956 draft; Heisman Trophy winner Paul Hornung and tight end Ron Kramer were the team's top two picks in '57; Nitschke, Taylor, Currie, and guard Jerry Kramer were drafted in '58. Green Bay almost lost Nitschke to the Canadian Football League, however, when he balked at a contract Blackbourn offered following Ray's appearance in the North–South Shrine game. The deal Blackbourn brought to Nitschke was for a $7,000 contract. When Nitschke heard what other college players were signing for, he took Green Bay's offer as an insult. Unimpressed with both the contract and Blackbourn's handling of the negotiations, he resisted the Packer coach's attempts to get him to sign quickly. Nitschke turned his attention from the NFL to the CFL. The Toronto Argonauts had also drafted him, and Nitschke booked a flight to Canada to talk with Toronto team representatives.

Before he left, however, Nitschke made a phone call that would change his life. Contacting Packer talent scout Jack Vainisi, Nitschke told him he was flying to Toronto to talk with Argonaut officials. Vainisi's response was immediate. Urging Nitschke not to go, he arranged to meet with Ray over dinner in Chicago.

Nitschke and Vainisi liked and respected one another, and the Packer scout offered a contract that, while worth only a little more money than the original deal Blackbourn had offered, also promised Ray a $500 bonus upon signing.

The fact that Vainisi had flown to Chicago to meet with him proved to Nitschke that the Packers really were interested in him and eventually proved more persuasive than the $500 signing bonus. Nitschke put the money to good use; he used $300 of it to purchase a 1954 Pontiac, then drove by the home of Al Herges, whose family had adopted Nitschke as one of their own during his playing days at Illinois. Spotting Al's son, Butch, playing basketball in the yard, Nitschke approached him with the remaining $200 of his bonus money in his hand.

"Buy your mom, your brother, your sister, your dad, and your aunt some clothes," Nitschke told Butch, then returned to his car and drove off.

Nitschke's quiet act of gratitude belied the Packer scouting report that labeled the Illinois linebacker "a mean cuss." It was an attitude that the rookie carried into training camp in 1958. He cruised into camp in his Pontiac, a big-city guy taking in a small town. He was still a loner, still carrying a chip on his shoulder, and his abrasive attitude soon alienated members of the town and the community. Nitschke talked too loud, drank too much, and started too many barroom brawls. His childhood insecurities, all stemming from the fact that his mother had been taken away from him, still dogged him. If he was in a bar and had a couple of drinks, Nitschke's mood turned dark and ugly. He would see another patron sitting close to him as an infringement of his privacy. If someone gave him a wrong look, Nitschke took it as a challenge. If someone smiled at him, he would see it as though they were laughing at him.

"Ray was a real loud, kind of obnoxious guy," remembered defensive back Bobby Dillon, a four-time All-Pro who intercepted a Packer team record 52 passes from 1952 to 1959. "He and his brothers would come up to Green Bay and raise hell from time to time. The stories were all around town."

Nitschke carried the same chippy attitude into the clubhouse. When he first arrived in camp, Nitschke saw that the Packers were a team divided. There were various factions on the club, four or five players in each group, all going in their own direction and fraying the fabric of team togetherness. Nitschke stood alone, off to one side, a faction unto himself. Whatever his problems away from the game, he was a determined, aggressive player once he took the field. Blackbourn had promised Ray he would get a shot at either defensive end or outside linebacker, but when the Packers fired

Blackbourn in the off-season and replaced him with assistant Ray "Scooter" McLean, Nitschke was used primarily as a backup to Bettis in Green Bay's four-three defense.

By 1958, the four-three had become the standard defense in the NFL and the middle linebacker was its linchpin. Great middle men like Sam Huff in New York, Bill George in Chicago, and Joe Schmidt in Detroit popularized the position, which grew out of the fertile mind of defensive strategist Steve Owen. As head coach of the New York Giants, Owen had sat in the stands in Philadelphia's Municipal Stadium on the night of Saturday, September 16, 1950, taking notes as the Cleveland Browns of the defunct All-America Football Conference destroyed the two-time NFL champion Eagles. Owen studied how the Browns attacked coach Greasy Neale's five-four "Eagle" defense by spreading them wide with sideline passes and pounding the thinned-out middle with 238-pound fullback Marion Motley. The result, a 35–10 upset by the upstarts, brought a revolutionary response from Owen.

With his team scheduled to face the Browns in two weeks, Owen drew up a six-one-four defense that had his ends, Jim Duncan and Ray Poole, flexed and dropping into coverage, and his middle guard, John Cannady, off-set from the line of scrimmage. With Duncan and Poole dropping to the flat to take away Cleveland quarterback Otto Graham's flare passes, and with the off-set Cannady providing a more difficult target for the Browns' trap blockers, Owen's defense opened in umbrella fashion and dealt Cleveland coach Paul Brown his first pro shutout, 6–0.

Owen's "Umbrella Defense" proved to be more than a one-game gimmick. He had used a similar scheme back in 1934, when he huddled with Columbia University coach Lou Little prior to the Giants' 1934 title game against the unbeaten Bears. The Bears romped into the frozen Polo Grounds as defending league champions. The year before, fullback Bronko Nagurski surprised the Giants in the NFL championship game with flip passes at the line of scrimmage to end Bill Karr, and Chicago's strategic passing paved the way to a 23–21 win. One year later, Chicago entered the '34 title game as the first unbeaten and untied team in NFL history. Owen looked to put an end to the Bears' 13-game win streak, and came up with a five-three-two-one defense in which he positioned a third linebacker, Johnny Dell Isola, behind the noseguard. Isola's presence over the middle took away Nagurski's short passes and proved pivotal as New York upset Chicago, 30–13. Owen's five-three-two-one defense remained popular in the NFL for the next decade, until pass-oriented teams like the Los Angeles Rams of the 1940s showed its vulnerability in the secondary. His Umbrella Defense, however, was better balanced and endured longer. By the end of the 1950s, virtually every NFL team was running the four-three-four defense that stemmed from Owen's Umbrella concepts, and the middle linebacker became the dominant defensive figure in the game.

Nitschke liked being in a position that was the focal point of the defense, but he struggled to learn the nuances of his new position. Middle linebackers were similar to tight ends in that they had to be hybrids. Just as tight ends had to be big and strong enough to serve as a sixth lineman on blocking plays and quick and agile enough to serve as receivers on passing plays, linebackers had to be strong enough to stop the run and quick enough to defend against the pass.

Nitschke's primary responsibility as a linebacker at Illinois had been stuffing the running games of Big Ten opponents. His defense against the run served him well in his first Packers' training camp, when he butted helmets for the first time with another rookie, Louisiana fullback Jim Taylor. Taylor was 6-foot-2, 215 pounds, and seemingly cast out of iron. One of the NFL's early practitioners of weight training, he attacked defenders with his ferocious running style. Football, Taylor said, is a game of contact. As a running back, he had to make defenders respect him, and he did that by trying to punish them before they punished him. The idea, he said, was to give more than he got. "It's either them or you," Taylor said.

"Jimmy Taylor loved contact," said Dillon, who recalled a game against Chicago where Taylor broke through the line on his way to a touchdown. "He could have scored easily," Dillon said, "but he saw a Bear at the two-yard line headed for him and ran right over him. We said, 'What's going on with you?' and he said, 'Aw, you've got to sting 'em a little bit.'"

Taylor was all high knees and lowered shoulders, and Nitschke was impressed with the fullback's power and pistonlike leg drive. Nitschke said later that he hurt when he tried to tackle Taylor. To Nitschke, Taylor was a tiger, one of the toughest and most determined men he had ever encountered.

"Both of them went a hundred percent, all the time," Dillon said. "Taylor would just as soon run over somebody and Ray would just as soon hit you. That's what made them good ballplayers."

Nitschke's aggressiveness in camp turned off many of the Packers' veteran players, but it earned him the respect of the coaching staff. Prior to the last cut that summer, Nitschke approached McLean and said that if he was going to be released, could the coach let him know right away so he could try to catch on with another NFL team?

"Ray," McLean said, "we're going to keep you."

Nitschke was the fifth linebacker on a club that usually carried just four, but McLean liked what he had seen in camp. Nitschke was assigned to the special teams, the "suicide squads" of pro football. But when Bettis went down with an injury in the first exhibition game, Nitschke started the rest of the preseason and the season opener against the Bears. Nitschke's first official game in the NFL was played Sunday, September 28, before a sellout crowd of 32,150 in Green Bay's City Stadium. He played with a sense of wide-eyed wonder. In later years, he recalled the Bears' center Larry Strickland, "must have been six-foot-seven." Strickland, in reality, was 6-foot-4, but Nitschke's recollection indicates the awe that most rookies feel when playing their first league game in the NFL.

Chicago beat Green Bay, 34–20, and the loss proved to be a foreshadowing of the Packers' season. Green Bay tied with Detroit, 13–13, the following week, and lost to Baltimore and Washington before eking out a 38–35 win at home over Philadelphia. It was the Packers' first victory of the season—and their last. The team was young and inexperienced; against the Eagles, Green Bay frittered away most of its 38–7 lead before holding on for the win. McLean was too nice to discipline the veterans he had grown close to in his years as an assistant, and the players took advantage of their coach. The Packers followed their win over the Eagles with a humiliating 56–0 loss at Baltimore, and even an aggressive rookie like Nitschke saw no need for further optimism that season. Green Bay dropped its final seven games of the season to finish 1–10–1, and McLean was fired as head coach.

Nitschke was embarrassed by the Packers' season, and assessed his own performance with the same bottom-line approach. He had played aggressively, but his inexperience frequently left him out of position and he often ended up hitting the wrong people.

"Ray was a real active guy," said Dillon. "He was kind of wild, but he had a lot of ability. He liked to make tackles everywhere, and sometimes he was out of position."

Nitschke started the first four games of the regular season, and felt he made an immediate statement for his hard play in his debut game against the Bears. When Nitschke left the field that day, he hoped the Chicago veterans knew the name of the rookie playing middle linebacker.

Nitschke's final game as a starter came in Week Four against Washington. Redskins fullback Johnny Olszewski blasted his way to 156 yards rushing against the Packers, and Green Bay coaches blamed Nitschke for the 37–21 defeat. Nitschke wasn't so sure; he often found himself wrapping up Olszewski well beyond the line of scrimmage, indicating to him that the Packer front wasn't doing its job. Nitschke took the benching grudgingly and took out his frustrations the rest of the season as a kamikaze member of the suicide squad.

By season's end, the Packers were in shambles. "We had a terrible year," Dillon said. Center Jim Ringo thought the team was "a hellhole," and halfback Paul Hornung heard stories that coaches around the league were forever threatening their players with trades to Green Bay. "It was the Siberia of pro football," Hornung said.

Amid the team's turmoil, Nitschke felt he had played hard enough to look back with some pride on his rookie campaign. On December 28, he settled back along with millions of other nationwide viewers to watch NBC's telecast of the NFL championship game between the Baltimore Colts and New York Giants in historic Yankee Stadium. The game became an instant classic, and by the time it ended with Colt fullback Alan "The Horse" Ameche galloping into the gathering darkness of the end zone in overtime, Baltimore's 23–17 victory had stamped the NFL on the nation's collective consciousness.

Pro football was about to enter a new era, and so were the Packers. One month to the day after he had served as the Giants' offensive coordinator in the championship game, Vince Lombardi was named Green Bay's new general manager and head coach. Nitschke's response to the hiring mirrored that of many others.

"Who the hell," he thought, "is Vince Lombardi?"

When Lombardi accepted the Packers' job, one of the first things he did was contact long-time friend Ed Breslin. Knowing Lombardi had grown tired of being an assistant coach and longed to be in charge of his own team, Breslin told him, "It's what you've always wanted."

"Yeah," Lombardi remarked, "and the first thing I'm gonna do out there is build a defense."

For much of his football life, Lombardi had concerned himself with the offensive side of the game. As a senior on the 1932 St. Francis Academy team in Brooklyn, he played halfback on offense and was a two-way guard. Though small by today's standards at 168 pounds, Lombardi was squat and powerfully built, particularly in the upper body. His hard hits earned the respect of teammates who had sought to test him—"This guinea (hits) like the Fifth Avenue El," one stunned teammate remarked—and Lombardi's no-frills, no-nonsense play as a two-way guard helped St. Francis finish the season with one of the best records among New York's private schools. The lone loss in their six-game schedule came in the season opener, when Lombardi and Co. were outdueled by Erasmus High School and its sensational sophomore quarterback, Sid Luckman. Luckman later went on to star for Columbia University and became a Hall of Fame quarterback for the Chicago Bears.

With the help of Dan Kern, a 24-year-old Fordham University graduate who tutored Vince in Greek, Lombardi gained a football scholarship to Fordham, at the time the largest Catholic university in the country. He became a member of the famous "Seven Blocks of Granite" line and was coached by a staff that included head coach Jim Crowley and line coach

Frank Leahy. Both Crowley and Leahy were protégés of Notre Dame legend Knute Rockne. Crowley was one of Rockne's "Four Horsemen" and Leahy later became one of the most successful coaches in Fighting Irish history. After graduating in June 1937, Lombardi played guard for several semipro teams, including a Wilmington, Delaware, squad that met NFL teams like the New York Giants and Washington Redskins in exhibition games. He later became head coach at St. Cecilia High School in Englewood, New Jersey, winning 32 straight games with the brutal single-wing power plays made famous by Jock Sutherland at the University of Pittsburgh. Lombardi's education in offensive football continued when he became an assistant at West Point, learning the innovative passing game as taught by Army assistant Sid Gillman, whom Lombardi replaced in 1949, and overall team preparation from head coach Earl "Red" Blaik.

Lombardi left West Point in 1954 to become offensive coordinator of the New York Giants. In his five-year stay in New York, he helped coach the Giants to two Eastern Conference titles and one NFL championship. His first season as offensive coordinator saw New York improve its record from 3–9 to 7–5 and their point production from 179 points to 293. In 1956, the Giants won the Eastern Conference with an 8–3–1 record, and Lombardi's offensive game plan helped New York romp past Chicago in the NFL championship game. Two years later, in Lombardi's final season with the team, New York beat Cleveland in a playoff game to decide the Eastern Conference, then dropped a 23–17 decision to Baltimore in the overtime classic.

Because he had spent the majority of his career on the offensive side of the ball, Lombardi didn't understand the techniques, the steps and drops, of defensive football. In 1957, he had spent a long afternoon on the sidelines watching a San Francisco defense coached by coordinator John Phillip (Phil) Bengston frustrate his offense in a 27–17 defeat. The date—Sunday, December 1—is significant because it is generally regarded as the birthday of the blitz. The memory of 49er linebackers Karl Rubke, Matt Hazeltine, and Marv Matuszak swooping in on New York quarterback Charlie Conerly and forcing five fumbles remained prominent with Lombardi, and when he was named head coach and general manager of the Packers, the first assistant he hired was Bengston.

A tall, chain-smoking Swede, Bengston became the ice to Lombardi's fire. He had begun his coaching career in the 1930s at Missouri under Don Faurot, the father of the Split-T offense. In the forties, Bengston coached at Stanford under Clark Shaughnessy, who had introduced the Man-in-Motion-T. Bengston broke into the NFL in 1951, when 49ers coach Buck Shaw named him San Francisco's new line coach. Shaw was fired following the '54 season, and Bengston then worked under Red Strader for one season and Frankie Albert for two. When Albert quit coaching at the end of the '57 season, the 49ers named Howard "Red" Hickey his successor. Hickey and Bengston were cordial to one another, but there was little chemistry between the two men. The day after Hickey was named head coach, Bengston walked into Hickey's office, congratulated him, and following an awkward moment of forced smiles, said what both men were thinking.

"It isn't there," Bengston said. "It just won't work."

By the time the 49ers announced later that day that Bengston would not be back with the club, he had already cleared out his desk and was heading home to Minnesota, his coat pocket stuffed with a list of NFL teams who might be in the market for coaches.

Bengston contacted the Packers about their head coaching vacancy and was assured by club president Dominic Olejniczak that he would be seriously considered for the position. When the Packers named Lombardi their new head coach and general manager, Bengston phoned Vince. Lombardi wasn't in, so Bengston left a message. Shortly thereafter, Bengston's wife, Kathryn, took a call, and handed the phone to her husband. On the other end of the line was the former Giants' assistant coach, whose voice was tinged with an unmistakable New York accent.

"How *ah* you, Phil? This is Vince *Lombahdi*."

Lombardi told Bengston he was putting together a new coaching staff in Green Bay and needed someone with experience to handle the defense.

"We're going to start from the bottom up and build a winning team here," Lombardi said. "If you're interested, why don't you come out to Green Bay for an interview?"

When Bengston joined the Packers, he was 45 years old, the same age as Lombardi, and had the reputation as a "career assistant." His long tenure in San Francisco and thinning black hair earned him the nickname "Old Dad." Bengston and Lombardi shared some similarities—both were Catholic, both had been successful assistants in the NFL, both were students of the game who demanded excellence from their players. But it was their differences that made them such a dynamic coaching duo. Lombardi's interest lay in coaching offense; Bengston's in defense. Lombardi was passionate, Bengston calculating. Lombardi was volcanic, Bengston placid as a mountain lake.

As a tactician and defensive strategist, Bengston has never received his full due from NFL historians. Mostly, he's remembered as the man who replaced Lombardi as head coach in Green Bay and presided over the fall of the Packer dynasty. It's an unfair legacy, since Bengston was inheriting an aging team wrung dry by years of Lombardi's emotional coaching style and pressure-packed games. In many ways, Bengston's situation in taking over the '68 Packers resembled that of Ray Handley in taking over the '91 Giants from Bill Parcells. Like U.N. troops at the Yalu River, they were tired veterans trying to hold off fresh attackers with depleted forces.

Bengston was not only Lombardi's chief lieutenant during the Green Bay glory years; he was chiefly responsible for fielding a unit that ranks among the greatest in history and has sent five of its members to the Pro Football Hall of Fame. In 1967, when the Packers won an unprecedented third straight title and second straight Super Bowl, nine of the eleven members of the unit Bengston put on the field had been named all-pro in their career.

During his stay in New York, Lombardi had worked side by side with Tom Landry, a quiet, intellectual Texan whose work with the Giants defense led many to consider him the leading defensive strategist in the game. A former defensive back and assistant coach with the Giants in the early fifties under Owen, Landry had fine-tuned his coach's Umbrella scheme and come up with the modern four-three. For five years in New York, Lombardi's offensive unit scrimmaged Landry's defense in Giant practices, and Lombardi watched the four-three in action on a daily basis.

When Lombardi left for Green Bay, he took his working knowledge of Landry's defense with him and implemented it as the base defense for the Packers. A symbolic seed had been taken from New York to Green Bay, and when Bengston was hired as defensive coordinator, he immediately refined Landry's version of the four-three to his own personality. Bengston taught his cornerbacks to play seven yards off the ball, backpedaling at the snap in a concept he called the "Fisherman Theory"—like patient fishermen, Green Bay corners had to wait until the precise moment to break on the ball and make their catch. The Packers also employed what Bengston called the "Victory" formation, a zone pass-coverage scheme employed in end-game situations.

When Bengston studied film of the Green Bay defense throughout the winter of '59, he found the Packers to be a collection of talented but tentative players. Because they had been burned by big plays for so many years, Green Bay defenders developed a safe, cautious approach. They were defensive in every sense of the word, Bengston said, the Switzerland of pro football defenses.

The challenge, as Bengston saw it, was to change the Packers' approach on defense from conservative to aggressive. Bengston had coached an attacking defense in San Francisco, and he planned to instill in his Packer players the belief that a modern defense must have an aggressive mindset. Defenses were equipped with their own formations, plays, and strategies. They could score points, win games, and ultimately win championships. Most importantly, Bengston thought, a successful defense must have a morale of its own, must have its own leader, its own goal, and its own reward.

Bengston's philosophy of an attacking defense fueled by an aggressive leader blended seamlessly with Lombardi's vision of the four-three. In New York, Landry's unit had been geared to Huff, and both Lombardi and Bengston believed that for the Packer defense to be as successful as the Giants' unit, Green Bay would need a dominant middle linebacker in the mold of Huff.

"When Lombardi left, he took the New York Giants' defensive playbook to Green Bay," Huff remembered. "In later years, Ray and I could talk the same language because we played the same position. In the four-three, your middle linebacker will be your leading tackler, and he should be because you're playing both sides of the field and in the middle. So you don't want to put a guy in there that doesn't like to tackle. And Ray was a hitter."

The Packers' new philosophy fit Nitschke perfectly. He had watched Green Bay's collapse the previous season. The team had a loser's complex, and Nitschke felt that some of the players lacked that extra spark. He believed the Packers lost late-game leads because they didn't believe they were good enough to win. Even though he was a rookie, Nitschke's assessment was an accurate one. Fellow linebacker Dan Currie later remarked that players hadn't expected to win in '58, and that it was understood that even when they tried their best they would most likely lose. The main objective, Currie said, was just to keep the game close.

Lombardi's staff, which studied more than 20,000 feet of film of the Packers and their opponents that first winter, recognized Green Bay's defeatist attitude and realized it was an outlook they needed to change when they met with their players for the first time in the training complex at St. Norbert College.

"Gentlemen," Lombardi began, "I have never been associated with a losing team and I don't intend to start now." Speaking in a deep, rough voice that halfback Paul Hornung thought sounded like authority itself and that sent chills up and down the spine of linebacker Bill Forester, Lombardi told his team they were going to start winning because they would outwork, outexecute, outblock, and outtackle every team on their schedule. Lombardi spoke at length about the need for professionalism, pride, and paying the price to win.

"I'm going to find thirty-six men who have the pride to make any sacrifice to win," he said. "If you are not one, if you don't want to play, then get the hell out."

The speech fired up his players. Forester felt ready to run outside and scrimmage without pads. Tackle Bob Skoronski said later he thought Lombardi's emphasis on professionalism had more to do with making Green Bay champions than anything Vince did from a coaching standpoint. Lombardi later confided to split end Max McGee that he had been "nervous as hell" about delivering that speech. He was worried, Lombardi said, that he would return the next day and find only a couple of players still in camp. Issuing his trademark alligator smile, Lombardi told McGee he was relieved to find that the entire team hadn't left him.

Nitschke was in the army during training camp, and didn't catch up with his new coach until the Packers' exhibition game against the Washington Redskins in Greensboro, North Carolina. Ray's reputation, however, did precede him, and when he arrived, Green Bay equipment manager Dad Braisher pulled him aside.

"Watch yourself, Ray," Braisher told him. "Don't do anything you're not supposed to be doing. This Lombardi is really tough."

After spending six months in the army, Nitschke wondered how much tougher Lombardi's camp could be than what he had just been through. He was quickly filled in by the other players. Players had been vomiting on the practice field the first couple of days, and the squad as a whole lost an average of 12 pounds per man. On the first day of practice, Lombardi took one look at Bettis and defensive tackle Dave Hanner and told them to lose 20 pounds in two weeks or "get the hell out of camp."

Bettis made weight, a fact that Ray realized later kept him from possibly becoming a starter earlier than he eventually did. Six weeks of army conditions had kept Nitschke in shape, but the second-year pro soon realized that while he may have been in shape by U.S. military standards, he was not in shape by Lombardi standards. To compensate, Nitschke drove himself physically and mentally. "You pushed yourself as hard as you could," he said, "and then you had Lombardi pushing you that much more."

Nitschke remained second-string behind Bettis and was confined largely to the special teams. Because he had missed the opening days of training camp due to army duty, Nitschke felt like he had not had a full opportunity to show Lombardi and Bengston what he could do on the field. All they had to go on, Nitschke thought, were films of Green Bay's games from the previous season, films showing Nitschke as an active, if overaggressive, rookie.

"The guy was so fast and so smart, but he was so eager he made a lot of mistakes," Dillon said. "He'd leave his position of where he was supposed to be and that would hurt the team sometimes."

The Packers opened their 1959 regular season on Sunday, September 27, against the Chicago Bears in Green Bay. A crowd of 32,150 filled City Stadium on a gray, wet afternoon. Lombardi had bolstered the Packers with a number of off-season signings and trades. He drafted Colorado quarterback Boyd Dowler and converted him into a flanker; the rookie went on to lead the team in receptions that season with 32. Lombardi dealt Billy Howton—an all-pro end and Green Bay's second-leading receiver the season before—to Cleveland in exchange for defensive end Bill Quinlan and defensive tackle Henry Jordan. In retrospect the deal was a steal for the Packers. Howton led the Browns in receptions that season but was out of football following the '63 season. Quinlan and Jordan went on to anchor the right side of the Packer defense through the early years of their dynasty, and Jordan has since become a Hall of Famer. Lombardi furthered shored up the defense by acquiring another future Hall of Famer, safety Emlen Tunnell from the Giants, and picked up offensive guard Fred "Fuzzy" Thurston in a trade with Baltimore coach Weeb Ewbank.

Trailing the Bears 6–0 midway through the fourth quarter, the Packers rallied to score nine points in the final seven minutes. Slogging through the mud, Taylor followed pulling guards Thurston and Jerry Kramer on a sweep left from five yards out to give Green Bay a 7–6 lead, and Jordan and Nate Borden combined to trap Bear quarterback Ed Brown deep in the end zone for a safety. Nitschke played a role in clinching the victory. On Chicago's free kick following the safety, the Bears kicked it short hoping to recover the ball, but Nitschke fell on it, securing the win as Green Bay ran out the clock.

For a team that had made a habit of losing close games and hadn't beaten the arch-rival Bears since 1957, the dramatic victory was cause for celebration. Lombardi was swept off the field on the shoulders of his players, and the *Green Bay Press-Gazette* lauded the first victory of the new regime with a headline that read "Gutty!" In his game-day story, Art Daley of the *Press-Gazette* wrote that the Packers' performance showed much promise for the future.

"This was more than just a triumph over Green Bay's archrival," Daley wrote. "It was the beginning of the new and fiery regime headed by thunderous Vince Lombardi, who was carried off the water-logged field by the joyous Bays after the game."

The Packers followed with wins over Western Conference foes Detroit and San Francisco. After three weeks of the regular season, Green Bay was giddy over a team that sat alone atop the conference standings. Reality resurfaced, however, in the form of a five-game winless streak. With a losing season staring him in the face, Lombardi switched quarterbacks, benching starter Lamar McHan and replacing him with backup Bart Starr. The move may have smacked of desperation at the time, but it was a master stroke. Green Bay swept to victory in its final four games, finishing with a 7–5 record to tie for third place in the conference.

Though the team celebrated its first winning season since 1947, Nitschke didn't see much room for joy. He had received little meaningful playing time and felt it was Lombardi, rather than Bengston, who wasn't giving him an opportunity to show what he could do. Game after game, Nitschke would sit on the bench, hoping the Packers would get so far ahead the coaches would be forced to put him in just to give Bettis a rest and prevent an unnecessary injury. Week ten, however, demonstrated to Nitschke just how little the coaching staff thought of him.

Leading Washington 21–0 in the fourth quarter, Nitschke waited for the call to get in the game. With time running out, he approached Bengston on the sideline and asked to be put in the game. Bengston shook his head.

"No," Bengston said. "We want the shutout."

As he sat on the sideline, Nitschke tried to see his benching as a learning experience. He watched how Bettis and opposing middle linebackers—Chicago's Bill George, Detroit's Joe Schmidt—played the position. Other times, however, Nitschke sulked. At the end of the '59 season, Lombardi and Nitschke were clearly at odds, and the 1960 season would see the second-year middle linebacker on the verge of being traded away from Green Bay.

FOUR

TO VINCE LOMBARDI, Ray Nitschke was the rowdy of the Green Bay Packers; big, rough and belligerent, with a love of contact.

"He has the proper temperament for a middle linebacker," Lombardi explained in his 1963 book *Run to Daylight*, "but maybe too much of it."

Lombardi acknowledged at the time that Nitschke had been "a problem to coach." The problems lay in Nitschke's behavior on and off the field. Still seething inside at the loss of his mother, Nitschke remained an undisciplined loner. His constant mistakes on the practice field infuriated Lombardi, who demanded perfection at all times. "Everyone makes mistakes," Lombardi would tell his players, "but not too many if you want to remain a Green Bay Packer."

"Great players have that instinct, you can call it a nose for the ball, and Ray had it," flanker Boyd Dowler recalled. "I used to laugh because he'd say 'I have a hunch, I have a hunch,' but then he'd run the wrong way, off on his own. He'd be extra aggressive because he wanted to show he should be out there playing. But it took him awhile to break into the starting lineup."

To defensive end Willie Davis, Nitschke's mistakes on the field were compounded by his problems away from the game.

"He was a guy who couldn't handle his alcohol and would get into trouble and barroom fights," Davis remembered. "He was frustrated those first couple of years until he really got his game underway. He was a guy with a pretty quick temper, and somebody would look at him and he'd be ready to punch him out. Some guys shouldn't drink because they can't handle the booze, and Ray was one of those guys.

"I think there was a point where Lombardi was ready to give up on Ray, because Ray had a tendency to make mistakes, and Lombardi detested mistakes. Some of Ray's more embarrassing moments came when he decided to play one of his hunches. He would go chasing out after a play he thought the offense was going to run only to have it be a different play. In the films, you would see him trying to sneak back to his position."

Nitschke's wild, undisciplined ways led to his becoming one of the team's whipping boys. "He needs it," Lombardi said at the time, "and he can take it." The team's coaching staff struggled to find ways to reach their backup middle linebacker. Lombardi chewed him out and Nitschke took it. But he frustrated Lombardi by turning around and making the same mistake over again. Bengston offered a different approach, often throwing his arm around the shoulders of his defensive players as he issued quiet instructions. Of his four linebackers—Nitschke, Tom Bettis, Dan Currie, and Bill Forester—Bengston thought Nitschke promised to be the roughest and toughest of them all. He also told Lombardi that Nitschke might someday become the Packers' starting middle linebacker.

Lombardi had his doubts. He could see Nitschke was talented, but the Packer boss questioned his young linebacker's motivation. "Vince was incredibly intense and driven," guard Jerry Kramer said. "He'd chew your ass out for anything. And he and Raymond had some exchanges. But I think Coach saw in Raymond the same thing he saw in me, an ability we weren't using. We were comfortable in having made the team, and Vince could see that."

Nitschke's seeming comfort masked what he later described as an inner turbulence. He was still drinking, and it would take just a couple of shots of whiskey for him to become loud and obnoxious. He would sit by himself at a bar, toss back a few drinks, and then, as he once recalled, "say the wrong things to the wrong people." Before long, Nitschke would be breaking up the furniture and brawling with patrons. Lombardi feared for Nitschke's future, feared getting a phone call some day from the police.

"I remember in the beginning, Ray didn't have a whole lot of discipline," Vince Lombardi Jr. said. "He had all the tools but it took awhile for my father's message to sink in, to make sense to Ray. But you could see he had a lot of passion."

Nitschke entered the 1960 season as the Packers' fourth linebacker. For the first time since arriving in Green Bay, he had decided to stay in town during the off-season and not return to Chicago. While many of his teammates caught the first plane out of town following their return home from a season-ending win December 13 in San Francisco, Nitschke stayed in town. He still considered himself a big-city guy, but other than his older brothers he felt there was nothing for him to return home to. As long as he was making his living in Green Bay, he reasoned, he might as well remain there. With its close proximity to his home in Illinois, and with its family-oriented, small-town feel, Green Bay was beginning to grow on the former Chicago street tough. "It was a pleasant area," he said, "nice people, the whole bit."

He still wasn't happy about his lack of playing time under Lombardi, but he respected his coach as a man and as a leader of men. Upon his arrival in Green Bay, Lombardi had broken up the cliques that had developed under Scooter McLean and done away with the players who had caused internal problems. The result, Nitschke thought, was a healthy atmosphere where no one on the team was satisfied with playing close games, as they had been the year before, but were concerned only with winning.

Kramer said the team's attitude prior to Lombardi's arrival was that if they won, fine. If they didn't, well, there were more important things to do after the game.

"We were just a group of guys who had a horseshit season and didn't know how to win," Kramer said. "But when you look back, so many of the guys who would have greatness thrust on them were already on the team—Jimmy Taylor, Paul Hornung, Jim Ringo, Forrest Gregg. And then along came Vince."

Lombardi defeated the Packers' losing attitude by instilling in his players the belief that in his life they ranked only behind God and family. His players became his extended family, "my boys" as he called them, and they bought into his beliefs of self-sacrifice and teamwork. Split end Max McGee played many games where he may not have had even one catch, or even had a pass thrown his way, but if he had thrown a good block for Taylor or Hornung and the Packers had won the game, McGee was happy.

Nitschke, the loner, welcomed the feeling of family that Lombardi brought to the locker room. Defensive tackle Henry Jordan may have joked that Lombardi treated everyone on the team the same—"like dogs," Jordan said—but Nitschke saw it as the truth. Lombardi, he said, didn't care about his players' race, religion. or political beliefs. America was on the cusp of the socially conscious sixties, and still in the distance were the struggle for civil rights; freedom marches in Selma and Montgomery, Alabama; the Watts riots; and uprisings in Detroit and Newark, New Jersey.

When Lombardi was hired in Green Bay, the Packers had just one black player on the team, defensive end Nate Borden. Emlen Tunnell, an African-American athlete who had forged a Hall of Fame career with the New York Giants and was brought to Green Bay by Lombardi in 1959, said Borden was staying in a rental room so dirty and run-down that Tunnell said he wouldn't have kept his dog there.

"Vinnie changed all that," Tunnell said later. "He gave the people who were renting the room to Nate hell and then moved him into a decent place."

In his first meeting on the field with his team, Lombardi laid down the law about race relations within the team. "If I ever hear 'nigger' or 'dago' or 'kike' or anything like that around here," he said strongly, "regardless of who you are, you're through with me. You can't play for me if you have any prejudice."

Sportswriter Jimmy Cannon thought Lombardi in his own way was a great social scientist. "His dignity and grace in racial matters was almost totally neglected," Cannon wrote. "He made black and white people some neutral color."

At a time when NFL teams had quotas for the number of black players they would have on their rosters—the Redskins' quota, for instance, was two, the Giants' was six—Lombardi proved progressive in drafting and trading for African-American athletes. Before the start of the 1959 season, Lombardi acquired Tunnell from the Giants and defensive end Willie Davis from Cleveland. Davis, who later became defensive captain of the Packers and a Hall of Fame defensive end, joined defensive end Bill Quinlan and tackle Henry Jordan as three outstanding players Lombardi acquired from Cleveland Browns head coach Paul Brown. It was later suggested by some that Brown had helped Lombardi build the Packers into a contender because he felt an obligation to see Vince succeed after talking him up so much to Green Bay's search committee back in January 1959. When Jerry Atkinson, who was an executive committee member, contacted Brown for a reference on Lombardi, the Cleveland coach was effusive in his praise.

"Lombardi is a great football tactician and he is also a scrapper," Brown told Atkinson. "He'll get the most out of his men. He won't let anybody dog him."

Atkinson told the Cleveland coach the Packers were looking to hire "a Paul Brown of Green Bay." Would Brown, Atkinson asked, work closely with Lombardi and assist in setting up the new regime? Brown said he would, and in the next two seasons, delivered to Green Bay three members of the defensive line that would start for Green Bay in the 1960, '61, and '62 NFL championship games, as well as return specialist Lew Carpenter.

Said Atkinson, "I'll never forget what Paul Brown did for us, for Green Bay."

The presence of Davis at defensive end, free agent Willie Wood at free safety, and rookie Tom Moore, the team's top draft choice, as a backup halfback helped give Green Bay a new look at the start of the 1960 season. To Nitschke, however, there was little difference between the '59 and '60 campaigns. Through the Packers' six exhibition games, all of them victories, Nitschke was still confined largely to the special teams. He had come to camp prepared to take the starting job from Bettis, but the biggest impression he made early on occurred during a September practice. It was a humid day, and the skies over the two practice fields on Oneida Avenue grew dark with the threat of an approaching storm. Because it was so hot, Lombardi told his players they could take off their helmets and shoulder pads. The players put their equipment on the ground near a 25-foot steel structure that stood between the fields. It was regarded as a photographer's tower, but the Packers believed it had been built to allow Lombardi to occasionally watch practice from above and yell down at them.

As dark clouds rolled in from the west, a gusty wind carried in the first drops of rain. Nitschke hustled back to the base of the steel tower where he had put his equipment, and began putting his pads on to protect them from getting wet. He put his helmet on too, and the instant he pulled the hard plastic shell down over his head, a strong gust of wind caught the tower and tipped it over. A thousand pounds of steel scaffolding collapsed on top of Nitschke, sending him sprawling to the ground. A steel bolt drove through his yellow-gold helmet, four inches above his left temple. NFL helmets in 1960 were constructed of plastic with a web suspension that provided an inch of space between the top of the helmet and head. The bolt that punched through Nitschke's helmet stopped just short of his skull. "I put my helmet on to protect this," Nitschke said later, pointing to his bald head. "If I hadn't, I might have spent the rest of the season in the cemetery."

When the scaffolding collapsed, Lombardi and the players went running to the site, unsure of who was beneath it.

"Who's that guy on the ground?" Lombardi yelled.

As the players dug the mystery man out from beneath the pile of steel rubble, quarterback Bart Starr shouted, "It's Nitschke."

Lombardi looked relieved.

"Nitschke? He's all right. Everybody back to practice."

After seven weeks of the regular season, Nitschke was still playing second-string, still running down punts and kickoffs. Nitschke's playing time had increased during that time, and the Green Bay press, taking note of Bengston's four-linebacker rotation, dubbed them the "Fearsome Foursome," predating the popularized use of the term to describe the Los Angeles Rams front four of the late 1960s.

Nitschke continued to learn from Bettis, whom he considered his best friend on the team, and continued to study other linebackers from the sidelines to pick up playing tips. Nitschke's aggressiveness and toughness impressed Bengston and Lombardi, and when Green Bay dropped a 33-31 decision to the visiting Rams in Week Eight, Packer coaches decided a change was in order.

The next game on Green Bay's schedule was the annual Thanksgiving Day meeting in Detroit against the Lions. The Packers were locked in a four-game race for the Western Conference title with defending champion Baltimore, Detroit, and San Francisco, and the Green Bay defense was showing signs of weakening, having given up 33 or more points in two of its last three games. At practice during the short week before the Thursday game, Lombardi pulled Nitschke aside and told him the middle linebacking job was his.

"Go out there and do the best job you possibly can," Lombardi told him. "We're going to sink or swim with you."

Kramer said Lombardi's short conversation with Nitschke was a turning point for Ray professionally. "Now he had a goal," Kramer said, "and he went from a guy who was happy to be a part of the team to wanting to be a great linebacker."

Nitschke heard later that part of the reason for his being promoted was a locker room flare-up between Lombardi and Bettis. Davis, however, recalled another reason why Nitschke was given the starting job at middle linebacker. Opposing quarterbacks, Davis said, were taking advantage of the 6-foot-2 Bettis by completing passes over the middle just beyond the reach of his outstretched fingers. At 6-foot-3 and 235 pounds, Nitschke was an inch taller and 10 pounds heavier than Bettis, and with his long arms and huge hands, presented a larger obstacle in the middle for quarterbacks to contend with.

Nitschke's first start since being benched following the loss to Washington in 1958 didn't signal an immediate turnaround for the Packer defense. Detroit defeated Green Bay 23–10, but the Packers responded the following week by beating Chicago, 41–13. Heading to San Francisco for their third straight road game, Nitschke spent a frustrating Saturday afternoon trying to chase down 49ers halfback Hugh McElhenny in muddy Kezar Stadium. A future Hall of Famer, McElhenny was dubbed "The King" by 49ers quarterback Frankie Albert, who called McElhenny "the king of all runners." An open-field artist who slashed from sideline to sideline with sudden bursts of speed and an assortment of swivel-hip fakes and sidesteps, McElhenny often ran forty yards to gain five. NFL commissioner Pete Rozelle once called him the most exciting runner he had ever seen, and McElhenny left a lasting impression on the young Nitschke. "He was something to behold," Nitschke said later.

Despite McElhenny's success eluding Nitschke, the Packer defense still managed to shut out San Francisco, 13–0. Green Bay's win, coupled with Baltimore's 10–3 loss in Los Angeles—the third straight defeat for the Colts—dropped the two-time defending NFL champions out of first place in the West and allowed the Packers to take a one-game lead with one game left.

The following week, the Packers flew to Los Angeles for the season finale against the Rams. A victory would give Green Bay the Western Conference title. The team was quartered in Santa Monica. Looking to unwind, Nitschke went alone to a restaurant across the street from the hotel and ordered a drink from the bar, violating a team rule. Prior to his arrival, several Packer players had gained reputations for their love of the nightlife; Hornung was called "Picadilly Paul" for his frequenting of a nearby nightspot. Knowing the reputation some of his players had among the citizens, Lombardi put out a strict order that first season prohibiting them from standing at public bars.

"I don't care if you're drinking ginger ale and talking to a friend," Lombardi told his team. "It just doesn't look good if a fan sees you in the place."

"Vince had a serious problem with that," flanker Boyd Dowler remembered. "We weren't supposed to be at the bar if we were in a supper club or a restaurant."

The alternative was for players to drink at a table or booth. Nitschke knew about the directive, but decided, as he later put it, to "take a chance." He was standing at the bar, drinking and minding his own business, when Lombardi, Bengston, and defensive backfield coach Norb Hecker suddenly strode in. Startled, Nitschke realized there was nothing he could do. As the three men walked toward him, Nitschke rasped, "Hi, Coach."

Lombardi said nothing, but as they walked past him, Nitschke could see the back of Lombardi's neck beginning to redden. When the coaches sat down at a nearby table, Lombardi grabbed a handful of peanuts from a bowl on the table and squeezed them so hard he shattered the shells.

A round of drinks was sent to their table—scotch, bourbon, and beer—and when Lombardi informed the waiter they had yet to order, he was told the drinks had been sent by a patron at the bar. Looking over, Lombardi saw Nitschke grinning back at him. The Packer boss seethed for a minute, then told Bengston and Hecker, "Let's get out of here."

As the three men walked by Nitschke at the bar, Lombardi, still looking straight ahead, shouted, "You're all done! You're through! Get out of town!"

Nitschke could tell by the tone of Lombardi's voice the coach meant what he said. His only hope was that Lombardi would calm down enough to change his mind. Nitschke had seen it happen before; Lombardi had once embarrassed Kramer on the practice field by calling him "a cow." Later that same day, Lombardi saw a despondent Kramer sitting by his locker stall. Throwing his arm around Kramer's slumped shoulder, Lombardi told him, "Son, some day you're going to be the greatest guard in the National Football League." The short pep talk immediately lifted Kramer's confidence, and he became, along with Fuzzy Thurston, one of the keys to Lombardi's lead play, the power sweep. Kramer was also arguably the greatest drive-blocking guard of the sixties, and his omission from the Pro Football Hall of Fame remains an ongoing mystery.

Lombardi, however, never wavered from his plan to trade Nitschke. Realizing the Packers were on the verge of clinching the Western Conference title and how important Nitschke could be to their defense, Bengston and Hecker tried to persuade Lombardi to keep him. Lombardi was unmoved. "Get rid of him," he replied. Eventually, Bengston convinced Lombardi of Nitschke's value to the team. Lombardi, however, was now in a situation where he had to back down without losing face. Shrewdly, he decided to leave Nitschke's fate in the hands of his teammates. Lombardi announced that if the Packer players voted to keep Nitschke on the team, he would go along with their wishes.

"Vince said, 'Well, it's not going to be my decision, it's your decision' and walked out of the room," Hornung recalled. "How were we going to vote him off the team? We would have to be crazy. So when Vince left the room I stood up and said, "Well, I think we ought to just vote him off the team.' I think Ray was about ready to choke me. He didn't think that was too funny."

The decision was a smart one on Lombardi's part, since he knew which way the team would vote. "We knew we had him then," Hecker said later. The next day, the Packers voted 39–0 to keep Nitschke.

"I think my father wanted to get rid of him to make an example out of him," Vince Jr. said. "It was probably the culmination of a lot of things that had built up, but cooler heads prevailed. Still, I think my father would probably have thought the better of it a day or two later and not traded him."

On the final Sunday of the regular season, Green Bay defeated Los Angeles, 35–21, in the Coliseum. The victory was the Packers' third straight, and allowed them to win the Western Conference with an 8–4 record, one game better than Detroit and San Francisco.

That night, 11,000 fans crowded Austin Straubel Airport and withstood 12-degree cold to welcome their champions home from the West Coast. The title was the Packers' first since 1944, and the *Press-Gazette* celebrated by publishing the newspaper's first "extra" edition in 21 years. It sold out within hours. Green Bay mayor Roman Denissen proclaimed the Packers' conference title to be "the most wonderful thing that has happened to Green Bay in a long time."

The 1960 NFL championship game was scheduled for Monday, December 26, in order to avoid conflicting with Christmas Day. That the

Packers were playing the Philadelphia Eagles offered a bit of irony for Lombardi. In January 1958, he had been offered the Eagles' head coaching job. Vince McNally, the Eagles general manager, met him at a Philadelphia train depot and offered a short-term contract with an option for an extension if the club performed well. Lombardi was excited about the opportunity to finally become an NFL head coach, excited about the opportunity to coach Eagles' quarterback Norm Van Brocklin.

"Every time I see that guy coming on the field," Lombardi said, "I start shivering."

When Lombardi took the Eagles' offer back to Giants' owner Wellington Mara, Mara talked him out of accepting the position. The Eagles, Mara said, were run by meddling stockholders who weren't going to yield control of the club. Mara told Lombardi that the short-term contract wasn't sufficient to rebuild the Eagles and that he might be fired before the job was completed. To further induce Lombardi to stay with the Giants, Mara raised Vince's salary and improved his insurance policy. There was also the understanding that once Giants' head coach Jim Lee Howell stepped down, Lombardi would be named his successor.

When Lombardi informed McNally of his decision to stay in New York, the Eagles hired Buck Shaw, Bengston's former head coach in San Francisco, to take over as the new boss in Philadelphia. Lombardi remained one more year with the Giants, then went to Green Bay. One year later, the paths of Lombardi, Bengston, and Shaw converged once more, this time in Franklin Field to decide the NFL championship.

Like the Packers, the Eagles' turnaround was a remarkable one. In 1958, they had finished 2–9–1 and tied for last in the Eastern Conference with the Chicago Cardinals. It was the second-worst record in the NFL outside of Green Bay's 1–10–1 finish, but the following season saw both the Eagles and Packers improve to 7–5. In 1960, Philadelphia dropped a 41–24 decision to Cleveland in the league opener in Franklin Field, but led by Van Brocklin and two-way star Chuck Bednarik, the Eagles went on a white-hot winning streak.

"We won nine games in a row," Hall of Fame flanker Tommy McDonald noted, "but we were behind at halftime in six of them. Nobody really picked us to finish near the top or anything like that. I would have to say that Cleveland and New York had better overall teams than we did. We were just an average team, but we always pulled the game out in the third and fourth quarters. And then we started a little saying, 'Okay, the third and fourth quarter is ours. It's the Eagles' time.'"

The Eagles clinched their first Eastern Conference title in 11 years with consecutive wins over the rival Giants, 17–10 at Yankee Stadium on November 20, and 31–23 in Franklin Field the following Sunday. The rivalry between the Eagles and Giants has long been one of the most intense in the league, and perhaps never more so than in 1960. Philadelphia had dominated the Eastern Conference at the end of the 1940s; New York at the close of the 1950s. Their mutual dislike dated back some three decades, and prompted Giants' team physician Dr. Francis Sweeny to state on one occasion that every time New York played Philadelphia, "we have to bring at least one of our players home through the window."

The reference was to the practice at the time to load injured players onto the team train via a stretcher through an open window. When the Eagles traveled to Yankee Stadium for their first meeting with the Giants in 1960 Philadelphia was challenging New York's two-year reign as conference champions. Six straight victories had lifted the Eagles into first place, and the Giants trailed by one-half game. A crowd of 63,571 jammed into Yankee Stadium and rocked the historic structure as the Giants jumped to leads of 7–0 and 10–7 before the Birds battled back to tie the game at 10 and then take a 17–10 lead late in the fourth quarter. With two-and-a-half minutes remaining, New York rallied. A Frank Gifford reception carried the Giants to the Eagles' 49-yard line, and Gifford followed by gathering in a pass at the Philadelphia 30. The Giants' flanker was still on his feet and looking for more yardage when defensive back Don Burroughs drilled Gifford low and Bednarik belted him high. The force of the double-blow resounded throughout the huge stadium and lifted Gifford off his feet, parallel to the ground. When he landed, his helmeted head slammed the hardened turf with a sickening impact. The ball squirted free from his limp hands, and Chuck Weber covered it for Philadelphia. Bednarik's tackle not only knocked Gifford out of football for the next two seasons, it virtually knocked the Giants out of contention for the conference title. Photographers rushed to get pictures of Bednarik exulting over the fumble recovery, but to New York fans it appeared the Eagles' linebacker was celebrating his knockout blow over the prone Gifford.

Bednarik in 1960 was the last of the 60-minute men, a two-way starter at center and linebacker. As the Eagles' center, the 35-year-old Bednarik would be matched against the 23-year-old Nitschke in the NFL championship game. Nitschke's youth and inexperience in big games symbolized the Packers' plight as they got ready for their first post-season game. For Lombardi, the NFL championship game was his third since 1956, but his first as a head coach. He drove his players and coaches hard that week, telling them, "we haven't got a thing really won yet until we win in Philadelphia." When assistant Red Cochran asked at a team meeting if the coaches could leave a little earlier than their scheduled departure of 9 P.M.—"maybe 8:30?" Cochran asked—in order to get in an hour of Christmas shopping, Lombardi exploded.

Pounding his fist on the table, he shouted, "Red, you wanna be Santa Claus or you wanna be a football coach? There's no room for both."

Lombardi followed his own dictum; he and his wife Marie didn't even put up a Christmas tree that week. He eased up on Christmas Eve, which the team spent in a Philadelphia hotel. Concerned about his players being away from their families, he arranged for presents to be brought to his suite, and the team gathered there to open their gifts.

As game day dawned in Philadelphia, the Packers remained tense. NBC had paid $200,000 to broadcast the game nationally, and as Nitschke ran onto the field for pregame warm-ups, his mood reflected that of his teammates. This was a big game not only for the players and coaches, Nitschke thought, but for the Packer organization, which hadn't been in an NFL title game since 1944. Nitschke knew Green Bay had outstanding players, but he also realized they were still a young team, a team he believed was just on the verge of becoming great.

Some of the Eagles shared Nitschke's sentiment. Van Brocklin could see the potential the young Packers had and knew as he looked at his own team that the Eagles' leaders were aging pros making their last stand. "If we're ever going to win the championship," the Dutchman told his teammates, "it better be today."

Bednarik saw the promise in the Packers as well. From watching films, he knew they were a strong team with a lot of physical talent. "And they executed even then," he remembered. "You could tell they had some kind of spark."

Still, the Eagles weren't convinced the spark came from Lombardi. Unlike future Packer opponents, Philadelphia didn't enter their championship game in awe of the Green Bay boss.

"Vince?" Bednarik asked. "In 1960 he was just another coach."

McDonald agreed. "I didn't realize how great Lombardi was going to be," he said.

Franklin Field sparkled amid a warm sun and unseasonably comfortable weather conditions as the two teams prepared for the kickoff. The sudden change in temperature favored Philadelphia; the field, which had been frozen for nearly two weeks, thawed and turned the stadium floor slick and muddy. The slippery bog slowed the Green Bay ground game, and a questionable decision early by Lombardi cost the Packers three points when he went for the first down on fourth-and-two from the Eagles' six-yard line. Taylor, betrayed by the slick footing, was stopped at the five, and Philadelphia took over.

Green Bay regained the ball on another turnover, Nitschke eluding Bednarik's block on a draw play and submarining halfback Ted Dean.

Nitschke's hard hit forced a fumble, and outside linebacker Bill Forester recovered for the Packers. Five plays later, Paul Hornung kicked a 20-yard field for a 3–0 lead. The Packers upped their advantage to 6–0 in the second quarter on a 23-yard field goal by Hornung, but Van Brocklin brought the Eagles back. From his own 43, the Eagles' quarterback found McDonald free on a slant for a 22-yard gain to the Green Bay 35. On the next play, Van Brocklin connected with McDonald again, this time down the right sideline, and the Eagles end carried it in for the score and a 7–6 lead. Bobby Walston's 15-yard field goal and a 13-yard miss by Hornung as time expired allowed Philadelphia to take a 10–6 lead into halftime.

"They dominated us statistically," Bednarik said, looking back. "But we hung in there."

Game films show Nitschke battling Bednarik throughout much of the afternoon. Since the Packers played a straight four-three alignment for much of the game, only on occasion sliding their tackles head-up over Bednarik, the Eagles' center usually had a direct path to the Packers' middle linebacker on running plays.

"It was strictly a defensive battle," Bednarik said, "and I know Nitschke did a helluva job out there."

Eagles receivers kept a constant eye out for the Packers' middle linebacker whenever they ran crossing patterns over the middle, a patch of turf McDonald referred to as "Nitschke territory."

"When you went across the middle on him, you better bring your lunch with you," McDonald said. "If he could hit you, he was going to hit you. In those days, there was no five-yard limit beyond the line of scrimmage. And if the ball was in the air, you better watch your head."

Green Bay's scheme defensively was to shut off the Eagles' passing game by pressuring Van Brocklin with an array of stunts and blitzes. At San Francisco, Bengston had developed the blitz in 1957 while preparing for Giants' quarterback Charlie Conerly. "I decided that if we were going to stop Conerly," Bengston said, "we'd have to do it in the pocket rather than at the receiving end."

Bengston devised the blitz, code-named it "Red Dog," and sent his linebackers pouring in on Conerly. The scheme caught Lombardi, then the Giants' offensive coordinator, by surprise, and Bengston revised the strategy to use against Van Brocklin in the '60 title game. Green Bay's defensive coordinator decided that if the Packers were to defeat the Eagles' passing game, they would have to defeat it at its source. That meant getting to the Dutchman. Films show Nitschke stunting and looping on several occasions, clawing his way past Eagles guards Stan Campbell and Gary Huth. Van Brocklin, however, continually beat the blitz by holding the ball to the last second, allowing his receivers that precious extra moment to run their patterns. From the Green Bay sideline, Starr watched in fascination as Van Brocklin made big play after big play despite pressure from the Packer defense. "I was really in awe of him that day," Starr said.

Green Bay gained a 13–10 lead in the fourth quarter when Starr, showing the same poise he admired in Van Brocklin, connected with McGee for a seven-yard score. But the Eagles responded on their next series. Dean returned the kickoff 58 yards to the Packers' 39 before Wood made a touchdown-saving tackle. A defensive holding penalty took the Eagles to the 32, and Dean and fullback Billy Barnes each gouged out six yards against the Green Bay defense. With the ball at the 20, Nitschke slowed the Eagles' drive when he sacked Van Brocklin for a loss of seven yards. It was a momentary setback only. The gritty Dutchman dropped back again, seemingly daring yet another Packer blitz, and hit Barnes for a 13-yard gain. Barnes and Dean alternated smashing into the Green Bay defense, Dean finally put the ball in the end zone when he skirted left end from five yards out for a 17–13 lead.

There was just under 10 minutes remaining when Green Bay got the ball back, but the Packers' drive was short-circuited when Bednarik jarred the ball loose from McGee at midfield and then recovered the fumble. Determined to run out the clock, the Eagles put together another march. But Nitschke, who had stopped an earlier Eagles' drive by dropping Walston with a shoulder tackle on a third-down slant pass, helped stuff Barnes on third-and-four.

The tackle forced an Eagles' punt, and the Packers took over on their own 35 with 1:10 left. Starr passed for two first downs, but had to use two time-outs in the process. With 17 second remaining, the Packers were on the Eagles' 22 with no time outs left. Dropping back to pass, Starr saw his primary receivers covered, then swung a pass to Taylor. The Packer back broke several tackles as he bulled inside the 10, where Bednarik, who had slid over from his left linebacker position, was waiting.

"He was coming right at me, running like hell," Bednarik said. "I knew I had to make the perfect tackle. . . . If he gets by me, he scores."

Fullback and linebacker collided at the eight, a clash of future Hall of Famers, and Bednarik wrestled Taylor to the dirt. Spitting mud from his mouth, Taylor was fighting to get up and run one more play. Bednarik, however, wasn't moving.

"Get off me, you son of a bitch," Taylor growled, but Bendarik remained in place, watching the final seconds tick off the stadium clock. When the clock hands got to zero—"Those big, beautiful zeroes," a grinning Bednarik said later—he released Taylor from his grasp.

"Okay, you son of a bitch, you can get up now," Bednarik said. "This damn game is over."

As the Packers trudged off the field, Bednarik caught up with Taylor and Hornung. He told the muddied Packer backs they had a helluva team, and that they'd be back in the title game. The words were of small consolation; some of the Packers wept openly in the dressing room. They had dominated the game statistically, owning huge advantages in first downs (22–13), total yardage (401–206) and plays from scrimmage (77–48). Unsure at first of what to tell his team, Lombardi called them together in the middle of the room.

"Perhaps you didn't realize you could have won this game," he said. "We're men and we will never let this happen again. We will never be defeated in a championship game again. Now, we can start preparing for next year."

Nitschke was stung by the defeat, stung more when he heard the comments emanating from the Eagles' victorious locker room. According to Nitschke, Van Brocklin told reporters that the Packers' middle linebacker had been out of position at times, allowing the Eagles to create big plays. Nitschke, who felt he had prepared himself to play the game as well as he could at that stage of his career, believed he was getting blamed for the loss. Nitschke knew his aggressiveness had caused him to make mistakes during the game, but felt he had played as well as he could against a more experienced team.

In the days that followed, Lombardi, perhaps seeking to shield his players from too much blame, acknowledged he had made some coaching errors in the game. Of the decision to go for a first down rather a field goal early in the game, Lombardi told reporters, "I made the wrong guess."

Nitschke appreciated his coach's public stance and adopted the attitude that whenever the Packers again played a big game, he would play as if he had something to prove. He would prove, Nitschke said, that the loss to the Eagles was not his fault.

Pocketing the loser's share of the title game money, which in 1960 was $3,105.14, Nitschke returned home to Chicago for the off-season. Teaming up with Robert and Richard, the Nitschke brothers celebrated Ray's homecoming. The brothers never looked for trouble, Robert said later, "but a lot of guys in Chicago and the suburbs wished they'd never seen us."

The three drank and brawled together; if one got into a fight the other two quickly joined in. Unsuspecting street toughs soon realized that if they got into a fight with one brother, they soon had what Ray later called "eight hundred pounds of Nitschkes" on their hands.

The Nitschke brothers didn't always come out on top. Hornung remembered a time when the brothers were drinking and popping off around members of the Packers team. It was a mistake. Defensive end Bill Quinlan and linebacker Dan Currie, tough guys in their own right, carried the argument outside.

"Quinlan and Currie beat the shit out of them," Hornung recalled. "The Nitschke brothers didn't get the best of that one."

Ray's attitude at the time reflected his lifestyle. He didn't care what anybody thought of him; he had no real purpose in his life other than to have three square meals a day, a place to sleep, and a chance to tackle the guy running with the football on autumn Sundays.

Nitschke didn't know it, but his outlook on life was about to undergo a dramatic change.

FIVE

THROUGH the first 25 years of his life, Ray Nitschke's life had been influenced most heavily by the untimely deaths of first his father and then his mother. Everything that he was as the new year of 1961 dawned stemmed from his past. By his own admission, Nitschke was undisciplined, selfish, adolescent, and lacking confidence. He was plagued by serious personal problems, all of which had turned him into a loner who seethed with anger at what he believed was a "dirty trick" that life had played on him.

Nitschke's private frustrations led to public outbursts, and his reputation made him an unsavory character in Green Bay. He was considered by some a rowdy, a bully, someone people wanted to stay away from once he began drinking. People who knew Nitschke realized that even one drink could alter his personality and behavior; before long he would grow loud and obnoxious, and on occasion, vulgar. By 1961, Nitschke's reputation preceded him whenever he strolled into Green Bay bars and restaurants; some patrons would get up and leave at the sight of him coming through the front doors.

"I used to worry I might have bad breath," Nitschke said later, explaining the rush to the exit doors whenever he entered a Green Bay bar.

"He was crazy as hell," said Emlen Tunnell, who played safety for the Packers from 1959 to 1961. Chuck Lane, who served as the Packers' director of publicity in the 1960s, said over the course of an evening, when Nitschke was slightly over-served, he would start pitching folks through the windows of saloons and breaking bar stools over people's heads.

"He did a lot of things," Lane said, "that tended to discourage business."

Mike Manuche, a New York restaurant owner who was friends with Green Bay head coach Vince Lombardi, felt Nitschke's troubles were due in part because he had trouble expressing himself. "He would become violent and tear everything apart," Manuche said.

Green Bay halfback Paul Hornung thought Nitschke was headed for serious trouble. "He had a bad act early on," Hornung recalled. "We all stayed away from him because he was a pain in the ass."

Green Bay flanker Boyd Dowler knew about Nitschke's past, knew he had a rough upbringing in Chicago. "He was kind of a wild kid," Dowler said. "He was aggressive and outgoing, and he could get irritated and upset. And there were times early in his career when he'd be out roaming the streets. If he had kept drinking the way he was, it probably would have developed into a problem and it could have caused him serious trouble."

Because of his reputation, Nitschke found it difficult getting to know a waitress he had taken notice of in a Green Bay restaurant. The waitress was Jackie Forchette, a farm girl from Ewen, Michigan. One of seven children, Jackie was a middle child with two brothers and four sisters. Her father was a woodworker, and after moving briefly to California following her high school years, she returned home to be close to her ailing father. Ewen sits some 40 miles from the west end of the Upper Peninsula, and some 200 miles from Green Bay. Like most of Green Bay's citizenry, Jackie had heard about Nitschke, and she wasn't interested in meeting him.

She had grown up a practicing Catholic, and her first marriage had ended when her husband left her in New Mexico. After moving to Green Bay, she began dating again and was seeing someone when Ray first took an interest in her.

"At first, my mom didn't want to have anything to do with my dad when he started pursuing her," said Amy Klaas, the youngest of the couple's three children. "She had heard of him, she had heard of the way he had acted, and she didn't want to be associated with that kind of behavior and that kind of drinking. That's basically what it came down to."

Despite Jackie's lack of interest, Nitschke still pursued her. The first time he had seen Jackie, he had fallen for her. She was strikingly pretty, dark-haired with a pleasant smile and pleasing manner. One night, while Jackie was at a restaurant with her date, Ray walked in and sat down at the couple's table.

"So," Nitschke said to the man, "why don't you tell Jackie about your wife and kids?"

As the man sat there stunned, Nitschke told him, "Pay the bill on your way out."

"My dad had done some research on this guy and found out he was married and had some kids, and she didn't know anything about that," Amy said. "My dad stayed and had dinner with her, and the rest, as they say, is history. I guess she figured then that this guy isn't so bad."

By 1960, Jackie and her brother, Bruce, had taken an apartment in Green Bay. After Ray dropped Jackie off on the night of their first date, Bruce was in the apartment when he heard someone pounding on the front door.

"Who is it?" he called.

"It's Nitschke."

"Well, whaddya want?

"Your sister's got my car keys."

Bruce had yet to meet his sister's date face-to-face, and after he answered Nitschke in a way that was unsympathetic to his plight, he was shocked to see the size of the man outside his door. "He could have torn me up like nothing," Bruce recalled.

Other members of Jackie's family were not so easily impressed. When she took Ray home to Ewen to meet her father, Jackie introduced her new boyfriend as a pro football player.

"Well," her father answered, "he must not be any good. I've never heard of him."

Bruce could see the feelings developing between the couple. They both had been through rough times—Nitschke from his childhood days and Jackie from a failed first marriage.

"Ray had a hard upbringing," Bruce observed. "He didn't trust a lot of people. But he liked Jackie right off the bat. She was personable; if she was in a room and met 50 people, she could remember the name of every one of them."

Ray and Jackie were married on June 26, 1961, and later made their home on Neufeld Street in Green Bay, not far from Lambeau Field. The change in Nitschke was dramatic. He gave up drinking entirely, having realized that he was one of those people for whom even one drink is one too many. The turning point in his decision to stay away from alcohol had come prior to his marriage, when he was out with Jackie and the two survived a horrific traffic accident.

"It was a pretty good car wreck," Jerry Kramer remembered. "I think he rolled the car a couple of times. The story was, he almost killed Jackie. From that point on, he changed."

Nitschke quit alcohol cold, just as he had quit tobacco cold in college, and realized that just as he had disliked smoking, deep down he had disliked drinking just as much. It had been a crutch to cover up his loneliness and insecurities, a crutch he no longer needed now that he had Jackie. He had grown tired of getting into fights, tired of waking up the next morning feeling foolish and embarrassed by his previous night's behavior. Now that he was married, he realized he was no longer just representing Ray Nitschke; he was representing Jackie as well. It was time, he thought, to wise up, set a good example, and become a man.

Together, Ray and Jackie began planning for a family. Because Jackie could not have children of her own, they agreed early in their marriage that they would adopt. In 1963, they brought home a boy, John. Richard was adopted in 1966 and Amy in 1972. Nitschke became the father he had never really known. He doted on his children, and along with Jackie they gave him the love and support that had been missing from his life since his childhood.

"Having a family," Nitschke said later, "really solidified my life. Before I got married I was kind of runnin' them streets."

"He was a good dad," said Richard, named after his father's second-oldest brother. "He didn't get really involved with a lot of things we did because of the type of work he did. He was pretty tied up during the four or five months of the football season. But when he was around during the summer, we did things and it was good."

As children, John, Richard, and Amy heard the stories of their father's wild days, heard how he had reformed after marrying their mother. "My father was kind of rowdy, let's put it that way," Richard said. "He wasn't the kind of guy that you really wanted to go out drinking with. So after he got married and adopted my brother John, he quit drinking. He realized he had choices to make in life. He was going to be a father or he was going to be a bum. He made his choice and stuck by it."

And did so with the help of Jackie and Vince Lombardi.

"I think my mom really did have a big part in him simmering down," Amy said. "Her and Lombardi. Obviously, they were the two people my dad looked to at the time for any kind of guidance and strength."

Family life helped Nitschke focus on what was important to him, which was having someone to love and having someone love him. He was no longer concerned with himself only; now he was looking out for his wife and children. It was something he needed, he said. To care for somebody, to worry about somebody else.

"I know it had been hard for him growing up," Amy said. "And I think that's why he made it a point to make family such a big thing. We always had to eat dinner together. There wasn't any of that 'I'm going to eat now and sit up in my room later.' We *had* to eat dinner together. And there were times we had to do family things and couldn't get out of it."

As young children, John, Richard, and Amy learned to share their father with the people of Green Bay. It was disturbing at times, Richard said, but they eventually became accustomed to it.

"It was hard to go out to eat sometimes," he recalled. "You couldn't sit down to have a normal dinner like most people. I'm not saying it was real bad or anything; we got used to it, I guess. I know I became accustomed to it. My dad would just tell the people, 'Hey, my food's here now. When I get done eating you can come back.' "

Amy said the reason her father was so obliging was that when he was younger he couldn't imagine anyone ever wanting his autograph. "He told me once that when he was 16 or so he could never have believed that he would become what he did," she remembered.

Richard recalled times when his father would become angry at the sight of pro athletes refusing to sign autographs for kids. "Dad would sign anything for anybody," Richard said. "He would get aggravated by that, because without the fans, my father would say, you're nothing. You're out there doing your job, but they're writing your paycheck. Without their support, the club doesn't exist and you're out the door. In this day and age, I don't think that would happen, but when my dad played, that's the way it was."

The Nitschkes lived on Neufeld Street in Green Bay until the fall of 1970, when they moved to Oneida, where their home sat on the border of four different school districts. John went to a private school in Green Bay; Richard to a public school located in Pulaski some 25 miles away. Both played high school football, and while their father was supportive of their interests he never tried to push them in any particular direction.

"Just do what you want to do," he would tell them, "and do the best job you can."

He and Jackie regularly attended the boys' Little League baseball games and at home loved hanging out with the neighborhood kids. The boys would spend summer days playing wiffle ball in the street, and on those occasions when the ball would go down the sewer, the kids would call for Mr. Nitschke. Out Ray would come, and he would lift the sewer cap with one hand and hold it while one of the boys jumped down to get the ball. He and Jackie hosted barbecues, and Ray would cap the day by loading all the kids into the family station wagon and taking them out for ice cream. He loved to hold children—he would pick nine-year-old Bill Toogood up with one hand—but when he and Jackie brought Amy home in April 1972, Ray confided to friends he was afraid to hold his baby daughter because she was so small.

The change in Nitschke's off-field personality impressed those connected with the team. Lombardi said that marriage had settled Nitschke down, and teammates noticed the difference as well. The first couple of years when Nitschke wasn't married and wasn't playing much, Hornung said, had left Ray disgusted and hard to live with. Teammates didn't want to be around the brooding middle linebacker; at times, Nitschke seemed to want to fight his own teammates at the drop of a harmless crack.

"He was a nasty guy," Hornung said. "Shit, he didn't know what he was doing half the time. He thought he could drink, like all drinkers do. But we didn't want to be out with him when we he was drinking so we kept our distance.

"But once he stopped drinking, all that changed. When he got with Jackie, she straightened his act out. He stopped all that bullshit and became a great guy."

Al Pahl, a friend of the Nitschkes, thought Jackie had saved Ray from himself, and Kramer agreed.

"It all started with Jackie," Kramer said. "You have no idea how mean and nasty he was. When he had too much to drink, he would literally slap some lady in a bar and knock her on her ass. Anyone who was happy, he didn't like. But when Raymond met Jackie, he found love, and she brought a lot of good things into his life."

Kramer's relationship with Nitschke had been strained from the start. The two first met at the College All-Stars practice in the summer of 1958. Kramer was a guard from the University of Iowa and had been drafted by the Packers in the fourth round, one round behind Nitschke. Nitschke had been the 36th pick in the draft; Kramer was the 39th. At the All-Stars camp, Kramer made a half-joking reference to Nitschke's intelligence; a "smartass remark," Kramer said later, about Nitschke being a mental giant, a genius. Nitschke, who didn't need much prodding, didn't like Kramer's joke and jumped out of his chair. In a loud and menacing voice, he challenged Kramer to back up his remarks. Realizing he was wrong, Kramer backed down. When the two rookies reported later that summer to the Packers' training camp, their relationship remained strained. Nitschke hadn't forgotten the insult and always looked at Kramer as if he was a dog that had once bitten him.

The two had several verbal confrontations in their early years at Green Bay, and the situation finally reached a physical standoff at a team party. Both men had been drinking, and this time it was Nitschke who instigated the trouble. As he often did when he drank more than he should, Nitschke began spouting off. Sparks flew, and Nitschke asked Kramer if he wanted to take it outside.

"Hell, yes," Kramer said, then had second thoughts as he headed toward the door and saw Nitschke right behind him. Kramer had battled Nitschke in scrimmages and knew the power of Ray's forearms. "Oh, self," Kramer thought, "you are in trouble!"

Realizing that matters were about to get serious, Kramer figured he had better get his bluff in first. Turning around quickly, Kramer grabbed Nitschke by the throat, backed him up against a brick wall, and told him he was ready to tear his head off. "All right, you son of a bitch," Kramer told Nitschke, "I'm crazy enough to fight or drink. Whichever way you want it."

Nitschke looked at Kramer for a moment, then relaxed. "Naw, man, you're my teammate," Nitschke said. "I don't wanna fight you."

"We went back inside," Kramer remembered. "Fortunately for me."

The truce between Kramer and Nitschke remained an uneasy one, and through their years together in Green Bay, which ran from 1958 until Kramer's retirement in 1969, the two all-pros engaged in various scrimmage wars. By the mid-sixties, Kramer was arguably the best guard in the game; Nitschke the dominant middle linebacker. Every time they scrimmaged, Kramer knew Nitschke would be waiting for him, waiting with what Kramer called "that damned forearm of his."

Nitschke's forearms were ferocious weapons. Thick and meaty, he intensified their size and clubbing power by wrapping them in pads and fastening them in place with yards of tape. Films of Nitschke in the sixties show him using his forearms like scythes to cut through a cordon of enemy blockers and punish the ball carrier.

"You buckled it up when you went to see Raymond," Kramer said. "The first time he'd hit you, you'd be ticked off about it. But the next time you buckled it up because you knew he was going to deliver a hit."

"He and Jerry had some moments," defensive end Willie Davis remembered. "Ray made practice a little more aggressive than it should be, and Jerry would say, 'Why'd you do that, Ray?' And Ray's first reaction would be, 'Hey, man, just gettin' ready to play!' And the next thing you know Jerry would be saying, 'All right, you son of a bitch, let's get ready to play.' And it would get to be a real heated thing. But that was Ray. He had an attitude about the game and he played that way. He took no prisoners, and he fully expected that he was going to have some fights. And when someone would knock the crap out of him, he'd take it."

If Nitschke seemed ultra-violent on NFL Sundays, he was just as tough on teammates during the week. Center Bill Curry, who joined the Packers in 1965, said that Nitschke didn't care if it was Bart Starr or Paul Hornung, if they ran near him during a contact scrimmage, he was going to hit them. "He almost tore my head off a few times," Hornung remembered. "So I went after his knees. He had bad knees, and he got ticked off. I said, 'Bullshit, you're not going to tear my head off.' This was a Tuesday practice, and I said, 'Let's put the pads on and go full speed if we're going to do it this way. I'm not going to let him tear my head off.'"

"Lombardi said, 'You will *not* go after his knees.'

"I said, 'Bullshit, I won't. If he comes in after me I'm going for his knees. Let's all put the pads on and go full speed. That damn Nitschke runs around and tries to tear your head off.' But that's the way Ray was."

Red Cochran, who was the Packers backfield coach under Lombardi from 1959 to 1966, called Nitschke "gruff as hell" and thought he practiced the way he played. Cochran knew Nitschke didn't realize there was such a thing as half-speed, but he still took issue with Nitschke's rough treatment of Packer backs.

"Dammit, Nitschke," Cochran would shout during scrimmages. "Lay off my running backs!"

Green Bay tackle Forrest Gregg said if Packer linemen weren't careful when they scrimmaged Nitschke, they'd get one of his big forearms in their teeth. Kramer thought Nitschke used his forearms the same way Dillinger used a pistol—to intimidate people, to stop them.

At times, Kramer thought of Nitschke more as an opponent than a teammate. Nitschke, he said, seemed incapable of letting up, even against his own teammates. "He was always grabbing people, hitting people, throwing elbows," Kramer said.

Dowler used to look for Nitschke during practices, look for the elbows that were sure to come his way whenever his pass route carried him into Nitschke's territory.

"We're running our pass offense and I'd be going across the middle and Ray would throw a forearm at me," Dowler remembered. "I'd say, 'What the hell are you doing out here?'

"'Just making you better,' he'd say."

Like fullback Jimmy Taylor, Nitschke didn't know how to ease up when playing football, didn't know how to "brother-in-law it," the Packers' term for toning it down against teammates. And he never apologized for his aggressiveness. "I came to play," Nitschke said. "I came to practice."

Nitschke and Taylor were alike in their approach to football, and Nitschke looked up to Taylor. Just as Nitschke would explain his explosive charge into a running back by saying, "You want the ball carrier to be a little shy, and a little shyer the next time," Taylor adopted the same attitude toward defenders.

"You've got to sting 'em," Taylor would say. "If you give a guy a little blast, maybe the next time he won't be so eager."

In practice, the two men often collided in the Packers' nutcracker drill. On one occasion when Taylor was the ball carrier and it was Nitschke's job to stop him, Nitschke was screened by the blocker and Taylor galloped by, untouched. Lombardi stopped the drill and announced, "Mr. Nitschke, I have read that you are the best linebacker in the NFL. But after watching you just then I find it hard to believe. Now do it again!"

On the next play, an angry Nitschke grabbed the blocker by the shoulder pads, lifted him off the ground, and tossed him back into Taylor. Lombardi was sufficiently pleased. "Next group," he shouted. Cornerback Herb Adderley recalled the practice collisions between Nitschke and the running backs, recalled the short tempers that occasionally flared.

"Hornung, Tom Moore, Elijah Pitts, any of the running backs, Nitschke would jar them just to let them know, 'Hey, this isn't touch football,'" Adderley said. "At least once a week we'd have to pull Ray Nitschke and

Jimmy Taylor apart. Both of them were tough guys and they always wanted to prove that they were tough. So they would get into some kind of scuffle during the practice session."

Davis remembered days when Nitschke would be keying Taylor on a scrimmage play and after chasing him down, deliver a hit. "Ray was going to manage a little push or a whack that Jimmy thought was more aggressive than it should have been and the next thing you know they would be pushing and shoving," Davis said. "It was in their competitive juices. Those two could get into a pushing match over who wanted to stand in a particular spot."

Kramer recalled the scrimmage conflicts between Nitschke and Taylor, and thought that the occasional flare-ups stemmed from the fact that the two men were so much alike in their approach to the game.

"Raymond and Jimmy got pretty damn close to a fight a couple of times," he said. "Raymond was that kind of a practice guy, and Jimmy was too."

By 1961, Taylor had developed into one of the most punishing fullbacks in NFL history. "He'll kill you for a yard," one opposing player said. Once, when five Ram defenders piled on and drove him out of bounds, Taylor leapt from the pile, clapped his hands, and shouted, "Way to hustle, guys!"

"Taylor was a tough, mean S.O.B," remembered Eagles' linebacker Chuck Bednarik. "Tough and mouthy. When we beat them in 1960 and I made that tackle on him, I was excited and I looked at him and said, 'You can get up now, this damn game is over!' So they came back and played us two years later and just beat the shit out of us. And Taylor let me know it. He would come up to me and say, 'Hey, how do ya like that shit, heh?'"

To Giants' middle linebacker Huff, Taylor was like Nitschke in that they both played with a linebacker's mentality. "Jimmy Taylor loved to run over you," Huff said. "He'd kick you in the head with those knees."

Like Nitschke, Taylor had endured a tough childhood, one that involved the untimely death of a parent. Born in Baton Rouge, Louisiana, on September 20, 1935, Jimmy was still in grade school when his father passed away. His mother worked in a laundry to support her three sons, and Jimmy pitched in by taking on two paper routes. One required him to get up early every morning and deliver papers before school; the other saw him delivering papers immediately after school was over.

"I must have pedaled my bike a million miles," Taylor said later, and credited the hard work with developing his tremendous leg drive.

"Jimmy will let you grab a leg," Green Bay offensive line coach Bill Austin said at the time, "then ram it through your chest."

Taylor's upper body development began in high school, when he hired on as a roughneck on an offshore oil rig. Taylor's job involved handling heavy pipes, and he would sometimes be out on the boats for 10 to 12 hours before returning to shore.

"Toughest thing I ever did," he said.

Taylor played well enough at Baton Rouge High School to earn a football scholarship to Louisiana State University. Poor study habits caused him to flunk out following his freshman year, and he spent the next two years at Hinds Junior College in Raymond, Mississippi. Taylor reapplied to LSU, and played his final two seasons of college ball under head coach Paul Dietzel. Despite sharing the same backfield with Heisman Trophy winner Billy Cannon, who would go on to become the first superstar of the American Football League, Taylor impressed scouts as a fullback, linebacker, and place-kicker. As a senior he ranked among the nation's leaders in rushing and points scored. The Packers chose Taylor in the second round of the '58 draft, and he arrived in camp with the reputation of being absent-minded. Taylor had trouble remembering his new Packer teammates' names, and solved his problem by calling everyone "Roy" or "Rick" or "Reno." He took over as the Packers' top fullback on Sunday, December 7, 1958, in San Francisco, in the penultimate game of the regular season, and remained in the starting lineup until leaving the team following Super Bowl I.

Taylor often engaged in what Lombardi referred to as "jive talk," and his manner of speaking confused his head coach. When Lombardi would question him in film sessions about a missed block on a linebacker, offensive tackle Steve Wright said Taylor would reply, "Uh, well, Coach, I was standing around and I cut to the right and he was standing there right in front of me and I didn't know which way to go because I saw his fromish and then his kribish and when the tackle froused, you know, it happened so quick."

"What?" Lombardi would ask incredulously. "Does anybody know what he's saying?" Lombardi later complained to writer W. C. Heinz that Taylor "uses jive talk I can't understand."

Taylor angered Lombardi by smoking cigars in the back of the darkened room during film study. Wright thought Taylor smoked during the meetings because he knew it blew Lombardi's mind. Taylor would light his cigar, take a few puffs, and then hear Lombardi's voice cutting through the darkness. "Taylor, put that damn cigar out!" When Lombardi chastised Taylor for failing to carry out a fake properly, Taylor would infuriate his coach by taking a long drag from his cigar, flick the ash off the end of it, and remark, "Guess I'm washed up, Coach."

No one, however, found anything to complain about when Taylor carried the ball. He stood 6-foot and weighed 215 pounds and was one of the first players in the league to devote himself to a rigorous weightlifting and isometric training program. Taylor trained himself with the same monkish fanaticism that Marciano had used to rule the heavyweight division in the 1950s, and his body looked like it had been chiseled out of granite. Lombardi would bump into Taylor by accident and walk away feeling as if he had just bumped into a cast-iron statue. "Nothing gives," Lombardi said, and the Packers' head coach noticed that Taylor's neck and shoulder muscles were so heavily developed that when he wanted to turn his head he would have to turn his whole upper body as well.

Taylor's devotion to physical fitness impressed Nitschke. He was amazed that in camp during two-a-day practices Taylor would lift weights early in the morning before the first practice then lift again before the afternoon practice. Two-a-days under Lombardi were an annual period of agony for the Packers, but Taylor was the one player who seemed unfazed by the grass drills and contact scrimmages under the blazing sun. Despite being someone whom Nitschke thought didn't have too much natural ability, Taylor really pushed himself in an effort to become the best fullback in the game. To Nitschke, Taylor played the game as if he was convinced there was no one better than he was, and his determination and desire had a profound impact on Nitschke. If Taylor could play that hard on offense, Nitschke thought, then he could play that hard on defense.

Nitschke's decision to dedicate himself to getting the most out of his potential paid off in the summer of 1961. Before Lombardi welcomed his Western Conference champions back to camp, he issued a sobering warning to his players. "Football," he said, "is a hard-headed, cold business. If a player isn't as good as he was last year when he won the championship for you, he's got to go."

Since success could make players "fat-headed," they would have to come to camp with a singleness of purpose, a dedication to victory. "I can assure you," he told the media, "that our staff and players will have that again in 1961."

Green Bay added three key rookies in Adderley, defensive tackle Ron Kostelnik, and halfback Elijah Pitts. The Packers went 6–0 in the preseason for the second straight year and outscored opponents by a combined score of 146–69. They stumbled in the regular season opener, losing to Detroit 17–13 before a crowd of 44,307 in Milwaukee, but then won their next six games and nine of their next ten. The Packers won despite having Nitschke, Hornung, and Dowler called into the service due to the Berlin crisis. The fall of 1961 had seen tension between the United States and Soviet Union escalate over access to Berlin, and President John F. Kennedy responded by calling up U.S. Armed Forces Reserves and National Guard units. The buildup resulted in more than two dozen players from the NFL and AFL joining their respective units on active duty.

Nitschke and Dowler reported to Fort Lewis, Washington; Hornung to

Fort Riley, Kansas. Nitschke, along with a lot of other men from Wisconsin, was assigned to the 32nd Division. He was paid $85.80 a month to carry sacks of potatoes. Nitschke joked later that the army must have thought he had the muscles for such an important job. His biggest problem at first was finding a uniform shirt that would fit; the army had to special order one with a size 18½-inch neck.

Lombardi fretted over the loss of three front-line players to military service, and he pulled favors from the Kennedy White House to get them weekend passes so they wouldn't miss any games. Lombardi was on good terms with the Kennedys; in the 1960 Wisconsin primary, Vince and his wife Marie had gone to see JFK speak in Green Bay. The two men met, and Lombardi told the Democratic candidate, "I'm with you all the way." Ethel Kennedy said later that Lombardi's endorsement helped the Kennedy's cause in what was a key primary state. "A grateful President," she said later, "never forgot."

Nitschke ended up missing two games that season, and because he was often absent from practice, split time at middle linebacker on game days with Tom Bettis. Yet the everyday absence of three regulars was just one problem the Packers faced in 1961. Defensive tackle Dave Hanner underwent an appendectomy, but 10 days later was back in the lineup. Hanner, Nitschke said, had Lombardi's reluctant permission to miss one game. Kramer broke his leg during the season and Lombardi was forced to alter his offensive line. Gregg slid over from right tackle to Kramer's spot at right guard, and backup Norm Masters took over at the tackle position.

Despite having to juggle their lineup, the Packers won the games they had to win. In Week Two, they faced conference rival San Francisco and the famous "Shotgun" offense installed by 49ers' head coach Red Hickey. A top pass receiver during his playing days, Hickey had watched the solid defensive units in Green Bay, New York, Detroit, and Baltimore stunt the scoring of the standard T-formation offenses prevalent in the NFL in the early 1960s. Hickey's Shotgun formation involved a spread offense, with two wingbacks and a tailback playing quarterback. With its tailback plunges and wingback reverses, the Shotgun was fully loaded for the '61 season. The 49ers defeated Washington 35–3 in their season opener, and when Hickey brought the 49ers to Green Bay in Week Two, 38,669 jammed City Stadium to see if the Packers could jam the Shotgun. Green Bay did, winning 30–10, then followed with a 24–0 shutout of Chicago, and a devastating 45–7 victory over Baltimore in a game in which Hornung personally accounted for 33 points by scoring four touchdowns and kicking a field goal and six extra points. Prior to the annual Thanksgiving Day game in Detroit, Lombardi switched Adderley, who had been playing halfback, to cornerback. Because of the short week, Adderley received a three-day crash course in playing his new position from defensive coordinator Phil Bengston. Proving himself a quick study, Adderley turned the game against the Lions around with an interception that started the Packers on their winning drive in an eventual 17–9 victory.

The win over the Lions moved the Packers to within one game of their second straight Western Conference championship, and Green Bay hosted the Giants on December 3 with a chance to clinch the title outright. Both teams entered the game 9–2, and sportswriters called the showdown of the two conference leaders a preview of the NFL title game. Before a crowd of 47,012 in Milwaukee, the Packers staged a come-from-behind, 20–17 win to repeat as conference champions. Green Bay split their final two games to finish with a league-best 11–3 record, then prepared to rematch with the Giants, who behind star quarterback Y. A. Tittle had won the Eastern Conference with a 10–3–1 record, one-half game ahead of second-place Philadelphia.

The Packers had played in five NFL championship games prior to 1961, yet none had ever been held in Green Bay. Packer fans responded to the event, adorning store windows with signs that read "Titletown, U.S.A." When Huff saw the gold-and-green signs and car stickers, he laughed. "How about that," Huff said. "The hicks don't even know how to spell 'Tittle.'" Giants' fans came bearing signs of their own—"Tittletown, U.S.A." Sportswriters pointed out that the Packers and Giants had finished atop the league in both offense and defense. Green Bay's offense led the league in points scored with 391, and New York was second with 368. The Giants' defense led the NFL in fewest points allowed with 220, while the Packers were second with 223. Green Bay fans looking for good omens remembered that the Packers' previous NFL championship had come against the Giants, a 14–7 win in 1944.

The return of Nitschke and Hornung to the locker room for the title game lifted the spirits of the team. Hornung's personality, his rare combination of nonchalance and determination, inspired his teammates. He was the rogue son who could tweak Lombardi, the team's disciplinarian father figure. Hornung's free-and-easy lifestyle kept the Packers loose. Prior to a big game in San Francisco against the rival 49ers, Hornung followed a stream of emotional team speeches by standing up and saying, "Look, I came out here for two reasons. I took care of the first last night, now let's go out and beat the 49ers."

When Lombardi finished a chastising of Hornung by shouting, "What do you wanna be? A football player or a playboy?" Hornung wasted no time answering.

"A playboy!" he shouted back.

Hornung was handsome, and his blond, curly hair and blue eyes added luster to his nickname, "Golden Boy." He was also glib, and once, during his college days at Notre Dame, was caught by head coach Frank Leahy snuffing out a cigarette with his shoe.

"Do you see what I see near your shoe, Paul?" Leahy asked.

"Yeah, Coach, I see. But you take it. You saw it first."

Hornung loved the single life, and his advice to those getting engaged was to never get married in the morning. The reason? "You never know who you'll meet that night," Hornung said. When Hornung eventually married, he broke his own rule and was married before noon. But he had his reasons. "If it didn't work out," he said, "I didn't want to blow the whole day."

On bus trips to the stadium, Lombardi always demanded that his players be in their seats 15 minutes before the scheduled departing time. Lombardi's seat was in the front of the bus, at the right elbow of the driver, and latecomers invoked his wrath. When Hornung and teammate Max McGee, who also liked the nightlife, arrived late, Lombardi fumed.

"Where have you two been?" he asked.

Without breaking stride, Hornung replied, "Church." The remark broke Lombardi up.

Nitschke looked past Hornung's playboy ways and saw a player who was a tremendous field leader and clutch competitor. The bigger the game, Nitschke thought, the bigger Hornung played.

Game day in Green Bay brought sunny but sub-freezing temperatures, and a New Year's Eve day crowd of 39,029 filled City Stadium. On the field below, 50 stadium workers had spent the early morning hours clearing the field of 14 inches of snow and then covering it with 20 tons of hay to preserve footing before the warm-ups. To combat the 21-degree cold, infrared heating units were placed along the bench areas of both teams. Across the country, a national television audience settled in to watch the game on NBC, which had paid a record $615,000 for the exclusive rights to the game.

Unlike the previous year, when Nitschke had taken to the Franklin Field sod uneasy about the Packers' inexperience, he ran onto the frozen turf of City Stadium confident Green Bay could beat the Giants. Packer practices during the week had been crisp and precise, and the team was peaking, physically and emotionally. Nitschke knew he wasn't as sharp as he could be because of his missed practices, but splitting time with Bettis and playing on special teams had helped keep him reasonably well-prepared.

Running onto the field, Nitschke barely acknowledged the cold. He was concentrating on Tittle, whom the Giants had acquired from San Francisco in a trade. Tittle replaced Charlie Conerly as the starting quarterback in Week Two and had thrown for 17 touchdowns and 2,272 yards. Having coached in San Francisco when Tittle was there, Bengston knew all of his former quarterback's tendencies. He knew what pass patterns were Tittle's favorites, what play Y. A. was likely to call in a certain situation. As the Packers' middle linebacker, Nitschke would be engaging in a game of mental cat-and-mouse with Tittle. Knowing Tittle's habits beforehand gave Nitschke an advantage, and he took the field believing this title game was going to mark one of the great afternoons of his life.

Nitschke made his presence felt on the game's first play. A tape of the '61 championship shows him hustling downfield on the opening kickoff and slamming Giant return man Joel Wells to the frozen field. On NBC radio, play-by-play announcer Ray Scott provided the call on a play that helped set the game's tempo:

> *This crowd is really coming alive as Ben Agajanian comes toward the ball and this championship game is under way. . . . It is off to the left, it is going to land at the 15-yard line, picked up by Wells, gets away from one man, he's to the 20, 25 and he is collared from behind and flipped down around the 30-yard line. . . . Ray Nitschke makes the tackle. . . .*

Nitschke and Bettis spent the afternoon alternating at middle linebacker, where they stared across center at Tittle. The key to stopping New York, Nitschke knew, was to prevent Tittle from completing his deep passes to streaking ends Kyle Rote and Del Shofner, and holding fullback Alex Webster in check. The Packer defense was successful on both counts through a scoreless first quarter, but they gained a break when Rote slipped past the secondary only to drop Tittle's pass.

Green Bay broke the game open in the second quarter, scoring 24 straight points. Hornung had been cleared from army duty on special orders from JFK—"Paul Hornung isn't going to win the war on Sunday," the president said, "but the football fans of this country deserve the two best teams on the field that day"—and Green Bay's glamour back scored the first points of the game when he veered off right tackle from six yards out on the opening play of the second quarter. Nitschke followed with an interception of a Tittle pass that had been tipped at the line by defensive tackle Henry Jordan. Backpedaling into the secondary, Nitschke clutched the fluttering ball and returned it eight yards before Rote dragged him down from behind.

Scott made the call on NBC radio:

> *A spread formation now for New York. . . . Fading to pass is Tittle, he is looking, he's throwing, the ball is batted. . . . Intercepted by Nitschke! He's at the 34-yard line. Ray Nitschke intercepts a ball that was batted near the*

line of scrimmage. . . . Ray Nitschke, who had moved in at middle linebacker, carried it back to the Giant 34-yard line and the Packers are in great position. . . .

Nitschke's interception set up Green Bay's second touchdown, a 13-yard pass from Starr to Dowler. Taking advantage of a New York secondary that was forced because of injuries to play offensive halfback Joe Morrison at safety, Starr followed with a 14-yard touchdown pass to tight end Ron Kramer. Desperate to put points on the board before halftime, the Giants replaced Tittle with Conerly, a championship quarterback from years past. Conerly drove New York deep into Green Bay territory, but Nitschke and the Packer defense responded to the challenge. Fighting off the block of center Ray Wietecha, Nitschke combined with defensive end Bill Quinlan to shut down halfback Phil King's alley to the end zone at the Packers' 8-yard line. Nitschke then teamed with left linebacker Dan Currie to stop Webster's drive through the middle at the 6. Two plays later, halfback Bob Gaiters ran right on an option and overthrew Rote in the back of the end zone.

Nitschke and the Packer defense had held, and Hornung closed the half a short time later with a 17-yard field goal to give Green Bay a 24–0 lead. Nitschke opened the second half by taking Pat Summerall's short kickoff at the Packers' 18-yard line, and displaying the running style he had showed years before as a fullback at Illinois, tucked the ball under his right arm and barreled 18 yards upfield before slipping on the icy turf and being downed at the 36.

Nitschke's run brought a chuckle from Ray Scott, who opened the second half with the following call:

The sun is shining, but don't get me wrong, there's no heat wave in Green Bay. All things considered it's just about as much as we could hope for. We're ready to go. . . . Summerall comes to the ball, his kick is high and fairly short. It will land at the 20, be picked up and taken to the 25, 30, 35 and down falls . . . Ray Nitschke, I do believe. That's right, Ray Nitschke, who played some fullback in his football career but (is) known in professional football as a linebacker, takes a short kickoff, moves it to the 36-yard line where, trying to cut, he falls down. . . .

The Packers added 10 more points in the third quarter on a 22-yard field goal by Hornung and Starr's second TD pass to Ron Kramer, a 13-yarder that made it 34–0. Hornung's 19-yard field goal in the fourth closed the scoring at 37–0 and he finished the game with an NFL championship record 19 points. The Packer defense had done its job as well. Webster, who had rushed for 928 yards that season and averaged 4.7 yards per carry, was held to 19 yards rushing, and Tittle was limited to six completions in 20 attempts. Nitschke hounded Tittle all afternoon, and the result was that the Giants quarterback threw for just 65 yards while splitting time with Conerly. By game's end, New York's vaunted air attack had been limited to six first downs and 130 yards of total offense.

Giants' rookie Greg Larson played right tackle that day, and was shaken by the ferocity of Nitschke and the Green Bay defense.

"When we fell behind they knew we had to pass," Larson said after the game. "When they knew that, they came in swinging fists and elbows and yelling and looking crazy in the eyes. They came in screaming and screeching. It was the most frightening thing I ever saw in a football game, absolutely terrifying. We had no way to stop them. It was unending. They were like wild men. Play after play, pounding and slapping and punching. It was enough to make a man cry from the physical brutality of it all."

At the final gun, Lombardi was hoisted on the shoulders of his players. "Today," he told them, "you are the greatest team in the history of the National Football League." Later, as a cold dusk descended on Green Bay's New Year's Eve celebrations, Lombardi received a telegram from President Kennedy. "Congratulations on a great game today. It was a fine victory for a great coach, a great team, and a great town."

In the crowded Green Bay dressing room, defensive backs coach Norb Hecker paid special tribute to Nitschke. A review of the radio broadcast of the game reveals that Nitschke was credited with four solo tackles and one QB pressure. Hecker said later that it was Nitschke's hard hits that inspired the Packer defense.

"It sort of rubs off on the rest of the men and makes them want to hit harder," Hecker said. "You know how it is when you're in a fight and someone on your side gets in a big punch? It swings things your way. That's the way it is when Nitschke flattens someone."

Bengston thought Nitschke's hitting had given the Packers' middle linebacker a presence on the field, a presence opponents were becoming increasingly aware of. "It gets so they want to know where Nitschke is lined up on every play," Bengston said. "They become quite conscious of his presence."

Nitschke was overjoyed with the victory. He found it hard to describe the depth of feeling he was developing for his teammates. Strangers to one another not so long ago, they had been molded by Lombardi and the coaching staff into a group of men with a singleness of purpose and confidence in one another. A team that Nitschke knew had been on the verge of greatness since 1960 had realized their goal in one afternoon of near-perfect football—an afternoon, Nitschke felt, that couldn't be improved upon.

The Packers returned for the 1962 season seeking a second straight NFL championship and a third consecutive Western Conference title. For the third straight season they won every preseason game, then won their first 10 games of the regular season. The defense excelled, claiming consecutive shutouts in Weeks Two and Three and allowing just 14 points combined over the first four games. Even with Hornung below par physically because of a sore knee, the Packer offense scored a total of 100 points in its first three games, including finals of 34–7 over Minnesota and 49–0 over Chicago.

The Packers were strong, Jerry Kramer thought. And Lombardi went through that season with a gleam in his eye, a gleam that Kramer thought meant the Packers had better not do anything wrong. It was the gleam of a successful man seeking additional success.

Driven by Lombardi, the Packers reached their peak as a team. They were tough and experienced, and like the DiMaggio Yankees of the forties and early fifties, featured a clubhouse filled with H.A.s, the Yankees' term for "Hard Asses." They were hard men playing a hard game, a family of rough, rowdy brothers who battled opponents, and at times, each other. If Nitschke missed a tackle, for instance, Wood would let him know it in the huddle.

"Don't you ever let those running backs get to me again!," he would scream at Nitschke. From his free safety position, Wood had the best view of the play as it unfolded in front of him, and he didn't see why he had to make the tackles Nitschke should have been making. "He was getting paid twice as much as me," Wood said.

Wood stood 5-foot-10 and weighed 170, but he withered teammates with hard stares. Even Nitschke was frightened by Wood's cold looks. "I hate to miss a tackle," Nitschke said at the time, "because if I do, I know I'm gonna get a dirty look from Willie. He'll kill you with that look."

Some of the Packers, like Starr, were angelic assassins. Off the field, Starr was soft-spoken and courteous. But Zeke Bratkowski, who became Starr's backup in 1963, said once that Starr's personality changed once he lined up under center. "On the field, he'll cut your heart out and show it to you," Bratkowski said.

Starr ran an offense geared to power sweeps and off-tackle blasts; Lombardi called it "grinding meat." *Time* magazine described it as "rugged, old-fashioned blocking to open holes for rugged, old-fashioned ball carriers." Starr would slap the ball into Taylor's rock-hard stomach some 20 times a game, Hornung would take it 12 or 13 times, and Starr would throw the ball 25 times. "That was our offense," Hornung said.

"Those Packer teams of '61 and '62 were just fantastic football teams, if not the greatest of all time," Huff remembered. "There was no way you could go into Green Bay and beat 'em. They had Hornung and Taylor in the backfield, two Hall of Famers, and their line could *block*. They had to, because they had Lombardi coaching them and he made them a tough team."

Opposing coaches knew what the Packer offense was going to do; it was always Hornung into the strong side, Taylor into the weak side, and Starr carving up the defense with a ball-control passing attack. Otto Graham, who coached the College All-Stars from 1958 to 1963 and the Washington Redskins from 1966 to 1968, said it was never difficult to prepare a game plan for the Packers because they rarely tried to surprise opponents with anything new. "They just dared you to stop them," Graham said.

"The offense made it very easy for us," said Currie, an all-pro at left linebacker. "They'd get the ball and go eight-and-half minutes for a touchdown, and when the opposition can't get their hands on the ball, it kills them. It makes it very frustrating for them. "

At the heart of the Packers' precision offense was the power sweep. In the playbook, the call was "49-Sweep" when Hornung ran it to the right side; "28-Sweep" when Taylor ran it to the left. In time, it became known simply as the "Lombardi Sweep." It was Green Bay's bread-and-butter play, their top-priority play, the play they had to make go and the one opponents had to stop. Every team in the NFL had their own signature play. Chicago ran the pitchout for speedy halfback Willie Galimore and Cleveland the toss sweep for fullback Jimmy Brown. In Detroit, the Lions favored the fullback slant for Nick Pietrosante; in San Francisco, the 49ers ran the screen pass better than anyone else.

In Green Bay, the Packers ran the sweep, a play that had become a part of Lombardi during his days as a guard at Fordham, when he played against the single-wing sweep as run by the great Pittsburgh teams of Jock Sutherland. Lombardi's sweep incorporated the same qualities as Sutherland's, the same guard-pulling techniques, the same cutbacks by the ball carrier. Lombardi had run the sweep in New York when he had Frank Gifford, and when he took over in Green Bay, he saw in Hornung a halfback who was a bigger, stronger version of Gifford. The sweep was the first play Lombardi put into the Packer playbook, and he taught it with such force he sometimes punctuated his remarks by snapping the chalk in two.

"What we want," Lombardi would tell his team, "is to get a seal *heah*, and a seal *heah*, and run this play IN THE ALLEY!"

The Lombardi Sweep became the dominant play of the decade and served to influence a generation of future head coaches. Don Shula's Miami Dolphins featured the sweep in the 1970s, with Mercury Morris running strongside in Hornung's footsteps and Larry Csonka pounding the weakside just as Taylor had before him. The trend continued in the 1980s with Bill Parcells, Mike Ditka, and Bill Walsh running their versions of the Lombardi Sweep.

"That damn sweep worked because everybody on the team did his job," former Baltimore Colts coach Don McCafferty said once. It was a matter of Packer execution, McCafferty said, and it was the defenses who were getting executed. When a reporter asked if there was anything mysterious about the Packers' success with such a simple play, McCafferty shook his head.

"Just too damned good," he said.

In practice, Nitschke would watch as Green Bay's guards pulled from the line and began their calvary charge around the end with Hornung and Taylor hot on their heels. "Dapper! Dapper!" Nitschke would call out to Currie amid the thunder of cleats. "Look out, Dapper! Here they come!"

The Packers ran the sweep relentlessly in practice, and while other NFL teams finished each practice day by running wind sprints, the Packers closed their practices by running the sweep. Nitschke and the Green Bay defense saw the sweep so much in practice they grew to know the intricacies of it as well as the offense. That hard-earned knowledge paid off on game days. When opposing teams would try to sweep the flanks against Green Bay, the Packers' instant recognition of the play allowed them to shut it down. Nitschke consistently shot the gaps left by the pulling guards, and films show him running down Baltimore's Lenny Moore on a sweep right in Green Bay, wrapping up New York's Phil King on a sweep left in Yankee Stadium.

As a team, the Packers peaked in 1962. When they rematched with the Eagles in Philadelphia in Week 11, they rolled up 628 yards in a 49–0 win. Green Bay linemen whip-sawed Bednarik, their old antagonist, with powerful, precision blocks. It was payback for the '60 title game, Bednarik thought, and Packers' defensive coordinator Phil Bengston didn't disagree. "We had learned the lessons of 1960," he said.

Walking off the field at halftime, a weary Bednarik called out to Green Bay assistant coach Tom Fears.

"Hey, Tom, when are you going to put in the scrubs?"

Looking right through Bednarik, Fears replied coldly, "Chuck, we don't have any scrubs."

Watching Nitschke on that November 11 afternoon, Bednarik realized that the linebacker the Eagles had seen two years earlier in the NFL championship game had returned to Franklin Field as the veteran leader of the Green Bay defense.

"A linebacker is like a general," Bednarik recalled. "He's a guy that calls the defenses, he can see what the hell's going on from behind the line. He could actually grade those guys while the game's going on. You know, 'What the hell are you doing?' You're like a teacher behind there too, you know, 'Why don't you do this? or 'You've gotta do this.'

"I could see Nitschke was a helluva football player, and he did a helluva job at middle linebacker. He really stood out."

Lombardi called Nitschke "the spearhead of our defense," and recognized the importance of the position. Modern middle linebackers, Lombardi said, had to be mobile because they had gone from 300-pound giants rooted to the trenches to 230–240-pound freelancers who comprised the second line of defense. They also had greater opportunities for fame since they were now out in the open, where fans could see them taking shots at the ballcarriers. "It has made Sunday heroes," Lombardi said, "of the Schmidts, Nitschkes, Huffs, and the rest."

Lest Nitschke or any player get too comfortable with his new-found fame, Lombardi kept them in line. He reminded his team throughout the '62 season that since they were on top, everyone was looking to knock them off. "This is the real test," he would say. "This year you find out whether or not you're really champions."

On the practice field, in the film grading sessions, Lombardi pounced on every mistake. Jerry Kramer said Lombardi rode them unmercifully that season. As an assistant at West Point under Red Blaik, Lombardi had picked up the habit of addressing the young cadets as "mister." By the time he reached the NFL, he had developed a way of saying the word in the most cutting fashion. When one of the Packers made a careless mistake, Lombardi would look at him with disgust. "You really are something, you are *mister*," he would say with derision.

Lombardi's tough coaching methods insulated Nitschke and the Packers against outside pressure. Even a 26–14 loss in Detroit on Thanksgiving Day, the Packers' lone defeat of the season, failed to rattle them. For one of the few times during the Lombardi years, the Packers failed to match the intensity of their opponent. Several Packers had been left bloodied and dazed by the beating the Lions handed out that afternoon, and Detroit had run out to a 26–0 lead in a performance that ranks as one of the greatest in franchise history. "They came out of the chutes like they'd gone crazy," said Starr, who was sacked 11 times on the day. "It looked like there were 50 of them playing us instead of 11."

The Packers stopped the onslaught with two late touchdowns, but by game's end, they were physically beaten. When Starr asked his receivers late in the game which one could get open, McGee asked, "Why don't you throw an incomplete pass and *nobody* will get hurt." The remark left the battered Packers laughing in their huddle, and Bengston thought the moment proved Green Bay had turned the corner as a team. Even a loss as humiliating as this one had been, he said, had been just a momentary lapse, another step in the team's character building. Starr agreed. "We showed something in the second half," he said.

Lombardi later accepted the blame for the loss, calling it "coaching stupidity" for not adjusting to what the Lions were doing. Nitschke thought there was another reason. The Lions had all the momentum that day, he said. Detroit had been pointing to the rematch since October 7, when a late turnover led to a 9–7 Packers' victory in a game the Lions believed should have been theirs. Green Bay guard Fuzzy Thurston's mother had died before the Thanksgiving Day rematch, and his somber mood reflected that of the team. Green Bay was due for a letdown; they had won 18 straight games, including post-seasons and exhibitions, dating back to 1961, and they finally came up flat.

Still, Nitschke thought the Thanksgiving Day loss to the Lions helped the Packers. They were determined, he thought, not to let it happen again that season.

Confident that no defeat could destroy them, the Packers rebounded to win the conference title with a 13–1 record and became the first NFL team since the 1934 Bears to win 13 games in a season. Taylor led the NFL in rushing by pounding out 1,474 yards and an NFL-record 19 touchdowns. Starr led the league in passing and Wood led in interceptions. Eleven Packers were named all-pro, including four of their five starters on the offensive line.

In the East, the Giants repeated as conference champions, finishing first with a 12–2 record. For the second straight year, New York and Green Bay would meet to decide the NFL championship. For the second straight year, Nitschke would be matching wits with Tittle, who after 14 years of pro football, had suddenly become an overnight sensation by throwing for a league-record 33 touchdowns. It was a game that had been building for a full season, and when the Giants wrapped up their regular season with a 41–31 win over Dallas on December 16, a crowd of 62,694 fans rocked cavernous Yankee Stadium with a singular, tribal chant.

"Beat Green Bay . . . Beat Green Bay . . . "

SIX

GOOD AFTERNOON, everyone. We are waiting for the Packers and the Giants to come out of the dugouts now, as 62,000-plus fans are on hand at Yankee Stadium. Repeating the weather situation, the temperature here is 20 degrees. There is a northwest wind, about 25 to 30 miles an hour, with occasional gusts. And down on the surface it becomes a problem, because it does swirl around.

"The Green Bay Packers are now being introduced individually as they take the field. . . ."

Listeners to NBC Radio announcer Ken Coleman's 1 P.M. broadcast of the 1962 NFL championship game on Sunday, December 30, 1962 could hear the thunderous boos that accompanied Yankee Stadium announcer Bob Sheppard's baritone introductions of the Packers' offense:

"At *quahteback*, Number 15, *Baht Stah* . . . "

In the visitors' dugout, Ray Nitschke stood with members of the Green Bay Packers defense a waiting their turn to take the field. To Nitschke, it was a miserably cold day, and as he ran gingerly across the field in his white Packer uniform with the yellow-gold helmet and pants, the howling wind rippled his warmup cape and churned up cyclones of dust from the dirt infield. The Packers' appearance on the Yankee Stadium turf also churned up memories of last year's 37–0 title game victory over the Giants, and the standing room-only crowd of 64,892 shook the stadium with chants of "Beat Green Bay . . . " as members of New York's famous defense were introduced.

For more than a week, New York City had become engulfed in the intense buildup given the Packers–Giants rematch. Newspaper stands were filled with issues of that week's *Time* magazine, whose cover carried a picture of a grinning Vince Lombardi. Across the cover were the words, "The Sport of the '60s," and if the NFL was in the process of gripping the imagination of the American sporting public, it was the bitter rivalry between dynastic teams like Green Bay and New York that was helping shape pro football's transformation. For the Packers, the '62 title game marked their third consecutive appearance in the NFL championship game. For the Giants, it was their second straight title game appearance, their fourth in five years and fifth in seven years.

From the moment Don Chandler's 16-yard field goal cleared the uprights at 4:10 P.M. Central Standard Time on Sunday, December 2, 1962, giving the Giants a 26–24 win over the Chicago Bears at Wrigley Field and the Eastern Conference title, the attention of New York's players and coaches turned automatically to one thought.

"Another showdown," New York quarterback Y. A. Tittle said, "with the Green Bay Packers."

For almost a full year, the Giants had lived with the memory of their shutout loss to Green Bay in the 1961 NFL championship game played the previous New Year's Eve, lived with the memory of Packer backs Jimmy Taylor and Paul Hornung combining for 183 yards rushing, with quarterback Bart Starr's precise passing game, with a Green Bay defense, led by Nitschke, that had both beaten up and shut down the most prolific offense in the Eastern Conference. When it was over, when the Packers had carried head coach Vince Lombardi off the field on their shoulders and Green Bay fans chanted "Titletown . . . Titletown" and tore down the goalposts, the Giants' mood was symbolized by a solitary New York player. Covered in ice and dirt, the player slumped wearily in front of his locker stall as reporters raced into the locker room. Amid the muttering and swearing, the despondent Giant offered what *Newark* (New Jersey) *Star-Ledger* sportswriter Jerry Izenberg later recalled as the only printable quote from the loser's side. Looking up at the horde of reporters crowding into the visitors' locker room, the battered Giant snarled, "Shut the damn door."

Tittle remembered the Giants' post-game locker room as an "awful scene." New York was a team of great pride, Tittle said, and to have been crushed as they were was a terrible blow. Everyone on the club showed the emotional strain of such an embarrasing defeat; head coach Allie Sherman's eyes were moist, and he was flushed with anger and humiliation.

Now, the Giants geared for their chance at revenge. They had been hoping for a second shot at Green Bay, Tittle said, "and now we had it." New York was gripped with championship fever. There was talk of little else during the days leading up to the game. Between periods of a New York Rangers' game at Madison Square Garden, ice hockey fans began the chant, "Beat Green Bay." Tittle recalled the chorus being picked up all over town. Every time he turned on the radio, the balding, 35-year-old quarterback heard disc jockeys repeating the phrase. Store windows in Manhattan were filled with Christmas decorations and signs that read "Beat Green Bay." Fans stopped Giant players on the streets, in restaurants, or Christmas shopping in the stores, and implored them to "Let's go, beat Green Bay."

The Packers were the pick of oddsmakers to repeat as NFL champions. Green Bay had the best record in the league at 13–1; New York was second at 12–2. The Packers led the league in points scored with 415; the Giants were second with 398. Green Bay also led in defense, allowing the fewest points with 148, but New York had Tittle, who took over as the Giants' offensive leader following the retirement of quarterback Charlie Conerly.

Tittle highlighted the Giants' season in Week Seven, when he threw for 505 yards and seven touchdowns in a 49–34 win over the Washington Redskins. Though his aging appearance sometimes led to mistakes off the field—an airline stewardess had stopped him from getting on the team's chartered plane with the statement, "I'm sorry, sir, this flight is only for the football players"—there was no mistaking Tittle on the field.

Middle-aged among NFL players, Tittle would retreat into the protective pocket and, denying the furious rush of the defense, survey the field for a receiver. If he wasn't firing bombs to split end Del Shofner or flanker Frank Gifford, who had returned from a one-year retirement following the concussive hit by Philadelphia linebacker Chuck Bednarik, Tittle was backpedaling before onrushing defenders and beating blitzes with screen passes to fullback Alex Webster. Near the goal line, Tittle crossed up defenses by bootlegging his way to the end zone, his black high top cleats carrying his thin legs to paydirt.

Tittle's emergence at quarterback and the return of Gifford had made the Giants a more dangerous offense than they had been the year before, and they were confident they could score points on the Packer defense. Gifford was a charismatic veteran, a hero of Giant victories of the past, and he spoke for the team when he said everyone on the club "wanted revenge for the clobbering [the Packers] handed us the year before."

While the Giants were sky-high for the rematch, practices in Green Bay that week lacked the intensity Lombardi was looking for, and he pulled Nitschke aside on the Wednesday prior to the game.

"Hit those guys, Ray," Lombardi said. "Hit those guys like they're Giants."

Nitschke nodded, and when he looked at the members of the Packer offense in practice that day, he saw the Giants instead. Green Bay center Jim Ringo became New York center Ray Wietecha, and in a scrimmage, Nitschke drilled him with his huge forearms, leaving Ringo with a severely pinched muscle in his neck.

Ringo's nerve problem reached deep into his right arm, which grew numb from the force of Nitschke's hit. When he found he had trouble centering the ball, Ringo didn't think he'd be able to play against New York. He didn't want to hurt the team by trying to do something he was physically unable to. The Packers arrived in New York on Friday, and following a workout at Yankee Stadium, *Newark Star-Ledger* sportswriter Dave Klein was in the visitors' locker room looking to interview some of the Packers. The room had been mostly cleared, but on the other side of the lockers, Klein could hear a conversation between Ringo and Lombardi.

"How's the arm?"

"I can't feel it at all, coach."

When Lombardi saw Klein in the room, he exploded in rage. Ringo was a bit more calm. He explained to Klein that if the Giants knew about his injured arm, they might take shots at it, and then he ran a risk of permanent injury. Ringo promised Klein that if he didn't write about the injury beforehand, he would give him an exclusive afterward. Klein agreed, and when the Packers took the field on game day, Klein could see that Ringo's right arm at times hung limply at his side.

Ringo's injury soon became secondary to the game-day conditions. The night before the game brought wet but mild conditions, but early-morning churchgoers on Sunday were blasted by icy winds that gusted up to 40 and 50 miles an hour. By kickoff, the temperature was 14 degrees and dropping. Hot coffee froze just minutes after it was poured at stadium concession stands. The field was hard-packed and full of pebbles, and the grass had been eroded by a season's worth of games. Coleman did, however, point out one plus to his NBC listeners.

The sun keeps peeking in and out from behind the clouds of the east end of this great stadium. . . .

Among those seeking warmth down on the field was Packers' photographer Vern Biever. He started covering the Packers in 1941 as an 18-year-old stringer for the *Milwaukee Sentinel*. Two years later, he was an army photographer with the 100th Infantry Division, rolling into France and then Germany. When Biever returned to Green Bay following the end of World War II, he looked up Jug Earpe, the Packers' public relations director, and proposed a deal.

"You want a record of your games?" Biever asked. "Give me a field pass and I'll give you some pictures."

Biever became the NFL's first team photographer, and since then has provided a visual record of Packer legends—Don Hutson, Tony Canadeo, and Curly Lambeau; Lombardi, Starr, and Nitschke; Mike Holmgren, Bret Favre, and Reggie White. Biever has photographed 16 NFL championship teams, 15 Hall of Famers, and every Super Bowl game.

When he started covering the Packers, Biever would be accompanied by a maximum of three or four other photographers doing the game for the various wire services. He soon gained a reputation among the players as being quick on his feet and wily. Though he was positioned close to the action on the sidelines, he never got "rolled up," the players' term for being knocked off his feet by plays along the sideline. With his 4X5 Speed Graphics camera, Biever captured the game as it was played, using tight, focused shots and portrait-style close-ups.

Through the early years, Biever always wished there were more sideline photographers at each game, if for no other reason than to cut the wind that came howling through the old stadiums. His wish was never more fervent than in the 1962 championship game, when the wind gusted through Yankee Stadium with vicious intent.

"I always say this, they talk about the Ice Bowl being cold, but I felt colder at the 1962 championship game than I did at the Ice Bowl," Biever said. "That wind was dominating and more penetrating than the Ice Bowl. The Ice Bowl was cold, but this game here, the wind was such a factor."

The Giants won the toss and elected to receive, and as the two teams tried to loosen up on the sidelines, Lombardi sought out Nitschke.

"Give us some hits right away, Ray," he said. "Get the boys started hitting."

Nitschke started the hitting, teaming with left tackle Dave Hanner to stop halfback Phil King for a two-yard gain on the game's first play from scrimmage. On NBC Radio, Coleman made the first of what would be many mentions of Nitschke's name that day:

> *The ball is spotted down at the 32 for New York and it is first down, ten yards to go for the Giants as Ray Wietecha leads them out. Webster and King are set in behind Y. A. Tittle and Shofner comes out wide on the left side. . . . Tittle takes and he gives it to (King), driving straight on and digging out a couple of yards. Ray Nitschke, the middle linebacker, and Dave Hanner, the defensive left tackle, are in there to make the play. . . .*

Coleman's reference to Nitschke as the "middle linebacker" was unique that day. At that time, the position was still referred to in many circles as the "middle guard," and on Coleman's next two references to Nitschke, he called him Green Bay's middle guard. Two plays later, Nitschke was fronting the Green Bay defense again, and game films show him spinning King to the ground after an 8-yard gain on a draw play. Packers' defensive coordinator Phil Bengston always told his team that the first five to ten plays were pivotal in determining how the opposition was going to play Green Bay on a given day, and Nitschke had gone out for that first series intent on showing the Giants he was going to be coming after them all day, hitting hard on every down.

New York stalled on their own 42-yard line, and following Chandler's punt, the Packers took over on their 20. On the sideline, Nitschke shivered amid the icy conditions. The bitter gales slapped exposed skin like a barber's blade on a strop. It pierced every fibre of Nitschke's being; he could feel it whipping through his uniform and heavy pads. It even seemed to find its way under his skin, he said later, and rattle the bones beneath. Nitschke had played in cold weather in Green Bay, but this day in New York was colder than any he had ever experienced. It was so cold that even Nitschke couldn't find any fun in being in Yankee Stadium that day.

Bundled against the cold with a fur collar pulled up around his ears, Lombardi thought the game-time conditions were the worse he had ever encountered. "It was the worst day I can ever remember for a football game," he said later. "I was half sorry to ask people to play in those conditions."

To compensate for a field as hard and frozen as the Russian steppes, Nitschke joined with Packer backs and ends in wearing ripple-soled coaching shoes. Packer linemen wore cleats, and right guard Jerry Kramer, who would be called on to replace a hobbled Paul Hornung and handle the place-kicking duties, wore a cleat on his right foot and a ripple-soled shoe on his left, or plant, foot.

As hard as Nitschke had hit the Giants on their first offensive series of the game, New York's defense hit just as hard on the Packers' initial drive. The memory of the embarrassment in Green Bay the year before had been burned into their brains, as had pregame talk of the Packers being a superior team.

"Bullshit," Giant defensive end Andy Robustelli snapped at a reporter before the game. "I've never been as anxious to play a game as this one. We will absolutely kill the bastards. It's the only way I'll be able to forget the one out there last year.

"It won't be enough to just win this game. We have to destroy the Packers and Lombardi. It's the only way we can atone for what happened to us last year."

Giants middle linebacker Sam Huff set the tone early. On the Packers' fourth play from scrimmage, fullback Jimmy Taylor took Starr's handoff and headed right for a pickup of 14 yards. As Huff chased him down, the two neared the New York sideline. Drawing a bead on Taylor, Huff thought, "Okay. It's live or die right now."

Mustering every ounce of his 230 pounds, Huff hit Taylor so hard he dented his own helmet. Both fullback and linebacker went sprawling out of bounds, and the die had been cast. New York had been humiliated the year before by Green Bay, Huff said. They were not going to let it happen again. The Giants, Huff said, went into the game with blood in their eyes, and they were going to let Taylor know from the start that they were going to knock him down, and knock him down hard.

Green Bay Press-Gazette sportswriter Lee Remmel thought Huff's fierce play was motivated in part by an Associated Press wire photo from the title game year before. The picture showed Huff lying on the ground and Packer linemen figuratively dusting off their hands. "That picture ran all over the country," Remmel remembered, "and as a result, Sam was hitting Taylor in bounds and out of bounds, before the whistle, after the whistle, you name it."

Green Bay drove 60 yards in 11 plays and capped its first series with a 26-yard field goal by Kramer. Initially, Kramer had thought his kick had gone wide, and he cursed under his breath. When he saw the referee signalling the kick good, Kramer turned to Starr.

"What the hell's he doing?" he shouted.

"Shut up," Starr barked, "and get off the field."

The Packers maintained their 3–0 lead through a viciously fought first quarter. Taylor engaged in a running exchange with New York's defense, challenging them. "Hit me harder," he would say, then gouge out a four-yard gain. "I only got four this time," he would tell Huff and Robustelli. "Next time I'm going to get more."

To Huff, Taylor was a maniacal competitor who would do whatever it took to win. "He'd kick you, gouge you, spit at you, whatever it took," Huff said. "It was a street fight."

Taylor ran low to the ground, and all Huff and the Giants saw of him was his lowered helmet and high knees. More than any other Packer, Taylor took to heart Lombardi's belief that a football player had to direct all his anger toward his opponent during the game. "I hated them, from the opening whistle to the final gun," Taylor said. "I loved to take the battle to them, to sting them, to go right at them and pick up the extra yard. I figured I couldn't out-cute them, so I just ran over them."

From the Packer sideline, Nitschke watched in fascination as Taylor took the battle to the Giants. Nitschke figured the Packers had gained their three-point lead on the strength of Taylor's determination. "Early in the game," Nitschke said, "Taylor set the tone."

Nitschke had seen that first sideline collision between Taylor and Huff, had watched Huff drive Taylor out of bounds, and as the two men skidded across the ice, had seen Huff using his knees and elbows on Taylor as they tumbled out of bounds.

When the Giants got the ball back, Nitschke returned the favor. He stuffed King for a one-yard gain on a draw play, then short-circuited the

Giants' drive. Defying both the gusting wind and the Green Bay defense, Tittle had completed three passes for a combined 38 yards to move New York deep into Packer territory. On a second-and-nine at the 15, Nitschke stared across the line at Tittle. As Nitschke and Tittle matched wits, a banner flapping from the railing at Yankee Stadium read "O.K. Y.A., Make Green Bay Pay."

Nitschke knew the Giants had done the bulk of their scoring through the air, and though Green Bay wasn't a blitzing team, Nitschke figured it was a good time to gamble. With Giant fans rocking the stadium with a breathless "Go! Go! Go!" chant, Tittle retreated into the swirling dust of the pocket. Nitschke waited for a second, then looped behind Hanner at left tackle on a delayed blitz. King cut over from his left halfback slot to pick up Nitschke, who was by now two yards deep in the Giant backfield, but he was too late. With his arms raised, Nitschke tipped Tittle's pass, and the deflected ball fell into the arms of left linebacker Dan Currie, who returned it to the 39 before his left knee buckled and he was downed.

Green Bay took over and drove to the New York 30. Taylor carried four times on the march, grunting and growling his way to short pickups on power sweeps and off-tackle slants. On the next-to-last play of the first quarter, game films show Taylor was going down when Huff plowed into him. The violent collision caused Taylor to bite his tongue. Swallowing blood and spitting ice, the Packer fullback climbed groggily to his feet. He was jack-knifed in pain, and Nitschke watched as Taylor steadied himself by grabbing Starr's arm. Taylor, who said later that Huff "is a great one for piling on," left the game for a play as Kramer's 36-yard field goal on the final play of the first quarter fell short in the swirling wind.

"That was a nasty game," Currie remembered. "Geez, Jimmy Taylor split his elbow and still played. The Giants were really up for that game, and there were almost some altercations there a few times. That was the nastiest game I've ever been involved in."

While Taylor continued his constant battle with the Giant defense, Nitschke engaged in his own war with the New York offense. Whether it was wrestling Webster to the rock-hard turf, colliding with King, or blitzing his way into the Giant backfield, Nitschke went after the Giants with a fury.

From the Giants' sideline, Huff watched as Nitschke blitzed Tittle, "blitzed almost at will," the Giants' linebacker said. The Giants became incensed when they claimed King was a full four yards out of bounds when Nitschke plowed into him. But it was that kind of a day in New York, and Huff admired the intensity Nitschke brought to the position.

"He was a great, great linebacker," Huff said. "A great hitter, and the intensity was there. I admired the great ballplayers. Sometimes ballplayers are jealous of one another. But I don't think Ray Nitschke was ever jealous of me and I was never jealous of him."

As the second quarter wore on, Yankee Stadium took on the look and feel of Siberia. The skies grew dark with clouds, and the stadium lights had to be turned on even though it was still early afternoon. Violent winds ripped dirt from the grassless field and funneled it into mini tornadoes. Strong gusts blew the passes of Tittle and Starr back into their faces and wreaked havoc with the passing game. Gifford remembered passes thrown by Tittle landing in front of him and behind him, and at times seemed to be aimed at anyone but him.

By the second quarter, Tittle's fingers were frozen and he had trouble gripping the ball. The wind was clocked at 50 miles per hour on the field, and Kramer noticed the currents were doing crazy things that day; it would blow one way at field level; then blow in the opposite direction just above the ground. The same was true depending on which end of the field the teams were at. The wind would gust in one direction at one end, and Kramer would look down the field and see the dust swirling in a completely different direction at the opposite end zone.

"That was a difficult game to play in because of the weather conditions," Green Bay cornerback Herb Adderley said. "It was extremely cold with the wind-chill factor."

Blizzards of torn paper littered the darkening field during play, and once, a sideline bench that was unoccupied was lifted by a gale and tossed 10 feet onto the field. On the sideline, Bengston thought the combination of the whipping wind and the chants of close to 65,000 Giant fans threatened to sweep the Packers out of Yankee Stadium.

Nitschke, however, provided a second turning point when he recovered a King fumble at the New York 28 with 3:06 remaining in the half. Currie, who was having a big game at outside linebacker, forced the turnover with a jarring hit on King, and Nitschke covered the loose ball.

On NBC Radio, Coleman made the call on a play many considered to be the game's turning point:

> *Second-and-five at the 34 of New York. Y. A. Tittle, on a draw play, gives to King again. . . . Fumble . . . scramble . . . and it is grabbed by the Packers! The Green Bay Packers have come up with the ball and Ray Nitschke is the man who fell on it at the 28-yard line. . . . "*

Nitschke's fumble recovery paid immediate dividends for the Packers. On first down, Hornung headed right on what looked to be a power sweep, then stopped and lofted a long pass that flanker Boyd Dowler gathered in on the 7. One play later, Starr kneeled in the huddle and called "Blue Right 37." The play was designed for Taylor to go off right tackle, and Giants left tackle Dick Modzelewski saw something in Taylor's stance that tipped where the play was going. At the snap, Taylor took Starr's handoff and veered right. Modzelewski followed, but when Kramer drove "Little Mo" further outside, Taylor read his block and cut back across the grain, through the middle. The game film shows Taylor eluding the diving grasp of Rosey Grier at the 5 and skating into the end zone for the score. A play that had been designed to hit the "7" hole off right tackle had actually hit the "0" hole over center. Huff, who knew Taylor was a great option runner, had been trapped out of position, and Taylor hit the end zone untouched and standing up.

"It was the only play of the game they didn't touch me," Taylor said later. "But they sure made up for it the rest of the time."

Up to that play, Huff had been telling Taylor in pile-ups that the Packers fullback "stunk." When Taylor crossed the goal line, he turned his head in Huff's direction. "Hey Sam," he yelled. "How do I smell from here?"

"He was that type of guy," Huff said. "He'd tell me, 'Yeah, you're just a big talker.' He brought the best out in you. He was an unusual player; a great player, but an agitator."

Kramer's extra point made it 10–0 Green Bay, and the score stuck there through the rest of the first half. As the cold intensified, so did the hitting. Nitschke watched as Taylor continued his personal war with Huff and the New York defense. Nitschke compared Taylor to a bull moose who knocked Giant defenders down, trampled them into the icy ground, and kept going. Several times, Nitschke saw Taylor pull himself up from a vicious hit, then turn and snarl at the Giants. "Is that as hard as you can hit?" Taylor would snap. To Nitschke, Taylor was defying the Giants, defying them even though he was getting smashed to the frozen ground and getting piled on by half of the New York defense.

"He was always shooting his mouth off on the field," Huff said of Taylor, and the verbal battle heightened with the hitting. On the films, Taylor can be seen screaming at Huff, and he later accused the Giants' middle linebacker of trying to cripple him by using his knees and elbows on him when Taylor was on the ground. Nitschke thought Huff played a game that bordered on being dirty, and recalled one play where Huff seemed to be twisting Taylor's head in a viselike grip even though the play was over. Taylor's battles weren't with Huff alone. Films of the game show him exchanging words and near punches with Robustelli, and Modzelewski claimed Taylor bit him in a pileup.

"They were beating on us," Packers wide receiver Boyd Dowler recalled, "and we were beating on them."

The hitting was so fierce the Packers fumbled five times; the Giants twice. Taylor put the ball on the ground three times, courtesy of a defense that Tittle thought was delivering some of the hardest tackles he had ever seen. Huff, Robustelli, and the rest were giving Taylor the same treatment they reserved for Cleveland fullback Jim Brown—maximum effort on every play. They were driving into Taylor, Tittle thought as he watched from the sidelines, and flattening him on the frozen ground.

"The ground was like concrete," Hornung said, "and I remember one time Taylor wanted to leave the game. I said, 'Bullshit, you get back in here.'"

Starr would hand off to Taylor, then watch as his fullback would fight for yards before being gang-tackled. It was terrible, Starr thought. The huddle would form and Starr would watch Taylor come back after run-ins with Huff and left end Jim Katcavage, would see his fullback bent over and holding his insides together. "I never saw a back get such a beating," Starr said.

"Taylor was really banged up," Remmel said. "He was bleeding from the mouth, he had a cut tongue, he had bruises all over his arms and I'm sure all over his body. The intensity of Taylor and Huff kind of matched the weather; it was a raw, very frigid day."

The half ended with Green Bay leading 10–0, and as the Packers ran for the locker room, Nitschke could hear them panting hard, trying to catch their breath in the cold. Once inside, the players lined up to get hot coffee or bouillon, and as the team separated into offense and defense to discuss strategy, the words of Lombardi and Bengston were interrupted by a loud yell from the back room. It was Taylor, whose elbows were scraped raw and whose forearm bore a wide gash. Team doctors were sewing him up, and Taylor was screaming in pain, the kind of scream, Nitschke said later, that a player makes when he's in agony. When the doctors finished, they taped his arm, but all Nitschke could think was that the Packers might have to play the second half without Taylor, who in Nitschke's opinion was the toughest guy on the team and maybe the toughest guy in the league.

"How are we going to go out there," Nitschke thought, "and play two more quarters?"

The third quarter resembled the first two. Nitschke continued to battle Webster and King, and Taylor continued his battles with Huff and the Giant defense. Klein thought the game had become one of "ground thrusts and vicious tackles." It was primeval football, he wrote. Taylor would hurl his pain-wracked body at the Giants defense, and they would hurl him back. When New York had the ball, King and Webster, two of the biggest and toughest backs in the NFL, would plunge into the line to be met by Nitschke, Jordan, and Willie Davis. From his right tackle position, Grier thought the game had dissolved into a "bone-crushing defensive duel." High above the stadium field, Coleman called the game "a bruising defensive battle." Taylor continued to spit barbs at the Giants defense, but by the second half, even the members of the Packers' offensive line were telling their fullback to "shut up." Huff said that the Packers realized that the more Taylor talked, the angrier the New York defense became.

"I hit him so hard I don't how the hell he got up," Huff said. "I didn't think I could get up either but I had too much pride to stay down. Most guys, rather than get hit, would run out of bounds. But I knew Taylor wasn't going to do it. I knew he was going to turn back into me and bury me. And I thought, 'One of us is going to die.' "

The Giants finally broke through when Erich Barnes blocked Max McGee's punt on the 15-yard line and Jim Collier covered the loose ball just across the goal line. Don Chandler's point-after cut New York's deficit to 10–7, but again, Nitschke helped regain the momentum for Green Bay. After the Giant defense dug in and forced Green Bay to punt on its next series, return man Sam Horner tracked the flight of McGee's punt against the steel-gray sky and then saw the spiral slip from his numb hands at the New York 35. A scramble ensued, and both Nitschke and Green Bay tackle Forrest Gregg dove for the ball. They were fighting for it under the pile at the Giants' 42 when Gregg shouted, "Who is it?"

"It's Nitschke."

On NBC Radio, Packer broadcaster Ted Moore, who was sharing duties with Coleman and had taken over the play-by-play for the second half, made the call:

> *The line of scrimmage is the Packers' 30-yard line. McGee standing on his 15. Ringo over the ball. There's the snap. McGee gets the kick away, a low one, coming down to Horner, who fumbles the ball. . . . Recovered, I believe, by the Packers. . . . There's a tremendous pileup down on the Giants' 41-yard line. . . . And the Green Bay Packers did recover. I believe it was Ray Nitschke. Nitschke coming up with the football finally for the Green Bay Packers down on the Giants' 42-yard line.*

Gregg released the ball, and Nitschke gained credit for the fumble recovery, his second of the game. With Taylor doing the bulk of the running, the Packers fought their way to the 22, where Kramer hit a 29-yard field goal to give Green Bay a 13–7 lead. Both sides suffered amid the brutal cold and equally brutal hitting throughout the second half. Taylor carried 31 times for 85 yards despite swallowing his own blood for much of the game, and Huff played with what was later diagnosed as a slight concussion. Hornung was knocked out of the game in the fourth quarter after colliding with the ground and the Giant defense on a power sweep, and Green Bay safety Willie Wood was ejected from the game after knocking down an official during a disputed pass inteference call.

Nitschke and the Packer defense matched the heightened emotion by ratcheting up their own intensity. For the second straight year, they prevented the Giants' record-setting offense from producing any points, and when Kramer lined up for another field goal attempt, a 30-yarder with two minutes remaining, he thought, "If you make it, it's all over. We've got the game won." Keeping his head down and allowing for the wind, Kramer's kick cleared the uprights. When he turned toward the Green Bay sideline, Kramer saw Lombardi with a clenched fist in the air. Green Bay now led 16–7, and Lombardi's clenched fist was the Packers' victory sign.

The talk in both locker rooms afterward focused on what remains some of the hardest hitting in NFL championship game history. Since then, there have been several great defensive duels, notably the Baltimore–Tennessee matchup in the 2000 AFC playoffs when Ravens middle linebacker Ray Lewis matched up against Titan running back Eddie George, but even that showdown failed to live up to the intense conditions of the '62 NFL title game.

The Giants defended their play against Taylor afterward. Cornerback Dick Lynch said Taylor "never stops defying you." Modzelewski called Taylor "a crazy runner," and Huff said that Taylor was a back who would do anything to gain an extra couple of inches; he would crawl on his hands and knees if he had to. Since a runner isn't officially downed in the NFL until the whistle blows, Huff figured that if Taylor was down in the frozen dirt fighting for extra inches, the Giants would be down there fighting just as hard to prevent him from getting them.

Nitschke had been fighting just as hard on the Packers' side, and a review of the original radio broadcast reveals he finished the game with 10 tackles to go along with his three forced turnovers. For his dominant play, Nitschke was named the player of the game by *Sport* magazine. Tittle said later that Nitschke had played an alert defensive game, recovering two fumbles and creating a third turnover when he deflected a pass for an interception, a pass Tittle thought would have been a sure touchdown since tight end Joe Walton was so alone in the end zone he was waving for the pass.

Nitschke was both surprised and pleased by being named MVP, which earned him a new Corvette, as well as recognition as the first defensive player in NFL history to win the award. Nitschke was most pleased, however, by the fact Green Bay had earned a second straight NFL championship, and the game's highlight film shows him standing in front of his locker talking reflectively to reporters.

High above the dark and now deserted playing field, league officials were scanning a play-by-play account of the game. It had been so cold in Yankee Stadium that the ink in the duplicating machine had frozen in the second quarter. Today, the play-by-play account of the second quarter can barely be read, and among all the dim lines, one seems dimmer than the rest:

King fumbled, Nitschke recovered on the Giant 28.

As New York writer Harold Rosenthal later noted, that single line might serve best to sum up the story of the '62 title game.

SEVEN

MR. NITSCHKE, are you connected with the government?"

Just hours after being named the Most Valuable Player of the 1962 NFL championship game, Ray Nitschke appeared on the CBS prime time game show *What's My Line?* A Mark Goodson-Bill Todman production, *What's My Line?* was a primetime fixture from 1950 to 1967. Hosted by John Daly, the show was filmed in CBS Studios in New York and included arguably the wittiest panel of celebrities in game-show history: Arlene Francis, Dorothy Kilgallen, and Bennett Cerf. Mystery guests were brought on the show, and with Daly serving as the suave moderator, the show's panelists would probe for their guest's occupation one question at a time. In a testament to the innocence of the times, guests received the grand sum of $5 for every "no" answer, and among the notables who appeared on the show and were asked by Daly to "Enter and sign in please . . . " were future presidents Jimmy Carter, Gerald Ford, and Ronald Reagan. It was on *What's My Line?* that panelist Steve Allen first uttered the now-famous query, "Is it bigger than a breadbox?"

Kilgallen opened the panel's line of questioning to Nitschke by asking if he was connected with the government, and Nitschke answered with a flat "no." Looking very businesslike in his dark-framed glasses and conservative suit and tie, he remained a mystery to the panel through the first two questions.

"He's very quiet and reserved," Francis said finally, "which would lead one to believe he'd be with the Giants, but I believe he's with the Green Bay Packers."

"We were really having some fun," Daly told his audience. "We thought with the glasses and Ray's very quiet nature that we might get away with it for awhile and we did actually. Well, Ray, needless to say we congratulate you and all your colleagues. It was a great game, we're sorry . . . to see our Giants lose but if they had to lose they certainly lost to a great team and to the greatest middle linebacker in the league."

Nitschke's performance on national television in the '62 title game elevated his status at a time when the NFL was dominated by Hall of Fame-caliber middle linebackers and fullbacks. In Chicago, Bill George is remembered as the first man to play the middle linebacker position on a regular basis. An All-America tackle at Wake Forest, the 6-foot-2, 230-pound George joined the Bears in 1952. At the time, most NFL teams were still running a defensive alignment of five down linemen, two linebackers and four defensive backs. As the middle guard in the five-two, George's responsibility on pass plays was to bump the opposing center and then backpedal into coverage. George played the position well enough to earn all-pro honors in both 1952 and '53. In a 1955 game against Philadelphia, however, George was being beaten regularly on passes over the middle. To compensate, the Bears changed tactics. Rather than have George bump the center before dropping into coverage, George would stand up and take a quick step back. The strategy worked immediately. On first down, he knocked down an Eagles' pass over the middle. On second down, he picked off the first of his 18 career interceptions. Four years earlier, Giants' head coach Steve Owen and defensive captain Tom Landry had developed the Umbrella Defense in response to the problems presented by the Cleveland Browns' offense. The position of an every-down middle linebacker was born in Chicago that December 11 against the Eagles, and by 1957, the NFL replaced middle guard with middle linebacker on its annual all-pro teams.

A strong, intelligent player, George was responsible for molding the middle linebacker position into one of field generalship; the counterpart to the quarterback. In 1956, when the Bears were running various defensive alignments under head coach George Halas, George was given the responsibility of learning them all. Bears' defensive coordinator George Allen, who went on to coach strong defensive units in Los Angeles and Washington, called Bill George the smartest defensive player he ever coached. "He called defensive signals for the Bears when they were at their best," Allen said. "He made as few mistakes as any player I've ever seen."

George's strength of mind and body—he wrestled running backs to the ground with techniques he learned as a wrestler at Wake Forest—provided a role model for future linebackers to follow. From 1955 to 1962, George was named to eight consecutive Pro Bowls and led the Bears to two Western Conference titles and one NFL championship.

While George is generally regarded as the game's first pure middle linebacker, Detroit's Joe Schmidt proved instrumental in making middle linebacker the most important position on defense. Relatively small for his position at 6-foot, 220, Schmidt used speed and intelligence to help lead the Lions to Western Conference championships in 1953, '54, and '57, and NFL titles in '53 and '57. A product of the University of Pittsburgh, Schmidt was drafted by the Lions in 1953. Because he had suffered through an injury-plagued career with the Panthers, Schmidt's arrival in Detroit was treated with indifference. But when injuries depleted Detroit's linebacking corps, Schmidt stepped in and became a starter. The Lions had won NFL championships in 1952 and '53 with a five-two defense anchored by 350-pound middle guard Les Bingaman. But in 1955, head coach Buddy Parker dropped the five-two alignment the Lions had been using and instituted the modern four-three. Moving from left linebacker to the middle, Schmidt flourished in the new formation, and was named to the Pro Bowl 10 straight seasons from 1955 to 1964. Like Bill George, Schmidt combined strength with strategy. "He's a great tackler and a strong leader," Lombardi said at the time. "He can diagnose a play in an instant."

Schmidt's heady style may have been most evident in his pass defense. He recorded 24 career interceptions and according to Parker, helped revolutionize modern defenses.

"His style of play brought about the zone defense," Parker said, "and the modern defensive look of pro football."

Pioneered by George and Schmidt, the four-three was popularized in 1956 with the emergence in New York of Sam Huff. Committing to the four-three as their base alignment, the Giants drafted Huff out of West Virginia in '56 for the specific purpose of patrolling the middle. But when head coach Jim Lee Howell hesitated on where to play the 6-foot-1, 230-pound rookie, Huff grew discouraged and walked out of camp. He was persuaded to return by Lombardi, the Giants' offensive coordinator at the time, and Huff took over at middle linebacker when starter Ray Beck was sidelined with an injury. Huff's emergence as a starter coincided with Landry's development of what he called his "Recognition Defense." Rather than following the rule of the day which saw defenses swarm to the ball carrier, Landry taught his players to recognize the play and avoid the blocking schemes before committing to the play.

Landry's restrained style reflected both his analytical mind and reserved manner, and it ushered in a new era of defensive play. The Giant defense of the late 1950s became the forerunner of the "Flex" style Landry would later introduce in Dallas, and because Landry's style was suited to freeing the middle linebacker to flow to the ball, it made Huff a national hero. He became the NFL's first glamour player on defense, was featured on the cover of *Time* magazine in 1959, and in 1960 was the subject of a CBS documentary titled "The Violent World of Sam Huff."

As the focal point of the defense, middle linebackers like Huff, George, and Schmidt became the defensive equivalent of quarterback. They were responsible for knowing the formations and responsibilities of each defensive play, called out signals, and countered quarterbacks by engaging in mental gymnastics in the seconds before each snap of the ball. Landry aided Huff by sliding his down linemen to the center-guard gaps, thereby freeing his middle linebacker to flow to the ball.

For five years, from 1954 to 1958, Lombardi worked alongside Landry in

New York, and when Lombardi moved to Green Bay in 1959, he took Landry's four-three principles with him. Just as Paul Hornung would become Lombardi's Green Bay version of versatile Giants' offensive star Frank Gifford, Nitschke became the Packers' defensive answer to Huff. Green Bay's success in winning three straight Western Conference crowns from 1960 to 1962 gave Nitschke the recognition usually reserved for Huff, George, and Schmidt. From 1962 to 1967, Nitschke earned nominations to at least one of the five all-pro teams of the time—Associated Press, United Press, Newspaper Enterprise Association, *New York Daily News*, or *The Sporting News*.

The increased responsibilities of the middle linebacker position brought increased study time for Nitschke, and he worked closely with defensive coordinator Phil Bengston to master his position. Green Bay at the time ran a base four-three defense with man-to-man coverage. Out of the four-three, they could shift to a four-three Over, where the down linemen slid one position over toward the strength of the offensive formation, and the four-three Under, an undershift away from the strong side. It was a simplified system, but the Packers also employed "pinch" and "stack" principles that were innovative for their time. To keep the center and guards off of Nitschke, Bengston positioned his tackles in the center-guard gaps and instructed them to "pinch" inside, thereby rendering a blocker helpless. The stack would become a staple of the AFL, and Green Bay used it as a mixer in their base defense by stacking either of their tackles head-up on the center, thereby preventing the cutoff blocks aimed at eliminating Nitschke. Green Bay also ran an array of blitzes that Bengston had formulated during his days as the defensive coordinator in San Francisco. Nitschke's middle linebacker blitz was usually coordinated with one of his defensive tackles. If Nitschke blitzed to the strong side of the offense, the strong side tackle would take an inside route and Nitschke would loop behind him. If Nitschke was blitzing to the weak side, the weak side tackle charged inside. A third blitzing scheme required Nitschke to charge straight up the middle, and both defensive tackles to take outside routes. Occasionally, the Packers also ran a double blitz, with Nitschke coordinating his charge with one of his outside linebackers.

In the Packers' system, Nitschke had four keys to follow on each play. His initial key was the movement of the center, followed by the fullback and two guards. The coordinated movement of those four players at the snap of the ball revealed to Nitschke what play the offense was running. Film study during the week preceding each game saw Nitschke learning the habits of the opposing offense in general and his four keys in particular as he searched for clues and tip-offs. Green Bay's film study was so meticulous that during the off-season, Lombardi and his offensive coaches would scout the Packer defense while Bengston and his defensive coaches scouted the offense. What each side was doing was searching for the smallest clue, the smallest tip-off to what the offensive or defensive call was. If Lombardi saw a Packer defenseman tipping the call, the information was noted and given to Bengston for correction in the next summer camp. If Bengston saw a Green Bay lineman leaning one way or the other and tipping the play, he would inform Lombardi.

On the field, Green Bay defensive tackles Dave Hanner and Henry Jordan helped by pointing out to Nitschke certain tips on what to look for from the opposition. The tips were usually of the smallest nature; if a linemen or back leaned ever so slightly to his right or left, Nitschke could count on the play going in that direction. If a linemen's knuckles were showing white from the pressure of his weight leaning forward, Nitschke knew the offense was getting ready to fire out on a running play. If the linemen was leaning lightly on his down hand and was back on his haunches, the Packers figured he was getting ready to retreat and pass-block, and would set their defense accordingly.

Green Bay's defensive plays were relayed from Bengston via hand signals. During his first few years in Green Bay, Bengston would wigwag his fingers, signaling either a change in formation or a blitz. In time, opponents began picking up on Bengston's hand signals and he adjusted by changing his signs from game to game. One week would find Bengston signaling plays in by adjusting the brim of his fedora; the next week the signs were relayed by the straightening of his tie or the toss of a tuft of grass in the air as if to check wind direction. Linebacker Bill Forester would relay the call in the huddle, and Nitschke would shout the offense's formations once they lined up. Because Green Bay's defensive plays were automatic depending on what formation the offense was in, Nitschke had to be certain his split-second diagnosis was correct. Offensive formations at the time included "Red" or "Split" in which the running backs are split to either side of the quarterback; "Brown" or "Opposite" where the fullback is behind the quarterback and the halfback splits slightly to the weak side; "Blue" or "Near" where the fullback is behind the quarterback and the halfback splits slightly to the strong-side.

NFL teams in the sixties also used early versions of the Shotgun, the Slot, the I, the Double Wing, and even a Triple Wing. Nitschke would study the formation just before the snap, and his call depended on where the tight end was lined up, since that indicated the strong side of the offense. If both backs were split behind the quarterback and the tight end was lined up next to the right tackle, Nitschke's call would be "Red Right." If the backs were in a Brown formation and the tight end lined up left, he would shout call out "Brown Left."

Because the Packers' defensive calls were prearranged, Nitschke knew once he went through his progression of keys what his responsibilities were. He knew instantly whether he should follow the fullback, blitz the quarterback, or drop into coverage. By 1962, Nitschke's study habits had him firmly entrenched as Green Bay's starting middle linebacker, the leader of a Packer defense that was the NFL's best. On the verge just two years before of being run out of town by his head coach, Nitschke impressed Lombardi so much the Packer boss was completely passing over middle linebackers in the annual draft. Nitschke still irritated his coach with mistakes made on the practice field, but Lombardi was resigning himself to the fact that at the very least, Nitschke was able to eliminate his own errors. Lombardi told writer W. C. Heinz that when he chewed Nitschke out, Ray took it like a child in the sense that he was repentant and didn't argue, but he would turn around and make the same mistake again. Criticism rolled off Nitschke so much that even Lombardi, the master motivator, wondered if he was getting through.

"You don't improve him," Lombardi told Heinz, "but happily he improves himself."

To Nitschke, Lombardi was an amazing man. As a player, Nitschke had found that he needed to pace himself emotionally as well as physically in preparing for a game. Lombardi, however, was always "up" emotionally. "He had extraordinary emotional drive," Nitschke said, and while Lombardi yelled a lot at practice, Nitschke thought it was, at times, an act for the benefit of the player he was yelling at. Lombardi had yelled a lot at him their first few years together, Nitschke said, because he was wild and he needed to be kept in line. Lombardi's demand for perfection and dedication had infected the Packers as a team, and even though Nitschke could see that his coach's rage was an act at times, he bought it anyway.

Nitschke's observation was an astute one. Lombardi did have to work to get himself emotionally ready for every practice, every film session. He worked himself into frenzies in the coaches' room beforehand, then announced to his assistants, "I'm just going to give these guys complete hell today. . . . Today is going to be one of those days."

"He really stayed on us," Nitschke said, and at the end of the day, Lombardi would wipe the sweat from his forehead with a handkerchief like a stage actor wiping off greasepaint and announce, "I really gave it to them today, didn't I?"

Lombardi's outbursts became predictable; he would cuss the team early in the week, guard Jerry Kramer said, and kiss them as game day approached. Nitschke was Lombardi's whipping boy, and he often took the public lashings with a grin. "He gave Nitschke a lot of hell," safety Emlen Tunnell said at the time. "He was trying to help the guy and he did. . . . Vinnie knew the guy was going to be a football player. He *knew*. He handled Ray just right."

Mike Manuche, a friend of Lombardi's, agreed. "Vinnie really did a job on him," Manuche said. Lombardi would tell Nitschke, "We don't need you!" but in reality he saw something in his tough middle linebacker that made him want to work to straighten his life out.

"He helped turn my life around as a person," Nitschke said later.

Nitschke's improvement as a middle linebacker came under Bengston's quiet tutelage, and the two men struck up a warm working relationship. Lombardi's occasional rage was tempered by Bengston's reserved approach; if one of his defensive players felt Lombardi's verbal lash, Bengston would soothe the player's hurt feelings with quiet words of encouragement. To Nitschke, Bengston was a cool customer, a quiet, dedicated man whom he admired. "There is no man I respect more," he said. Unlike Lombardi, Bengston was able to maintain his poise; when he did get angry, however, his players knew it because his voice level would go up. "When he yells, you jump," Nitschke said, "because you know he is really mad." As quiet as his defensive coach was, Nitschke felt that Bengston could still be just as tough as Lombardi.

Quarterback Bart Starr saw firsthand the interaction between Bengston and the members of his defense. "Coach Bengston was an astute coach," Starr said. "He was a great teacher and I think he was a very compassionate and understanding person as well. He had a sense and feel for different individuals, and I believe he had a great feel for Ray and how to work with him."

Bengston was a sound defensive strategist, and Nitschke benefited from his teachings. "He simplifies the defense and explains it better than any coach I ever saw," Nitschke said. Under Bengston, Nitschke learned more than ever how to study the game, how to apply himself. Nitschke learned to study not only the moves of his opponent but also his personality, and Bengston also taught Ray how to study his own moves. The two would watch Green Bay game films together, and Bengston would quietly show Nitschke what he was doing right and what mistakes he was making. He taught Nitschke how to react to a certain blocking pattern in a way that would allow him to get to the runner quicker. He saw things that Nitschke overlooked and made Ray aware of his role in the overall context of the game. By learning the fine points of his position, Nitschke became as much a heady player as he was a heavy hitter.

Defensive end Willie Davis said Bengston was instrumental in saving Nitschke's NFL career. "Phil simplified Ray's assignments, and Ray had enough talent to play through some of his mistakes," Davis said. "Phil was a very methodical guy and he really prepared you very well to play the game. And after Ray was in the starting lineup for a couple of years, the mistakes went away and he became a great linebacker."

Bengston referred to Nitschke as a "dynamic manifestation of the anti-quarterback." If an observer wanted a lightning review of the plays and formations an opponent would use against the Packers, Bengston suggested they first check with the enemy quarterback. If he's not available, Bengston said, then ask Nitschke. Film study allowed Nitschke to match wits with opposing quarterbacks, and Bengston would watch from the sidelines as Nitschke would follow the opposing quarterback's audibles with signal changes of his own. When both arrived at the same call, Bengston said, the result was a victory for his fast-guessing anti-quarterback.

Out on the Packers' practice field, Nitschke's victories were sometimes greeted with less enthusiasm by Lombardi. In 1962, Lombardi had installed a special series of tight end reverses out of a double-wing formation in preparation for a key early-season contest against Western Conference rival Detroit. As Starr led the offense to the line of scrimmage, Nitschke's raspy voice cut through the gray, wet air.

"Double-wing!" Nitschke shouted. "Double-wing!"

Lombardi, aware there may be Detroit scouts watching the practice, cringed. "Not so loud," he said, admonishing Nitschke.

While Lombardi would run the Packer offense in practices, he gave Bengston full control of the defense. To Nitschke and the other members of the Green Bay defense, Bengston was as much a student of the game as Lombardi.

"Phil Bengston always said, 'It's not the defenses that we call, it's the men implementing the defenses,'" left cornerback Herb Adderley said. "All we did was basic defense, believe me. We had ten pages in our playbook. When I went to Dallas (in 1970) their playbook was like the Yellow Pages. Bengston had the players, and we were a basic defensive team. It was just a matter of going out there and playing like we practiced."

Bengston's approach was to get his players to practice hard during the week to gain the confidence necessary to do their jobs on game days. To Nitschke, football knowledge seemed to just flow from Bengston. Later, Nitschke would say that he learned more about the game from Bengston than from any other coach he'd ever had.

"Phil was our coach," remembered Dan Currie, who played left linebacker for the Packers from 1958 to 1964. "Vince coached the offense. He'd come into the defensive meeting, start hollering, and then slam the door, just to let you know that he was the boss. But Phil manned the defense. He did the teaching and he was very good at it."

While Lombardi was more offense-oriented, his early years with the

Packers saw him concentrate on building a championship defense. Nitschke knew the offense was Lombardi's pride and joy, but he also knew that his head coach realized that if the defense didn't get the offense the ball often enough, the Packers weren't going to win. Since the team that gets the ball the most is going to win, Nitschke figured the job of the defense was a fundamental one. "To get that ball," he said.

The emergence of great middle linebackers like Nitschke, Bill George, Joe Schmidt, and Sam Huff paralleled the rise of power backs like Jim Brown, Jim Taylor, Alan Ameche, and Joe Perry. The NFL in the early sixties was a game of power, and there was a sense of moral balance to the game because winning teams were not only considered superior skill-wise but also superior in courage, character, and desire. In the early 1950s, the game's moral balance had been altered by point-a-minute passing games that cheapened the game with long bombs and quick scores. The man-to-man power game was being phased out in favor of finesse blocks and free-and-easy offenses. Defenses reacted by dropping their passive play in favor of an aggressive attitude. Coaches like George Allen, Chuck Drulis, and Clark Shaughnessy put their defenses on the offensive, and the result was a smashing array of blitzes and formations. A defensive coordinator for the Bears in the late '50s, Shaughnessy developed a dizzying system of combination blitzes and coverages. Drulis, who handled the St. Louis Cardinals' defense, sent wildman safety Larry Wilson crashing after quarterbacks as the eighth man in a terrifying eight-man blitz. In Los Angeles, Allen fielded a football-grabbing unit that gained fame as "The Fearsome Foursome."

"We want the ball," Ram linebacker Maxie Baughan said, "and we have more than 300 defenses we can use to get it."

By the early '60s, the ball-hawking monsters of the defense had helped restore the balance that had been missing from the game for almost a full decade. Bigger, faster defensive specialists were shutting down the end runs and long bombs, and when offenses found themselves faced with a shrinking field, the game was forced back into an elemental confrontation, back into a moral balance where winners were judged superior not only by their physical strength but by their strength of character, commitment, and desire.

Power struggles were waged along the lines of scrimmage, and at the forefront were the middle linebackers and fullbacks. Because they played in the same conference, Nitschke went helmet-to-helmet twice a season with Baltimore's Alan Ameche and San Francisco's Joe Perry. A 6-foot, 220-pound product of Wisconsin, Ameche was nicknamed "The Horse," and he galloped through NFL defenses in helping lead the Colts to consecutive world championships in 1958 and '59. He climaxed the famous '58 title game when he lowered his helmet and drove in from a yard out to give Baltimore a 23–17 overtime win against the Giants.

At 6-foot, 206 pounds, Perry wasn't as big as Ameche, but his power was undeniable. He was called "The Jet" for his explosive 9.5 speed in the 100-yard dash, but former 49ers' coach Frankie Albert had another, more apt description of his star back.

"Perry is like a bowling ball fired from a Howitzer," Albert said. "It whistles down the middle of the alley and sends the pins flying in every direction."

Perry's head-down, head-first plunges into the line didn't always pay off. In a game against the Giants, Perry lowered his helmeted head and plowed into the end zone, an irresistible force about to meet an immovable object. The collision caused Perry to stagger to his feet, where he saw Jimmy Patton, the Giants' little 183-pound safety, snarling at him.

"Run past me again," Patton said, "and I'll cold-cock you again."

Perry headed to the sidelines, still shaking the cobwebs from his head, and told coach Red Strader, "Did you see that little sumbitch hit me? He's murder."

Strader laughed. "It was the goal post, you dummy," he said. "Good thing you hit it with your head."

Nitschke responded to the challenges posed by the fullbacks of his day with a snarling, forearm-throwing intensity. To him, football was an instinctive game, and his instinct was to follow the man with the ball. "And then," he said, "you make them sorry they took the damned thing from the quarterback."

Nitschke's play was fierce but also fundamentally sound. Rams' linebacker Les Richter said at the time that it wasn't Nitschke's speed or his quickness in getting to a play that was most amazing. "It's a desire to make the play," Richter said, "an ability to get to the right spot ahead of everybody else."

Green Bay opened the 1963 preseason on a down note. Halfback Paul Hornung was suspended by NFL commissioner Pete Rozelle for violating the league rule that prohibits players from betting on the outcomes of games. Nitschke was injured in practice prior to the annual College All-Star Game, and was in traction at home when the Packers played the All-Stars on August 2 at Soldier Field, Chicago. The game would have represented a homecoming for Nitschke, but he settled for watching the game on television. To compensate for the absence of Hornung and Nitschke, Lombardi started Tom Moore at halfback and switched backup center Ken Iman to middle linebacker. Coached by Otto Graham, the All-Stars featured future Pro starters in tackle Bob Vogel and guard Ed Budde, defensive linemen Jim

Dunaway and Fred Miller, safety Kermit Alexander, and a linebacking corps of Bobby Bell, Lee Roy Jordan, and Packer draft pick Dave Robinson. "Greatest collection of talent ever assembled on a football field," Lombardi said.

Fueled by a fourth-quarter touchdown pass from Ron VanderKelen to Pat Richter, the All-Stars scored 10 points in the final 15 minutes to stun Green Bay, 20–17. The win was the All-Stars' first since 1958, and it left the Packers embarrassed. Lombardi was mortified, and Nitschke always believed that if he had been able to play, Green Bay would have won.

The Packers won the rest of their preseason games, then hosted the Bears in the regular season opener on September 15. Brilliant sunshine and temperatures in the mid-70s greeted a Green Bay crowd of 42,327 as they jammed into Lambeau Field. The Packers–Bears rivalry was an ancient one, dating back to their first meeting in 1921. The coaching matchup was classic sixties—Lombardi versus Halas. The Packers had won five straight over the Bears, including final scores of 49–0 and 38–7 in 1962. They had won 13 straight at home, and their roster featured 13 players who had been named All-Pro in 1962 or would be in '63; 10 of those players would eventually be inducted into the Pro Football Hall of Fame.

In addition, the Packers entered the game with what appeared to be a huge advantage on the right side of their now-famous offensive line. Right guard Jerry Kramer and right tackle Forrest Gregg were all-pro players. Across the line, the Bears had moved offensive lineman Stan Jones to left defensive tackle to replace Fred Williams, and put Bob Kilcullen at left end as a substitute for the injured Ed O'Bradovich. It was expected that the Packers would pound away at the left side of the Bear line with Taylor and Moore, and *Chicago American* columnist Bill Gleason picked up on the theme in the days leading up to the game. Jones was a schoolteacher in the off-season and Kilcullen was an artist, and Gleason in his column wrote the Chicago defense looked solid except for the schoolteacher and the artist on the left side.

Whatever perceived shortcomings the Chicago defense may have had were offset by two off-season developments. George Allen had been named the Bears' defensive coordinator and he immediately began charting the tendencies of opposing offenses by meticulously breaking down their game films. Bears' linebacker Joe Fortunato said that Allen realized that Green Bay had tremendous tendencies. One such tendency was picked up when the Packers ran the power sweep. Allen's attention to detail revealed that when Green Bay was planning a sweep left, Gregg would cheat out some six inches from his normal position in order to get a better blocking angle. The Bears picked up on it, and Allen planned to adjust his defense accordingly.

Described by writer Murray Olderman as owning "the grimacing mien of a coal mine paymaster and the devotion to detail of an old maid librarian," Allen spent the summer poring over Packer game films. He realized that since Green Bay's well-schooled blocking schemes were based on instant recognition of defenses, the Bears would seek to confuse them by playing odd-man fronts with a man over center Jim Ringo. Since Bart Starr was an excellent audible quarterback, Allen planned to disguise Chicago's coverage schemes by dropping his linebackers—Fortunato, Bill George, and Larry Morris—into short zones.

Allen's intense preparation was aided by an unlikely source. Linebacker Tom Bettis, whom Nitschke had replaced as Green Bay's starter back in 1960, had been traded to Pittsburgh after having words with Lombardi in 1962. The Bears picked Bettis up prior to the '63 season, and the former Packer proved more than eager to help Halas and the Bears prepare for Green Bay. "Halas picked my brains, for sure," said Bettis, who cooperated by giving the Bears a rundown on the Packers' player personnel, their plays, and their system.

From the day the Bears arrived in training camp in the summer of '63, Halas had them pointing toward the season-opener against the Packers. Bears' running back Ronnie Bull remembered Halas repeatedly telling his team, "If we win that game, we have a chance to go all the way."

A gentle, southerly breeze wafted through Lambeau Field as the game got underway, and the Chicago defense, primed for its confrontation with the Packers' precision offense, forced an early turnover when safety Richie Petitbon covered a Taylor fumble at the Green Bay 33-yard line. Three plays later Bob Jencks booted a 32-yard field goal to give the Bears a 3–0 lead, but the Packers tied the game on their next possession on a 41-yard field goal by Kramer.

For the remainder of the first half, the game settled into a defensive struggle. Game films show Nitschke battling Chicago guards Ted Karras and Roger Davis. To Karras, the way Nitschke played his position was different than the other middle linebackers of his day. Karras found that Nitschke always took his blocks head-on; he seemed to especially enjoy taking on the linemen, and he played tough, hitting and holding his ground. To Karras, Nitschke played the game with power, as opposed to a player like the Giants' Sam Huff, whom Karras thought was quick in trying to shed his blocker. Nitschke, Karras thought, tried to punish offensive linemen, which Karras said only served to make him more hated around the league.

"Ray was a tenacious competitor," Cleveland center John Morrow said. "He was a son of a bitch. But that's a center talking about a linebacker."

Minnesota center Mick Tingelhoff said Nitschke was a loud, intimidating presence when he hovered over the ball just before the snap.

"He'd be out there yelling," Tingelhoff said, "and he would try to intimidate you. He was very, very intense, a big, rawboned, tough guy. He'd knock your head off with that great forearm."

Nitschke had a stated desire to manhandle the opposition. In a conversation with Currie, he talked about the physical contact, the man-to-man challenge of playing pro football.

"That's what I like about this game," Nitschke said.

Currie countered by telling how he enjoyed the artistic, scientific side of the game. "With me," Currie said, "it's the tackle instead of just belting the other guy."

"Not with me," Nitschke responded.

Opponents may have hated Nitschke, but they also respected him. Bears' Hall of Fame tight end Mike Ditka, whose career lasted from 1961 to 1972 said Nitschke was the best middle linebacker he played against. As a rookie, Ditka made an immediate impression on Nitschke when they met in the 1961 Midwest Shrine Game, an exhibition played in Milwaukee. Ditka was running across the middle of the field when the whistle blew to end the play. In an attempt to pull up, the rookie put his arms out and ended up pushing Nitschke from behind. Ditka said Nitschke took the contact the wrong way, and after the game, the two met accidentally in a Milwaukee bar where members of both teams had congregated.

"You're a dirty player," Nitschke said.

"Fine," Ditka responded, and within moments the two had to be restrained by teammates. They continued their feud on the field the next two games, and carried it over into the '63 season opener. In the second quarter, Ditka got the better of it when he executed a perfect peel-back block that violently upended Nitschke and put him out of the game. If it had been another linebacker, Ditka said, he would have hit him high, but since it was Nitschke, he went low.

Films show Nitschke flying head-over-heels, but his stay on the sidelines was short. Not long after, Ditka watched in amazement as Nitschke came hobbling back into the game, the knees of his yellow-gold pants taped up.

Joe Marconi's one-yard touchdown run in the third quarter gave the Bears a 10–3 lead, and Chicago's defense made it stand up the rest of the way. Starr, who had thrown just nine interceptions in the entire '62 season, was picked off four times in one afternoon by the Bears. Allen's shifting fronts and zone coverages helped confuse the Green Bay quarterback, and the Packers' proud ground game ground to a halt. Taylor was limited to 53 yards rushing, Green Bay's offense gained just 150 yards total, and the Packers never advanced beyond the Bears' 33. Bettis' information on the Packer defense allowed Bears' QB Bill Wade to continually frustrate Green Bay's blitzing schemes. A Wade-to-Marconi pass on the Bears' touchdown drive came when Wade had caught Nitschke and the Packers in a blitz and beaten them with a short pass that went for a long gain.

Ditka said later that Nitschke had played a great game, but Ray didn't agree. His knee had been injured on Ditka's block, and he had been caught offsides—a rare occurrence for him—when Chicago center Mike Pyle saw Nitschke jump the line of scrimmage on a blitz and quickly snapped the ball before Nitschke could jump back. It was smart football on Pyle's part, Nitschke said, and as the referee counted off the penalty yards, Nitschke stood there, angry at himself.

Despite the disappointing defeat, the Packers responded by reeling off eight straight wins. The Bears had dropped a Week Six decision to San Francisco, and when the Packers arrived at Wrigley Field on November 17, the two teams were 8–1 and sitting atop the Western Conference. It was a hugely anticipated matchup; tickets priced at $2.50 were being scalped for $100. Because NFL games at the time were blacked out within a 75-mile radius, Bears' fans wanting to watch the dramatic showdown on television began a mass exodus the morning of the game to watch it in bars and motels outside the city's limits. Wrigley Field pulsated with a full-house crowd of 49,166, and as the Packers took the field they radiated confidence. Even though Green Bay entered the game minus Hornung and Starr, the latter having suffered a broken hand against the St. Louis Cardinals, the Packers were loose. *Sports Illustrated* artist and photographer Robert Riger had spent time with Kramer and Fuzzy Thurston two days before the game, and Riger told Bears' defensive end Bob Kilcullen there was no way the Packers thought they were going to lose this game.

Nitschke was confident as well. Privately, many members of the Green Bay defense just didn't think Wade was a championship-type quarterback. Nitschke felt that since the Packers had been able to get themselves up for big games the past three seasons, there was no reason to think they couldn't do it again.

George Allen had other ideas. Having held Starr and Co. to three points in their season opener, the Bears' defensive coordinator planned to welcome Packer backups John Roach and Zeke Bratkowski by adding yet another defensive wrinkle. Green Bay center Jim Ringo was a master of the cutoff block on the middle linebacker, and in the season opener, Allen had shifted his down linemen, Stan Jones and Earl Leggett in "Over" and "Under" sets to keep Ringo off middle linebacker Bill George. For the

November rematch, Allen instructed Jones and Leggett to line up in an "Over" defense at the start, then shift just before the snap.

"We were in an overshifted defense to the left," Allen said; "Before the snap of the ball we'd move into an undershifted defense to the right."

Allen had never been a big proponent of the odd-front defense, but in that November game against Green Bay, the Bears continually shifted from one odd-front to another. Chicago players came back to the sidelines and told Allen the shifting confused the Packers. Offensively, the Bears planned to attack Green Bay's right side, where rookie defensive end Lionel Aldridge had taken over after Lombardi had dealt Bill Quinlan following the '62 championship. The word out of Green Bay was that Lombardi had traded Quinlan because the two men didn't get along. Lombardi's decision thrilled the Bears, especially assistant coach Chuck Mather. Quinlan was a veteran player, and he had given the Chicago offense problems in the past. With Quinlan gone, Mather said the Bears planned their ground game to run at Green Bay's right side. The plan paid dividends in the second quarter, when halfback Willie Galimore took a handoff and veered left. With Nitschke caught blitzing, the Bears sprung Galimore, and his 27-yard touchdown gave Chicago a 13–0 lead.

"A lot of times Nitschke would guess and take a chance," Adderley said. "Most of the times he was right, but when he was wrong, look out. When Galimore broke one for a touchdown that helped Chicago beat us in '63, Nitschke played a hunch and went to the wrong hole. Galimore went to the other side and once he broke it, that was it."

The Bears continued to pound away at the Packers' right side, and Nitschke said later that it seemed throughout the day that he had no sooner reached the sideline following a tough defensive series when he would have to take the field again. The Bears built a 26–0 lead before settling for a 26–7 victory, and they finished with 248 yards rushing. Later, Mather said the Bears had success running to their left because Lombardi had traded Quinlan. "That was one time," Mather said, "when the Italian outsmarted himself."

The defeat dropped Green Bay a game behind the Bears in the conference standings, and the Packers followed with a win in San Francisco. When Chicago tied Pittsburgh 17–17, the Packers were just a half-game behind the Bears in the Western Conference. Nitschke knew that if Green Bay continued to win and someone could knock off the Bears, the Packers could take over first place. Nitschke's season, however, would end sooner than he had anticipated. Playing the Lions in Detroit on Thanksgiving Day, Nitschke was fighting off a block by halfback Tom Watkins when his right forearm collided with Watkins' silver-and-blue helmet. Nitschke heard a sickening cracking sound, then felt a sharp pain shivering up his right arm.

"My arm's broken, guys," he told his defensive mates. "I'm taking myself out."

Currie wouldn't hear of it. "Oh no, you aren't," he snapped. "Wait until this series is over."

Nitschke stayed in and tried to disguise the injury from the Lions. He had no feeling in his broken arm, but he still managed to get in on the next couple of plays. He broke his nose on the second play when he stopped 225-pound Lions' fullback Nick Pietrosante on a running play at the Packer 36.

That was all for Nitschke. Green Bay's defense had made its stand, and Nitschke headed off the field with a broken arm and broken nose.

"The guy had a lot of mental toughness," Adderley said of Nitschke, "and mental toughness to Lombardi was playing injured. Don't complain about it and don't go into the trainer's room laying up there on the table and getting all kinds of treatment. Because football, Lombardi always said, was not a contact sport. 'If you want contact,' he always said, 'go to Arthur Murray's.' Football is a collision sport, so you have to expect bumps and bruises. So mental toughness was playing injured.

"I saw Nitschke play with a broken arm in Detroit. He hit Tom Watkins with a forearm, like a clothesline shot, and he broke his forearm. And the guy was in a lot of pain but he played. He came out, and they didn't have x-ray machinery in the locker room, so the doctor looked at him and said, 'Well, you got pain here?' and he said 'Yeah,' and they wrapped it up, put some gauze on it and he went right back out there. It was snowing and cold in Detroit that day and he went out and played. I saw him play with pulled muscles where he could hardly get around, but he didn't miss any games.

"He was, no question, the toughest guy on our defense. Without a doubt. And it was inspiring to other guys to see him play that way. Other guys would get hurt and say, 'Hey, he's doing it, we've got to do it too.'"

Green Bay led 13–6 when Nitschke left the field for good, but Detroit rallied to tie the game. He remained on the sidelines as the Packers won their final two games to finish 11–2–1, but they remained a half-game behind the Bears, who went 11–1–2 and defeated the Giants 14–10 in the NFL title game at frozen Wrigley Field.

Lombardi said later that the '63 Packers were the best team he ever coached, and Green Bay defensive end Willie Davis thought the '63 squad was at least as good as the '62 and '66 teams that are generally considered the best of the Lombardi era.

Out of the championship game for the first time since 1960, Nitschke spent the off-season with his wife Jackie and their young son, John. In past years, Nitschke had always spent his winter months killing time and getting into trouble. As he looked at his young son, Nitschke knew his life had been changed forever. He was now a husband and a father, and just as John would soon be taking his first steps toward walking, Nitschke was taking steps of his own—steps on the road to maturity.

Nitschke had ended the season in much the same way he had begun it, sidelined by an injury. As frustrating as the 1963 season had been for him, the '64 season was even more so. Hornung had returned from his suspension, but the year away dulled the luster of Green Bay's Golden Boy. After opening the regular season with a 23–12 win over Chicago, the Packers lost three of their next five games because of missed kicks by Hornung. The offensive line had been weakened by the trade of all-pro center Jim Ringo to Philadelphia, a trade that despite the stories passed down through the years, had actually been requested by Ringo so he could be closer to his home.

With Ringo gone, left tackle Bob Skoronski was shifted to center, but the line became a shambles when Thurston was injured and Kramer was hospitalized due to stomach surgery. A 27–17 loss to Los Angeles in Week Seven dropped the Packers' record to 3–4, far behind the streaking Baltimore Colts. While the Green Bay offense struggled, the defense stepped to the fore. They led the NFL against the pass and were second behind the Colts in points allowed. Nitschke, Davis, Henry Jordan, and Willie Wood were named to the NFL's All-Pro defensive unit, but it proved small consolation to finishing in second place for a second straight year. Green Bay's 8–5–1 record was their worst since a 7–5 finish in 1959, Lombardi's first year. The Colts ran away with the Western title, fashioning a 12–2 record before being stunned by the underdog Cleveland Browns 27–0 in the NFL championship game. The Packers suffered a final jolt when they lost the Playoff Bowl to St. Louis, 24–17, just the second post-season loss for Green Bay during the Lombardi era. The game was played January 3 in Miami, and one week later Nitschke made his first and only appearance in the NFL's Pro Bowl game. Held January 10 in Los Angeles, Nitschke sparked a dominating defensive performance from the West squad when he returned an interception 42 yards for a score in a 34–14 victory. A film of the play shows Nitschke dropping into coverage, making the interception, and then veering to his right, where he displayed the running style that had marked his fullback days at Illinois.

Teaming with Merlin Olsen, Roger Brown, and Gino Marchetti, along with Packer mates Davis and Wood, Nitschke helped hold an East team lineup of Jim Brown, Bobby Mitchell, Charley Taylor, and Paul Warfield to just 47 yards in the first half.

Being named to the All-Pro team and playing in the Pro Bowl gave Nitschke added ammunition when he headed to Lombardi's office to talk contract. By 1964 Lombardi's negotiating skills were legendary. He sweet-talked some players; harshly criticized others. Most players, like Davis, signed whatever offer sheet Lombardi gave them. When Davis once approached Lombardi with an aggressive case for a substantial raise, Lombardi listened quietly, then interjected one thought.

"Willie," he said, "you forgot just one thing."

"What's that, Coach?"

"Willie," Lombardi said, "I made you."

After that, Davis would go into Lombardi's office at contract time, make some small talk, and accept Lombardi's salary offer.

Nitschke, however, would not. He and Jim Taylor were two Packers who argued loudly with their coach over contracts. Nitschke actually looked forward to the impending argument, but the women in the Packers' front office did not. When Nitschke arrived for negotiations, the secretaries would sit back and listen to the loud, angry shouting match between Nitschke and Lombardi.

"He'd start roaring and I would too," Nitschke said, and with that the office secretaries would leave their desks and head for the hallway. "Between us, we scared them out of their socks."

Nitschke's contract dispute remained unsettled as the Packers prepared for the '65 campaign. He had been voted the NFL's best middle linebacker by both the Associated Press and United Press International, and was put off by Lombardi's salary offer.

"They're paying the rookies too much and forgetting the veterans," Nitschke told a reporter. "I'm worth more money."

Nitschke told Lombardi he was going to play out his option, but when a reporter called to verify Nitschke's contract status, Lombardi brushed the controversy aside.

"Nobody on this ball club," he said, "plays out his option unless he's talked to me for the last time."

Nitschke eventually signed, then put together another All-Pro season. He was named to the UPI All-Pro team, along with Davis, Adderley, and Wood. As a unit, the Packers allowed a league-low 224 points and for the third time in four years led the NFL in pass defense. At the forefront of the great Green Bay defense was Nitschke, the team's spiritual leader and leading hit man.

Highlights from the Packers' season show Nitschke making numerous big plays:

• Blitzing Steeler quarterback Bill Nelsen off his feet in the season opener in Pittsburgh, then picking off a Nelsen pass to set up a score in a 41–9 win;

• Blocking *two* Colts while clearing a path for Adderley to score on an interception return of a John Unitas pass in the home opener against Baltimore, a 20–17 Packer win;

• Recovering a fourth-quarter fumble by Minnesota's Bill Brown to set up a touchdown in a 38–13 comeback victory over the Vikings;

• Escorting linebacker Dave Robinson through the Baltimore fog on a game-turning interception in Green Bay's eventual 42–27 win.

The Packers' win over the Colts came in the penultimate game of the regular season and gave Green Bay sole ownership of first place in the Western Conference. But when the 49ers rallied to tie the Packers 24–24 in Week 14 and the Colts defeated the Rams 20–17 in the L.A. Coliseum, Green Bay and Baltimore finished tied atop the conference standings. A special one-game playoff was scheduled for Lambeau Field on the day after Christmas, and a crowd of 50,484 ignored the 10 inches of snow on the ground and the cold, gray air to witness a game that Nitschke said no one would want to miss. After missing the title game for two straight seasons, this was a game Nitschke believed would decide whether the Green Bay dynasty was indeed dead, as was being written in some circles.

The Colts entered the contest short of quarterbacks—both Unitas and backup Gary Cuozzo were injured, so head coach Don Shula went with halfback Tom Matte. Armed with a plastic wristband listing play calls and a simplified offense relying on quarterback draws, sweeps, and rollouts, Matte had guided Baltimore to victory over the Rams the past week. Matte had been a rollout quarterback under Woody Hayes at Ohio State, and when Shula contacted Hayes to inquire about Matte's ability to play the position at the pro level, Hayes assured him he could. Hayes went on to say that NFL teams featuring a four-three defense couldn't stop a rollout or bootlegging quarterback. The reason, Hayes said, was defenses had to spread their ends wide to stop a scrambling quarterback, and that the best defense to stop an option offense was the five-two that college teams used. Bengston and Lombardi had met with Hayes in coaching clinics and were aware of his thoughts on the four-three. Bengston, however, decided to stay with his standard defense, and not make special adjustments for the Colts' newest quarterback.

The quarterback shortage grew more desperate on the game's first play from scrimmage. After faking a draw to Taylor, Starr found tight end Bill

Anderson for a short completion. But a crunching hit by cornerback Lenny Lyles forced a fumble and linebacker Don Shinnick scooped the ball up at the 25. Trying to make a stop on Shinnick along the sideline, Starr took a heavy blow to his right shoulder from cornerback Jimmy Welch and had to be helped off the field. He was sidelined for the rest of the game with a broken rib and replaced by Bratkowski. With just 21 seconds of time elapsed from the scoreboard clock, the Packers had not only spotted the Colts a 7–0 lead but also their starting quarterback as well.

"We evened things up for them," Lombardi said.

Shula, however, didn't quite see it that way.

"There was a big difference," he said. "Bratkowski had about ten years' experience. My guy had two weeks."

Lou Michaels' 15-yard field goal in the second quarter increased the Colts' lead to 10–0 at the half and Lombardi blistered the locker room walls at halftime. "If you go down today after coming so close," he said, "how hard do you think it will be to climb this high again?"

Green Bay battled back in the third quarter. A high snap from center Buzz Nutter prevented Baltimore's Tom Gilburg from getting off a punt early in the second half, and the Packers took over on the Colts' 35. Bratkowski found flanker Carroll Dale deep for a 33-yard pickup, and Hornung hammered in from the 1. With nine minutes left in the game, Green Bay began a 15-play march that ended with Don Chandler taking aim from a severe angle on a 22-yard field goal attempt. As soon as he kicked the ball, Chandler threw his head back in disgust, and Colt end Ordell Braase clapped his taped hands together in celebration. But Baltimore's joy turned to outrage when field judge Jim Tunney raised his arms to signal the kick good with 1:58 remaining in regulation.

Nitschke acknowledged later that Chandler's field goal, which appears on the game film to sail above the left upright, was a controversial call. Nitschke had watched the kick wobble toward the goal posts, which in 1965 consisted of the old, white double uprights. What happened after that, he said, depended on which team you were rooting for. On the field, Nitschke could hear the Colts cursing the call, claiming that the ball didn't go through the uprights. All Nitschke knew was that the officials had ruled it good, the game was tied, and Green Bay had new life.

For months following the game, NFL owners and coaches studied the game film of Chandler's field goal and sought suggestions on how to avoid such a situation in the future. One idea was to place a net between the uprights to catch the ball, but the rules committee decided instead to extend the height of the posts to 20 fee and paint them bright yellow rather than white.

The playoff ended in a 10–10 tie, and the two teams prepared for overtime. As he awaited the extra period, Nitschke could feel the combined effects of the game and the weather. It had been a bruising, physical battle, played out amid darkening skies and crackling cold weather. The field was frozen, and for Nitschke and the Packers, the game had been an uphill battle from the start. Lombardi called it a "street fight," and Gregg thought it was one of the toughest games he had ever played in. "They just kept coming," he said of the Colts. "You have to give them a lot of credit for the way they played."

As overtime raged on, it appeared as if Green Bay was on the verge of being beaten. Behind the hard running of Matte and halfback Lenny Moore, Baltimore drove to the Green Bay 37. The Colts were in field goal range, and to inch the ball closer they ran first Moore and then Matte into the guts of the Green Bay defense. Nitschke and the Packers responded, hurling Moore back for a one-yard loss and then stopping Matte two yards behind the line of scrimmage. In two plays, the Colts had been pushed back three yards to the Green Bay 40. Unwilling to risk losing any more yardage, Shula sent Michaels in on third down to attempt a 47-yard field goal.

Michaels had beaten the Packers the year before with a long field goal, and Nitschke knew that the Colts' left-footed kicker had the range to make it from 47 yards out. Desperate to prevent a Baltimore victory, Nitschke positioned himself over Colts' center Buzz Nutter. At the snap of the ball, Nitschke provided an extra push that he hoped would disrupt the timing of Nutter's snap. Michaels' kick was short, and Nitschke felt later that his push might have prevented the Colts from winning the game.

Packers' broadcaster Ted Moore called the pivotal play on WTMJ Radio:

The ball is on the hashmarks at the far side of the field. It is fourth down and five yards to go for the Baltimore Colts. Lou Michaels will attempt a 47-yard field goal. The angle is to the left. Bob Boyd will hold. . . . There's the snap, the ball is booted, it's in the air and it's going to be . . . short and wide to the right! It is no good. . . .

Eight minutes of overtime had elapsed when the Packers took over on their own 20 following Michaels' missed kick. Moore commented later that "sheer tension was riding on every play." Bratkowski, who would finish the game with 248 yards passing, jump-started Green Bay's drive to victory with an 18-yard completion to Anderson on a crossing pattern. Two plays later, Bratkowski threaded a pass through a crack in the Colts' zone, and Dale gathered it in for another 18-yard gain. With the ball on the Baltimore 26, Taylor and halfback Elijah Pitts carried three times for eight yards. Chandler trotted back on the field, and with 13 minutes and 39 seconds having elapsed in sudden-death overtime, ended what was at the time the longest NFL game in history when his 25-yard field goal sailed cleanly through the uprights.

On WTMJ Radio, Moore made the historic call:

> *Now the Green Bay Packers have a shot at it. They will be kicking from about the 25-yard line. The ball is slightly to the right side of the field. There will be a very slight angle to the left. The ball is on the 18-yard line. Bill Curry gets over the ball at center. Bart Starr will kneel at the 25-yard line. It's all up to Bart Starr and Don Chandler now. Starr stretches out the hand, there's the snap, the boot. The ball is in the air . . . it is good! The Green Bay Packers are the Western Division champions by a score of 13–10 over the Baltimore Colts.*

Green Bay's win clinched the Western Conference title, and amid the post-game celebration Nitschke's thoughts turned to the impending title game matchup with the reigning NFL champions, the Cleveland Browns. His thoughts turned, too, to the man who would be his personal responsibility, a man Lombardi believed to be the greatest player of all time.

Jim Brown.

F OR RAY NITSCHKE, the days leading up to the NFL championship game left him preoccupied with one primary concern—containing Jim Brown.

The Cleveland fullback was a phenomenon, a 6-foot-2, 232-pound power back gifted with sprinter's speed. His running style—a loose, shuffling gait that seemed to leave him gliding over the grass fields—is one of the more powerful images of the NFL in the 1960s. Content to run past opponents, Brown when cornered could punish defenders as well. His big shoulders would shrug free from an opponent's grasp; the tapered, 32-inch waist would twist away; and his thigh and calf muscles would drive him forward for additional yardage. At the end of each run, Brown would rise from the mountain of men who had brought him down, walk slowly back to the huddle in a manner that deceptively implied injury, then explode into the defense again on the following play.

Through it all, he maintained a stoic, Spartan approach to the game. His face reflected neither defeat nor victory, and in later years he scoffed at a writer's notion that he was "thrilled" when the Browns won the 1964 NFL championship by blanking the heavily favored Baltimore Colts, 27–0.

"I was a warrior," he said. "I didn't go around getting 'thrilled.'"

So how did he feel at the time?

"Potent," Brown said.

In a nine-year career that began in 1957, Brown posted numbers that were not only potent, they were without parallel in league history. His numbers were not only beyond comparison; they were beyond comprehension. There had been great NFL backs before him—Red Grange, Bronko Nagurski, Ernie Nevers, Steve Van Buren, Marion Motley—but Brown embodied the best of each of them. He was strength, speed, grace, and intelligence personified. He had all the makings of a fictional superhero, but to the defenses of his day, he was concrete fact, not comic-book fiction.

"I always thought Superman was white and wore a cape," one NFL defender said. "Then I found out he was black, wore Number 32, and played for the Cleveland Browns."

Brown led the NFL in rushing five consecutive seasons and in eight of the nine years he played. In 1963 he ran for a league-record 1,863 yards, a 14-game average of 133 yards per game. He rushed for more than 100 yards in a game 58 times and more than 200 yards four times. His 12,312 career rushing yards were nearly 4,000 more than his closest pursuer, and his 5.22 yards per carry average remains a record to this day.

"He was the most devastating ball carrier in the history of the NFL," Browns' radio announcer Ken Coleman said, and Brown did seem invincible. For nine seasons, he was a marked man on the field, the target of every defensive player he faced. He carried the ball a league record 2,359 times, and films from Cleveland's 1965 campaign show Brown enduring multiple hits every time he touched the ball.

Against Dallas, he took eight hits on a seven-yard gain.

Against St. Louis, seven hits on a 19-yard run.

Against Philadelphia, six hits on a 15-yard pickup.

Every defender in the NFL, Coleman said, was committing his body to an all-out war against Jimmy Brown. Eagles' linebacker Chuck Bednarik agreed, then remarked that even with five members of the Philadelphia defense converging on him, Brown would somehow still get the first down. Despite being the focal point of every defense, he never missed a game due to injury in his nine-year NFL career, and he always came back on the next play, sweeping the flank with that signature loping style, gliding through the line on ground-eating runs and warding off tacklers with a forearm whose power Mike Tyson would have envied.

New York Giants middle linebacker Sam Huff, who engaged in several memorable Eastern Conference duels with Brown, said the Cleveland fullback lulled defenders to sleep with his slow retreat to the huddle, then attacked them the next down with the speed and power of a freight train. Running full steam into Brown, Huff said, was like running full steam into an oak tree. Huff had the fillings knocked from his teeth on one attempted tackle against Brown, and Steeler cornerback Brady Keys was another victim, suffering a bruised sternum and broken ribs after Brown had run over him.

Green Bay cornerback Bobby Jeter felt Brown's power in a 1965 exhibition game. "He busted four of my ribs," Jeter recalled. "I was trying to tackle him and he dropped that big forearm—it looked like a tree trunk—and put it in my ribs and that was it. The next time I opened my eyes I was in the dressing room."

Hall of Fame halfback Bobby Mitchell lined up next to Brown in the Cleveland backfield for four straight seasons from 1958 to 1961. "Forty-eight straight games," Mitchell said, "and I watched this man in every type of weather, every type of situation, and he always came through. I saw him play football in a way that I never saw anybody else play. There's something about every runner that's exciting and tells you that he's a great runner, but they just don't step out on the field and everybody knows that the boss is there. But that's the way it was with Jim. He would pull on his pants and everyone would get excited, you know, 'The big man's ready to run.'"

Run in a manner never seen before or since. He combined the abilities of the all-time greats—the power of an Earl Campbell, the fluid motion of a Gale Sayers.

"He would run inside and turn it loose on the defense," Mitchell said. "And then once he started popping you good inside and got you set up, he'd pop outside and go 70 yards. He'd hit up in there, and he'd meet somebody like Bednarik and you'd hear that sound—*whack!*—and both of them would be standing there and all of a sudden Jim would take off again. Everything would be stopped, and in the next second Jim would be gone."

Coached by Blanton Collier, the Browns had displayed remarkable balance offensively in winning the '64 championship. Brown was still the ultimate ball carrier, but halfback Ernie Green and rookie Leroy Kelly lent variety to the running game. The offense was spiced by a passing attack that featured quarterback Frank Ryan firing to Gary Collins on the post and rookie Paul Warfield on the corner. Brown led the NFL with 1,446 yards and a 5.2 average, but when injuries crippled the Cleveland attack in '65, leaving Ryan nursing a severe shoulder injury and Warfield a broken shoulder, Brown's workload increased again.

Carrying the ball a league-high 289 times, Brown carried Cleveland to a second straight Eastern Conference title. He led the NFL with 1,554 yards rushing and rushed for 17 touchdowns in just 14 games. He was named the league MVP, and in the week prior to the '65 title game, he became the primary concern of the Packers' defense in general, and Nitschke in particular.

Studying film of Cleveland, Nitschke could see that Brown was a gifted athlete. Since he was the key to Cleveland's offense, Nitschke knew Brown had to be stopped and that it was his responsibility to stop him. Brown was a triple-threat back. Nitschke would watch the film and see Brown soaring for a short-yardage score against the Eagles in Week Three; swinging out of the backfield and spinning his way through the secondary against the Giants in Week Six; then pulling up on a sweep to spiral a 39-yard scoring pass to Collins against New York.

There were other highlights as well. Brown, hurdling one Eagles' defender and gliding past another; knifing through four Dallas defenders to score on a weak side sweep; ripping off the NFL's longest run of the season, a 67-yarder against Pittsburgh, and scoring four TDs in a 42–21 win over the Steelers that clinched the Eastern Conference three weeks before the end of the regular season.

As he watched the films, Nitschke could see that Brown was unique in that he played the fullback position like a halfback. Like Packer power back Jim Taylor, Brown could bend the defensive line with straight-ahead thrusts, but the Browns also featured him on wide running plays that required a halfback's speed. To Nitschke, Brown was a fullback with finesse. He ran with speed and read his blocks; he knew where his teammates were on the field and where his downfield help was coming from.

All those elements came together on the Browns' number one running play, the toss sweep. Run from a double-wing set, the play was designated as "Flip-8" in the Cleveland playbook when run to the right side; "Flip-9" when run to the left. Brown would take Ryan's pitch left or right, read the blocks of pulling guards Gene Hickerson and John Wooten, and glide through the defense.

"We only needed to give him a crack—18 inches—and he would be in the secondary," center John Morrow recalled. "But one way or another, he'd get the yards. Jim got the job done."

The Cleveland offense worked tirelessly perfecting the toss sweep. "The trick was to get the ball to Jim when he was in full speed," Ryan remembered. "Jim was so fast and so quick that if we could get the ball to him and he could get around end, he could be effective."

Brown loved the toss sweep because it gave him room to create, to perform freely in open space. Once he was in the other team's secondary, he was on his own, and he could take defenders on one-on-one.

"That's when I'd go into my bag of stuff," Brown said at the time. "They're in trouble now—I'm in their territory, 55 things happening at once. I'm moving, evaluating their possible moves, trying to outthink and outmaneuver them, using my speed, quickness, and balance."

In the open field, Brown would limber-leg one opponent, offering the leg then jerking it away when somebody grabbed at it, then high-step past another. Brown called it "instinctive football," but there were times when he took on the defense with strength and brute force. On those occasions, Brown battered defenders by using the straight-arm, the forearm, or a lowered shoulder.

Nitschke watched Brown and saw that he knew how each defensive player was going to attack him. For some defenders, he'd lower that shoulder and run over them. Against others he'd call upon quickness and finesse to outrun them. On almost every occasion, Brown would use his forearm to protect his legs. Film study convinced Nitschke that Brown had a sixth sense that allowed him to read on the run the reactions of the defense. Brown was an artist, Nitschke thought, a player who ran with a purpose, an aim, and defeated opponents not only physically but mentally as well.

One story previewing the game praised Brown as a "smooth, strong, sophisticated superstar," but Nitschke and the Packers were prepared to respond with a defense that was the NFL's toughest to score against. Green Bay's 224 points allowed were more than 50 fewer than the second-ranked Chicago Bears, and four members of Packer defense—Nitschke, end Willie Davis, left corner Herb Adderley, and free safety Willie Wood—had been named to various NFL All-Pro teams in 1965.

"We had a total team effort," Adderley remembered, "and Ray Nitschke was the leader of that team. The fullback was his responsibility, and whether it was Jim Brown or Bill Brown of Minnesota, it didn't matter. That was his responsibility as the middle linebacker and he took the challenge."

Nitschke and the Green Bay defense game-planned for Brown in film study and on the frozen practice field. Defensive coordinator Phil Bengston found it amazing that this late in the season, during the week between Christmas and New Year's, the Packers were still out on the same spot where training camp had opened the previous July, still working hard on fundamentals. His defense had just put together one of its finest seasons, and they were still out in the dark cold, drilling, working and adjusting as if it were summer again. But Bengston realized that consistent preparation and practice had taken the Packers to where they were in 1965, and only a constant and rigorous attention to detail could carry them past Cleveland in the championship game.

As the practice week drew to a close, Bengston pulled Nitschke aside. They met in a conference room adjoining the dressing area, and together worked on revising their defensive play numbers and signals. Bengston knew from watching film of the Browns' offense that Cleveland could do severe damage to the Green Bay defense if Brown was able to make his cuts into alleys created by the Packer linemen being drawn too far to the strong side and their onside cornerback being too far over as well. The way the Browns ran their sweeps, out of the double-wing, presented unique problems, and Bengston recognized what those problems were. He also recognized that this time, it wasn't going to be enough for the Packers to rely on experience and past reputation. Green Bay would have to prevent Brown from breaking free on the strong-side sweeps by having Davis combine with left outside linebacker Dave Robinson to turn Brown in so that Nitschke could catch up with him. Bengston told Nitschke to watch for his signals from the sideline; the finger wigwags and hat-brim touches Bengston made would indicate what adjustments Nitschke would call for whenever Cleveland lined up in its double-wing set. Those adjustments, Bengston told Nitschke, could make the difference in stopping Brown before he swung out and away.

Nitschke loved the challenge of facing Brown, and wished he could play every game during the regular season against a superior player like that. He also loved the fact that Lombardi had told him earlier in the week that Brown was his responsibility. Knowing that Brown could embarrass a defense heightened Nitschke's intensity. To stop him, Nitschke knew he was going to have to play his position at the highest level possible. In the days leading up to the game, he gave himself pep talks, asking if he was up to the challenge of taking on Jim Brown. "Brown's your responsibility," Nitschke would say to himself. "Are you big enough to handle it? Are you a big enough man to stop him?"

Members of the Packer offense looked forward to the showdown between Nitschke and Brown as well. "The structure of our defense was basically the same as the New York Giants at that time," Boyd Dowler recalled. "When the Giants played the Browns it was always Sam Huff against Jimmy Brown. And our defense was structured the same way as the Giants. The linemen would keep the blockers off the middle linebacker, and the middle linebacker either tackles Jimmy Brown or he doesn't. If he does, we win. If he doesn't, we lose. That's about what it amounts to.

"That's the kind of challenge that Ray, with his personality and everything, would really get up for. And he had Jimmy Taylor riding him all week, because Taylor was always scrambling to be the top fullback in the league. Ray knew what he was up against and what he had to do."

Davis could see Nitschke readying himself for the meeting with Brown, and the Packers' defensive captain could see too the impending collisions between two men considered at the time best in the game at their respective positions.

"We went into that game thinking we had to stop Jimmy Brown," Davis remembered. "He was their running offense. And because of that fullback–middle linebacker matchup, I could envision some occasions when those two guys—Jimmy and Ray—would go at it."

As Nitschke geared for the confrontation with Brown, Lombardi reemphasized to his team that just as the running game is the heart of offensive football, stopping the run is the heart of defensive football. The team that can force the offense to throw more than it runs the ball, Lombardi said, will win more often than not. In four previous playoff games, the Green Bay defense had allowed just one rushing touchdown, Eagle halfback Ted Dean's five-yard score amid the Franklin Field mud back in 1960. And that score, Lombardi reminded his team, was the one that gave Philadelphia the title.

Dean's run had been a sweep around left end, and the Packers made it a point through the years to clamp down on wide running plays. A team that cannot keep its opponent from running wide to the outside, Lombardi would say, is a team that has lost the control on which the defense of the

Receivers who ran over the middle and into Ray Nitschke's territory paid a heavy price. In a sight familiar to NFL fans of the 1960s, Nitschke towers over Washington Redskins end and fellow future Hall of Famer Charley Taylor after delivering a crushing hit.

Ray Nitschke and Packers head coach Vince Lombardi had a sometimes tumultuous relationship during their ten years together in Green Bay. But the two men respected each other, as shown here with Nitschke helping Lombardi maintain his balance following an out-of-bounds play.

The face that frightened a generation of NFL ball carriers. Nitschke's toothless, menacing visage symbolized the fierce Green Bay defense as coached by coordinator Phil Bengston.

Ray Nitschke receives a handshake from Packers trainer Bud Jorgenson following a Green Bay defensive stand.

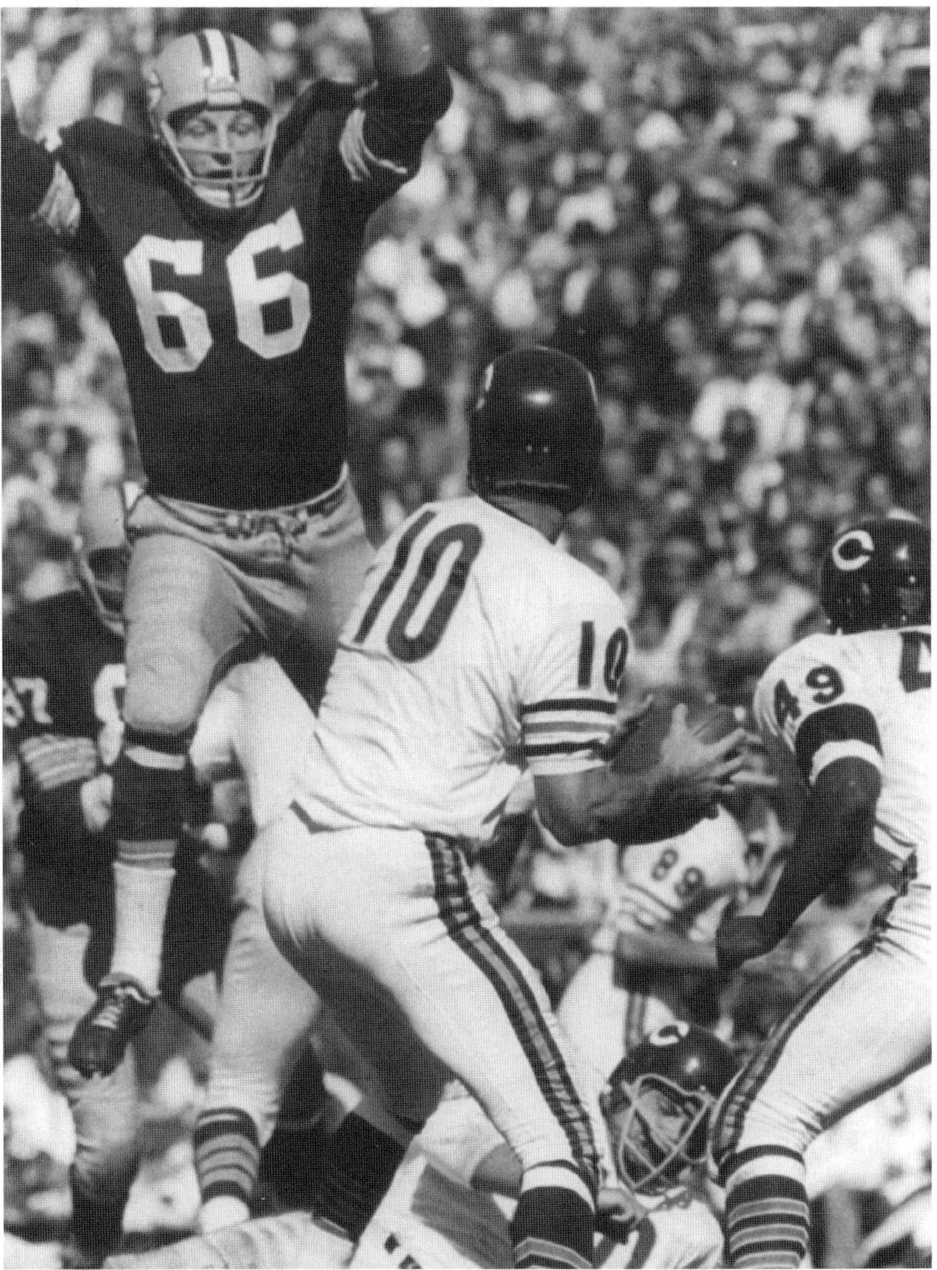

The Packers didn't blitz much under defensive coordinator Phil Bengston, but when they did, Nitschke proved to be a most able pass rusher. Here, the Packers' middle linebacker leaps high to block the passing lanes of Chicago Bears QB Rudy Bukich.

Even in the twilight of his career, Ray Nitschke (66) remained the focal point of the Green Bay defense.

Ray Nitschke Day at Lambeau Field. Ray and wife Jackie join with daughter Amy and son John in a ceremony retiring Nitschke's Number 66 jersey. To this day, Nitschke's jersey is one of just four retired by the Packers organization.

COPYRIGHT © VERNON J. BIEVER.

Always a doting father, Nitschke and son Richard enjoy a laugh together in 1968.

COPYRIGHT © VERNON J. BIEVER.

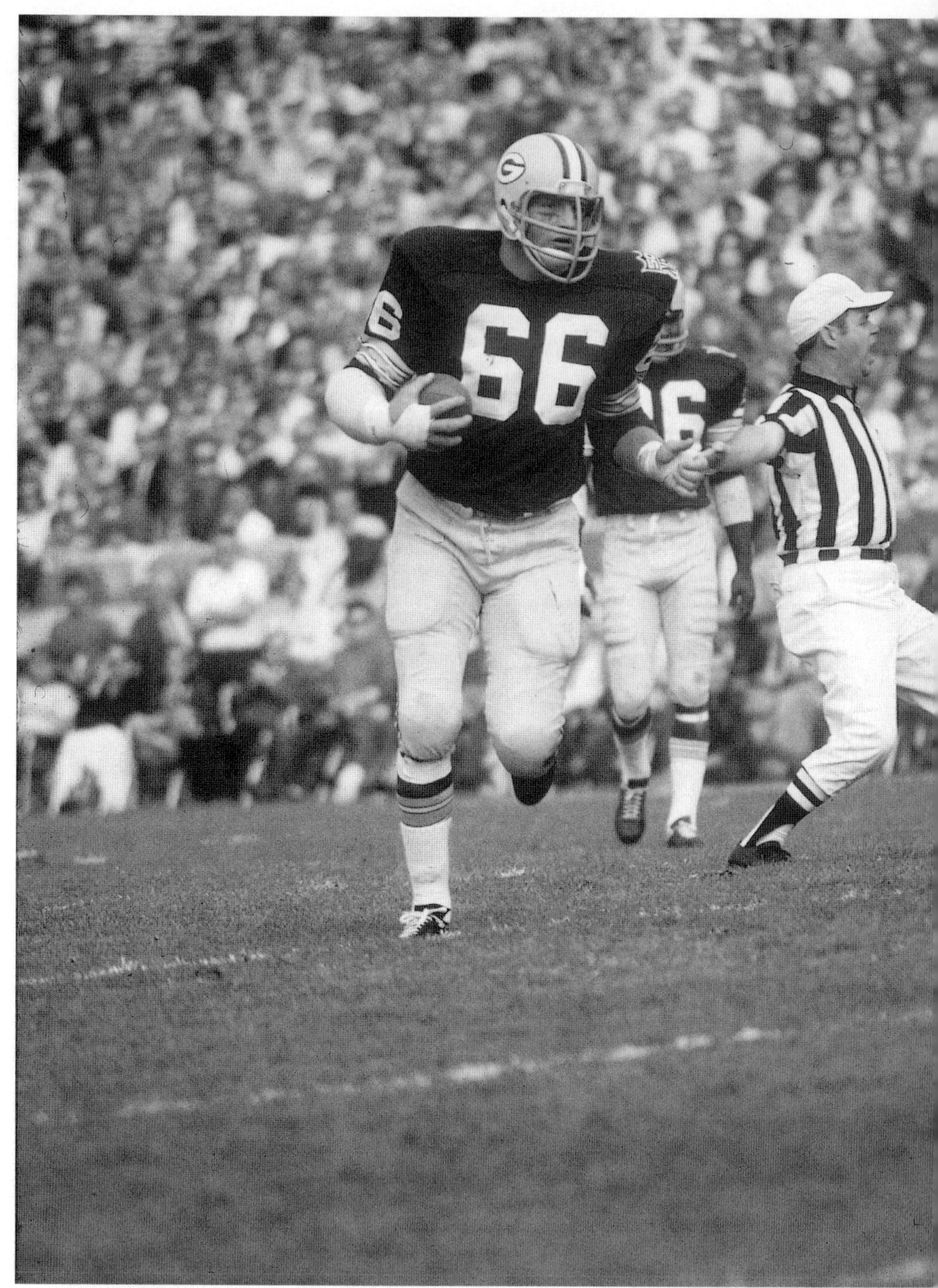

Whether it was hauling in one of his 25 career interceptions or recovering a fumble, Nitschke was known for his ball-hawking skills.

running game is founded. "The defense," he said, "must demolish every end run." As the end run was basically a power play off-tackle, if the ball carrier turned the corner cleanly the angle of pursuit was so great the defense could not hold the play down. The Packers' plan to stop the sweep was to turn the end run back to the pursuit men, and to turn it back early. Green Bay employed several different schemes to defense the sweep: the halfback force, in which the onside defensive back is responsible for stepping up and containing the play; the safety force, where the onside safety cheats and forces the sweep inside; the linebacker force, in which the strong side linebacker fights off the block of the tight end and takes a wide angle of pursuit; and the "tango" maneuver, in which the strong side defensive end and linebacker exchange responsibilities and rush lanes, with the linebacker charging inside and the end looping to the outside.

Since the left side of the Green Bay defense was so strong—Davis at end, Robinson at outside linebacker, and Adderley at the corner—the Packers dictated to the offenses of their day the direction their plays had to be run.

"We shut down the left side of the field," Adderley said. "We made the offense play on half a field. We helped (right linebacker) Lee Roy Caffey and (right cornerback) Bob Jeter make All-Pro and get to the Pro Bowl because we sent the business their way. Even Nitschke didn't make too many tackles on the left side of the field because by the time he got there he was yelling, 'Hold 'em up, hold 'em up! Let me get to 'em!' Too late, man, because Willie Davis had made the tackle and Dave Robinson and I came in to clean up. We'd tell Ray, 'We need you on the other side, man, stay away from this side of the field.' No team we played in the sixties could say 'We had success running the ball, we had success throwing the ball against the Packers' left side.' Uh-uh. Not against our left side, man. No indeed. They had no success. So Ray would cheat over to the right side."

Still, the Packers knew Cleveland was going to attempt to sweep both flanks, and because Brown was such an intelligent runner, Bengston planned to use each of those schemes in an effort to keep him from reading the Green Bay defense on the run. Nitschke figured Brown had his own theories about playing the Packers, and about playing Nitschke. No two men played their positions exactly the same; Nitschke played off his blocks differently than the middle linebackers Brown saw in the Eastern Conference, Sam Huff and Lee Roy Jordan for instance. So Nitschke knew Brown was studying the Packers' film to see how he played a certain defense, how he reacted to sweeps and traps. Since Nitschke had never been overpowered at the point of attack, he figured Brown wasn't going to try and run over him. He believed Brown would analyze him, then combine that knowledge with his natural ability once the game began.

"We played team defense and Ray was our leader," Jeter said. "Everybody knew what they had to do to stop Jimmy Brown, and Nitschke was the key ingredient."

By the eve of the game, Nitschke had sufficiently psyched himself for the challenge. Brown would get some yards, Nitschke thought, but he wasn't going to get as many against him as he did against other middle linebackers. Lombardi added one more bit of incentive for Nitschke, posting a sign in the locker room that read "Pursuit is the shortest course to the ball carrier."

Quarterback Bart Starr watched Nitschke pump himself up for the coming showdown with Brown and thought it was an indication of Nitschke's desire to succeed. "The man was a fierce competitor," Starr said.

Huff could relate to Nitschke's feelings as the Packers prepared to face Cleveland. From 1957 to 1965 Huff faced Brown twice every season because their teams were neighbors in the Eastern Conference. Like Nitschke, Huff saw the game as a personal challenge.

"My only fear was that if Jimmy Brown had a big day, everybody would say I was terrible," Huff said. "When you're playing Jim Brown, you don't sleep before the game. I couldn't wait for them to kick it off because I knew Jim Brown was my man. If he had the ball, I was going to tackle him. Hell, there wasn't any use in looking at anybody else. Just look at him. He was going to get the ball and I was going to have to get him.

"Jimmy Brown was so good he made you change your defense. Any other back, if he flared out for a pass, the outside linebacker would take him and you would take your regular pass drop, you cover inside and 10 to 12 yards deep. And if they throw that little flare pass out to the back, the outside linebacker comes up from the outside and I come up from the inside and we got 'em. Not with Jim Brown. When Brown came down that line I was right with him. And if the quarterback threw to him out there, I was isolated one-on-one with Jim Brown. And that was something you did not want to do. So you would get up close on him so the quarterback would see you and wouldn't throw the ball to Brown. You gave Cleveland the turn-in (pattern) so they wouldn't throw to Jimmy Brown."

The Browns spent the Saturday before the game, New Year's Day, working out at Lambeau Field. The turf was frozen and fast, and Morrow was confident the fast track would help the Browns' ground game. Game day, however, saw a bone-chilling wind whip from Lake Michigan through Green Bay. Swirling snow shut down Austin Straubel Airport in Green Bay and blanketed morning churchgoers in white. Governor Warren Knowles of Wisconsin had flown up from the capital in Madison to attend the game, but his plane couldn't land in the blinding storm. The governor returned to Madison and settled for watching the game on CBS. Packer fans, however, turned out by the thousands. A crowd of 50,852 made its way to Lambeau Field, and long lines of cars backed up traffic for miles around the stadium. The huge traffic jam frustrated the Browns, who were quartered in a Holiday Inn in Appleton, some 40 minutes from the stadium.

Collier had wanted his team to stay away from Green Bay to avoid being caught up in the city's frenzied activity that went with preparing for an NFL championship game and for the new year. When the Browns boarded their buses Sunday morning to head to the game, they were caught in the congested traffic. Cars were moving slowly because of the heavy snow, and because the highway crews that should have plowed the north-bound lanes had instead only cleared the south-bound lanes. The Browns' buses would creep forward, stop, then creep forward again along the 30-mile stretch of highway. The long line of snarled traffic inched its way toward Green Bay, so slowly that by the time the Browns made it to the stadium, some of their players were unnerved at having their pregame rituals upset. As the players left the bus, Cleveland sportswriter Hal Lebovitz noted that only Jim Brown seemed to have his game face on. Inside the stadium, Ryan watched as helicopters hovered just a few feet above the surface, blowing four inches of fresh snow off of the seats. Two bulldozers from the city's sanitation department were brought out just to find the field; within minutes they were pushing mounds of snow to the sidelines and piling it into large banks. Earlier that morning, a thick field cover of straw had been removed by men with pitchforks, and another crew had been busy rolling up the tarpaulin.

The snow had abated, and to Ryan, the playing surface looked lush and green. But when the Browns finally took the field, they were disgusted with the conditions. The snow had started up again, and it was now mixed with freezing rain. The mix of snow and sleet turned the once frozen field into a mud bowl. Ryan stepped on the field and thought it felt like mush. Brown, wearing a white Cleveland warmup jacket, ran gingerly for a few steps and then slid in the snow. His face was solemn; to sportswriter Jack Hand, Brown's look was one of disgust.

"The mud was coming up over our shoelaces," Morrow said. "That was a terrible day. Our running game was central to our offense, and their field was a quagmire, like soup."

Across the field, the Packers were grinning. Fullback Jim Taylor told guards Jerry Kramer and Fuzzy Thurston, "It's Packer weather." Green Bay fans agreed. They swept the wet snow from the seats, ignored the gray chill and filled every corner of Lambeau Field. Packer backers showed their fortitude throughout; one woman who slipped on the ice and broke her leg refused to go to the hospital until the game was over. Down on the field, the heavy snow was obliterating the yard lines, making it impossible to see the first down markers on the sidelines. So Mark Duncan, the supervisor of officials, began placing small red flags five yards apart along each sideline.

In the press box high above the field, Arthur Daley of the *New York Times* studied the muck below and thought no championship game should be decided under such conditions. Inclement weather had interrupted both the World Series and major golf tournaments in years past, Daley wrote, but only in pro football must the show go on.

"It was cold as hell and it was muddy," Hornung remembered. "But that was our kind of field."

Just to be perverse, the Packers opened the game by putting the ball in the air. Showing once again why he was one of the best big-game quarterbacks ever, Starr theorized that since the Browns had only arrived at the stadium a short time ago and had to get dressed quickly and get in a brief workout, he would keep them off-balance by throwing early in the elements. "We knew it had to be bad for them psychologically," Starr said after the game, "so we hit them right away."

Short passes to Taylor and Hornung led to a pair of first downs, and when Cleveland became conscious of Starr using his backs as primary pass targets, he drew the Browns in with a play-fake to Hornung and threw a towering pass to flanker Carroll Dale. Hampered by a heavily taped broken rib under his throwing arm, Starr's pass was underthrown, but when Dale stopped and came back for the ball, right cornerback Walter Beach and strong safety Ross Fichtner both slipped and fell to their knees. Dale skipped through an attempted tackle by right linebacker Galen Fiss, sidestepped free safety Larry Benz and raced into the end zone to complete a 47-yard scoring play.

Trailing 7–0, the Browns came out throwing on their initial series. Ignoring the wet snow and heavy ball, Ryan flared a first down pass to Brown. This was the same flare pass that had kept Huff awake at nights before facing Brown, and the big fullback wrestled the ball away from Robinson and turned upfield before being ridden out of bounds by Nitschke at the Green Bay 36. With a white hand towel draped from the back of his yellow-gold football pants, Nitschke rose from the sideline mush with the feeling that since the field wasn't in great shape, the poor footing might slow Brown down.

Following a game plan designed to emphasize the pass, Ryan found Warfield for a completion that carried to the Green Bay 17. Ryan followed with another pass, a 17-yard out pattern to Collins, who beat Adderley to the right corner of the end zone for the score. Bobby Franklin's bobbling of the center snap, however, prevented Cleveland kicker Lou Groza from attempting the extra point, and Green Bay maintained its lead, 7–6.

Cleveland engineered another first-quarter drive that eventually stalled when Ryan, scrambling from the pocket and skirting right end, tripped and was downed two yards shy of a first down by Nitschke. Groza's 24-yard field goal gave the Browns a 9–7 lead at the close of the first quarter, but Green Bay regained the lead in the second quarter when Don Chandler drilled a 15-yard field goal to put the Packers up 10–9. Another Chandler field goal, this time from 23 yards away, made it 13–9 Packers. With the heavy mud hampering the footing and making it difficult for receivers to run their patterns, both teams switched to their ground games. Game films show Brown taking handoffs from Ryan, then churning through the sleet and slush and into the heart of the Packer defense. Awaiting Brown amid the freezing muck and the meshing lines was Nitschke, who was trying to claw his way past Morrow to get to the Cleveland back.

"Ray won some battles and I won some battles," Morrow remembered. "He was trying not to get tied up too much in the line and I was trying to cut him off. On one play, we were going to pass and he knocked the crap out of me with his right elbow. I guess he just wanted to vent himself a little bit."

After each carry, Brown would rise from the slippery bog and head slowly back to the huddle. His white uniform, trimmed in orange and brown, was daubed with frozen mud. On the other side of the scrimmage line, Nitschke would adjust his half-cage facemask, then look to the sideline for Bengston's defensive signal. Future post-season games would feature other classic middle linebacker–running back duels—Jack Lambert and Earl Campbell in the 1978 and '79 AFC title games in Pittsburgh; Mike Singletary and Eric Dickerson in the '85 NFC championship in Chicago; Ray Lewis and Eddie George in the 2000 AFC semifinal in Tennessee—but Nitschke versus Brown was a confrontation carried out on a grander scale. In 1969, the Hall of Fame Selection Committee selected both Nitschke and Brown for the All-Decade team, and also named Brown the best fullback and Nitschke the best middle linebacker of the NFL's first 50 years. In 1965, both men were all-pros, both were in their prime, and both were the best in the game at their respective positions.

"The Packers pretty much freed Ray up to get to Jimmy," Ryan said, recalling the matchup. "Their defensive line allowed Ray to get to the point of contact against Jimmy."

On Cleveland's next series, Brown carried three consecutive times. Running a power sweep left, he picked up nine yards when Nitschke, taking an inside route on the linebacker force, was cut down by Hickerson. Wood and Henry Jordan combined to make the stop, and Brown followed by sweeping right, outrunning Nitschke to the corner and picking up 14 yards before Adderley and Wood jolted him out of bounds. On the next play,

Cleveland switched into the double-wing formation the Packers were most concerned about, and Brown ran a toss sweep to his left. Nitschke, bumped off stride by Hickerson, was taken out of the play and it was left to Jordan and Wood to once again bring Brown down, this time after an eight-yard gain.

Nitschke and the Packers were seeing first-hand the Browns' famed ground game. In three plays, Brown had run for a combined 31 yards, and CBS-TV sportscaster Ray Scott remarked that Brown was still "the big gun" in the Cleveland attack. Across the line of scrimmage, the Packer defense studied the movements of a man who had run for more yards and scored more touchdowns than anyone in pro football history, a man Scott said set a new record with every yard gained.

"We'd put a good hit on Jimmy, and he'd get up real slow like he was hurt," Jeter said. "Then the next play, here he comes again."

The success of the Browns' sweep relied on the quickness of its pulling guards. "On our sweep," Brown explained at the time, "we try to get our guards out front. If they get to the corner, you're going to make a gain."

On two of the previous three plays, Hickerson had pulled and taken Nitschke out of the play. Bengston's linebacker force was designed for Nitschke to chase the sweep from behind and cut into the backfield through the hole vacated by the pulling guard. With the Browns having success against the linebacker force, Bengston signaled to Nitschke to switch to a safety force play. When Brown swept right on a third-and-two, strong safety Tom Brown came up and forced Brown inside, where the pursuit was waiting. Robinson and left tackle Ron Kostelnik combined to stop Brown for a one-yard loss, and Cleveland ended a key series with a punt.

With less than two minutes to go in the half and the Packers clinging to a four-point lead, Bengston called for a linebacker blitz. Stacked behind Jordan, Nitschke looped around his right tackle, who took an inside charge and pressured Ryan. The Cleveland quarterback shook free from Nitschke but was sacked by Robinson for a five-yard loss. On third-and-15 from the Green Bay 35, Ryan flared a pass to Brown in the left flat. Nitschke chased from behind, then combined with Jeter to stop Brown one yard shy of a first down. The 14-yard gain set up a Groza field goal 53 seconds before the half, and his 28-yard conversion cut Cleveland's deficit to 13–12 at halftime.

Despite leading by a point at the break, there was cause for concern in the Packer locker room. Starr's ribs were aching, and several times in the first half Nitschke had winced on the sidelines when he saw Starr taking hits from the Cleveland defenders. Taylor was playing with a severe muscle pull and swollen ankle, Hornung was hampered by nagging injuries, and Dowler was starting despite a bad ankle and two damaged shoulders. Green

Bay's injury situation worsened when starting right cornerback Doug Hart left the game with an injury and was replaced by Jeter.

Defensively, Nitschke and the Packers were concerned about containing Brown. He had outmaneuvered the Green Bay defense on two pass plays in the first half, and the result was nine Cleveland points. Brown was having success sweeping the flanks and appeared on his way to duplicating his championship game performance from '64, when he barged through a Baltimore defense designed specifically to stop him for 114 yards rushing and another 37 yards receiving.

To keep Brown off the field, Lombardi made some hard decisions. Realizing the slick field was slowing the speed of their running backs to the hole, the Packers would go with straight running plays that would get Taylor and Hornung to the hole quicker. The Browns had taken away the power sweep in the first half by sending defensive ends Paul Wiggin and Bill Glass on wide rushes. Starr noted that Cleveland seemed willing to give the Packers the inside, and Lombardi ordered a steady diet of off-tackle slants and quick counters off a simulated sweep.

"The snow and mud were our allies," Lombardi said later. "When you have conditions like these, it's best to be basic, not fancy. And we're the most basic offensive team there is."

The Packers' second-half plan, Starr said, was to inch the Browns to death inside, and they put their plan into motion midway through the third quarter. Taking over on their own 10-yard line, the Packers put together a drive whose power would have made Patton's Third Army proud. Taylor, the toy tank, bulldozed his way to short but important gains. With Taylor running off-tackle slants to the weak side and Hornung hitting the strong side at a controlled trot, Green Bay took out a land claim on the football. Driving 90 yards, the Packers melted seven minutes off the clock and put seven more points on the board when Hornung swept left behind Kramer and scored from 13 yards out.

Packers' radio broadcaster Ted Moore called the game-turning drive on WTMJ Radio:

> *Starr is moving the club very well at this point. . . . Handoff to Hornung, slash over the right side and Hornung scampers across the 25, the 20, and down to the 15-yard line. The big hole was there on the right side. Beautiful blocking by Jerry Kramer and Forrest Gregg and Hornung drove through it. . . .*
>
> *Starr fakes, hands to Taylor up the middle, across the 15 to the 13-yard line on a straight-ahead smash. . . .*
>
> *Starr takes the ball, hands off to Hornung, sweep to the left side, he gets a block, he's inside the 10, at the five, cuts into the end zone for the touch-*

down! And there you saw the Green Bay Packer power sweep as in days of yore. Forrest Gregg cleared the way with a beautiful block, the two guards, Jerry Kramer and Fuzzy Thurston, doing a great job at the line of scrimmage. . . .

Trailing 20–12, the Browns looked to catch up quickly. From the Green Bay 40, Ryan sent Brown circling out of the backfield on a deep route down the middle of the field. Nitschke, his muddied white towel flapping from the back of his pants, gave chase. Brown was two steps ahead of Nitschke when he crossed the goal line, and had Ryan's pass in his hands for a moment. The touchdown would have pulled the Browns back into the game, and left them trailing by just 20–19. But Nitschke dove at the last second and dislodged the slippery ball from Brown's hands. It was a touchdown-saving play—and one of the key turning points of the game.

Nitschke said later that as he chased Brown down the field, all he could think of was that Brown was his responsibility, and that he couldn't let him make a touchdown. Nitschke knew Brown was faster than he was, but he had shadowed him down the field and felt he had a good angle on the ball. When he threw his arms up in the end zone, Nitschke felt the weight of the heavy ball hit as he batted it free.

From his position on the sideline, offensive tackle Bob Skoronski had seen the play, had seen Brown drop the ball in the end zone, and knew why he had failed to hold on to Ryan's pass. "Nitschke was all over him," Skoronski said, "hustling and hollering and screaming."

Dowler had watched along with Skoronski, had seen Nitschke hustling after Brown amid the freezing rain and slippery field. "They sent Jimmy Brown up the gap on a seam pass, and Brown could run awful fast," Dowler said. "Brown got a little behind him, and Ray was coming hard to knock the ball down in the end zone. They were both 30 yards downfield, and you know, that's a middle linebacker running with Jimmy Brown, who was one of the faster players in those years. Brown was awful big, but he was also awful fast, and Ray went right with him. Ray made a good play on the ball, and at the time, it would have been a big swing if they had scored there."

Knowing Nitschke and the Packers would gang up to stop Cleveland's ground game, Ryan said the Browns had entered the game looking to attack the Green Bay defense through the air.

"Ray was great against the run, and they really counted on him to plug holes," Ryan recalled. "We wanted to take him on by throwing the ball. It was not easy to find a weakness in their defense. They were just superb. They had very standard setups but they had such great defensive players. Their players were always where they were supposed to be."

Nitschke followed up on his great play against Brown by teaming with end Lionel Aldridge to wrestle a scrambling Ryan to the mud at the line of scrimmage, then joined with Jordan to thwart a Groza field goal that would have pulled the Browns to within five points. Just as he had disrupted the crucial center snap by Baltimore's Buzz Nutter on Lou Michael's overtime field goal in the Western Conference playoff the week before, Nitschke helped foul the Browns' attempt as well. Rather than line up directly over center, Nitschke got down in his stance in the gap between the center and massive Walter Johnson, Cleveland's rookie defensive tackle who was playing left guard on special teams. Nitschke shot the center-guard gap, and his charge caused Johnson, who should have blocked Jordan, to take a half-step to his right to block Nitschke. That small movement gave Jordan just enough of a crease to slip through the line, and he penetrated deep enough to get his right hand up and deflect Groza's field goal.

For the rest of the game, the Packers stuck with their simplified ground game, gouging out one grimy yard after another. Green Bay's line would knock the Cleveland defense back a yard or two, Taylor or Hornung would plow in behind them, and they would return to the huddle hitching their pants and shifting their shoulder pads. In his radio broadcast, Moore referred to Taylor and Hornung as "the thunder and lightning of the Green Bay backfield," foreshadowing by some 35 years the term used to describe the New York Giants' "Thunder and Lighting" tandem of Ron Dayne and Tiki Barber in the 2000 season. For the purists who loved power football, the Packers were putting forth a clinic in ball control. In the Green Bay huddle, second-year center Ken Bowman listened as his mud-caked teammates shouted, "Just like 1962."

"I guess," Bowman thought, "this is how they used to do it."

As the snow and sleet intensified, a heavy fog shrouded Lambeau Field. The stadium lights, which had been on all day, flared brightly in the bog, and amid a setting that seemed more suited to a filming of *The Hound of the Baskervilles,* the Packers put the finishing touches on their muddy, 23–12 masterpiece. Brown watched solemnly from the sidelines as Taylor, his competitive rival at fullback, ignored a badly swollen ankle and slanted and blasted his way through the Cleveland defense. When Cleveland had the ball, Taylor watched as Brown and Nitschke engaged in numerous collisions amid the dark mud.

"Our defense, Nitschke and them, always played tough against Jim Brown," Taylor said later. "They always rose to the occasion."

Davis said that once the Packers shut down the passing game, they could turn their full attention to stopping Brown. "Every time we played against Cleveland, Jimmy always presented that kind of a challenge," he said. "Everybody on our defense had the notion that Jimmy was the guy we had to stop."

Like Jordan, Davis was a former member of the Browns, and the duo always put forth an extra effort whenever Green Bay played Cleveland in those years. "We wanted to make the Browns regret having traded us," Davis said.

Against Cleveland in the '65 title game, Davis and Jordan were spurred on by Nitschke's chatter behind them. Every time Brown swept wide on the toss sweep, Davis could hear Nitschke yelling. "Here they come," Nitschke would yell. "Here they come!"

"He was our rah-rah guy, our chatterbox, and he was directing us where to go," said Davis, who was called "Dr. Feelgood" by his teammates. "It was always in the direction of winning the game, but he'd just start hollering at you. 'Hey, Dr. Feelgood, you gotta get in there! You gotta get to that passer.' I'd look at him like, 'Hey, what the—*You* get in there!'"

On one play, Brown veered outside and Davis gave chase. When Brown turned and headed into the hole, Davis realized he was suddenly in a one-on-one situation with the Cleveland fullback.

"Anytime you found yourself one-on-one with Jimmy Brown, you immediately looked for help," Davis recalled. "On this play, I was one of the first ones there to meet him and it was just Jimmy and me, and the one thing on my mind was, 'I've gotta stop this guy.' "

Davis did stop Brown; then heard the voice of Nitschke behind him. "Hey Doctor," Nitschke rasped. "That's the way to go."

Nitschke, his green-and-gold uniform splattered with gray mud, drew compliments for his play that day. Bill Curry, a rookie center for the Packers that season, recalled the game, recalled Nitschke having "a big afternoon" against Brown. Covering the game for *Sports Illustrated,* Tex Maule wrote that the Green Bay defense "read the Browns sweeps as though Nitschke were a party to their huddles."

Davis told Maule after the game that when the Browns came out in their double-wing set with Brown the lone back and tight end Jim Brewer and halfback Ernie Green set to the strong side, Cleveland was planning to sweep right. "So we flew out of there to turn Brown in," Davis said. "If we could turn him in, then he would run into Nitschke. . . . "

Peeling off his Cleveland uniform for the final time, Brown praised the Packer defense.

"Willie Davis is their leader in the line and they've got two great defensive backs in Herb Adderley and Willie Wood," Brown said. "As for Ray Nitschke at middle linebacker, well, he seems to know where I'm going before I know myself."

Jeter had the feeling that Brown, great as he was, hated to play against Nitschke. "Ray always brought his game up to another level when he played against Jimmy," Jeter said. "And I was glad about that, because it meant I wouldn't have to tackle Brown as much."

Brown had been held to 50 yards rushing and finished with less than 100 yards of total offense (94). In the second half, Nitschke and the Packer defense limited Brown to just nine yards rushing.

"When you can hold Jimmy Brown to less than 100 yards," Hornung said, "the middle linebacker has to be a big part of it."

Taylor, who for years had played in the considerable shadow cast by Brown, was named the game's MVP after finish with 96 yards on 27 carries. Hornung added 105 yards on 18 carries, and slogged through the slippery turf for one score.

In the somber Cleveland dressing room, Brown talked to reporters about the man who had been his most persistent pursuer. "I noticed that Ray Nitschke was keying on me," Brown said. "He's as tough as anybody."

Nitschke and the Packer defense, Brown said, were rough and skilled. But, he added, he thought they had received an assist from the elements. The field was ice and mud and left him bumping into defenders, Brown said, that he would normally have avoided.

When Nitschke read Brown's comments later, he smiled. He figured Brown was referring to a certain bald-headed defender that he had been running into all afternoon. Nitschke's meeting that day with Brown had been his fourth since becoming a starter. In 1961, Nitschke and the Packers held Brown to 72 yards on 16 carries in a 49–17 victory in Cleveland. In 1963, Brown gained just 56 yards on 11 carries in a 40–23 loss in the Miami Playoff Bowl. In 1964, Cleveland's championship season, Brown finished with 74 yards on 20 carries as Green Bay won again, 28–21, in Milwaukee.

Brown averaged an NFL-record 104 yards rushing per game in his career, but he never rushed for 100 yards against Nitschke and the Green Bay defense. Bengston's unit is the only NFL team that can claim that distinction against arguably the greatest running back in NFL history.

"That was because of Ray," Jeter said. "Ray Nitschke was Jimmy Brown's nemesis."

NINE

BEING NAMED to the NFL All-Pro team for the second straight season in 1965 helped further establish Ray Nitschke as one of the leaders of the NFL champion Green Bay Packers. But as the new year of 1966 dawned, Nitschke was becoming increasingly more interested in being a leader not only on his team but in the town as well.

Ray and Jackie adopted their second child, Richard, who was just 10 days old when the Nitschkes brought him home in 1966. John was three years old, and his growing family gave Nitschke a fulfillment he hadn't known since early in his own childhood. At Christmas, Nitschke would dress up in a full Santa Claus outfit, complete with red-and-white fur cap, and play Santa Claus for his young sons. Jackie decorated their house in a festive style and always arranged a miniature Christmas village complete with blinking lights and fake snow. She would then invite neighborhood children by to see the village and spend time at the house.

Nitschke didn't always have the time to spend with his family that he would have liked, especially since the Packers' seasons always ran long because of their annual appearances in the post-season. From 1960 to 1967, Green Bay played a post-season game every year for eight straight seasons. But Nitschke made up for lost time once the season was over, and family photos show him smiling broadly as he poses for photos with Jackie and plays with his children.

Getting married and settling down, Nitschke said, made him more concerned with being a man. "The responsibilities of family life turned me on," he said. "No matter what profession you have in life, you have to have happiness at home. I've had a happy family life, and I think it has helped me to go about my job in a better way."

The former street tough from suburban Chicago considered himself blessed to have what he described as "a wonderful wife and wonderful children." The man who once believed that everyone in the world was against him now looked to his family as his main source of strength.

"The family," he said, "is the single most important thing to me because of not having a very sound family life in my youth."

Nitschke became famous for his hugs, and one of the enduring memories that his children have of him is the strength of his embrace. John

Nitschke once recalled his father's bearhuglike hug as "pretty neat stuff." Green Bay defensive coordinator Phil Bengston said Nitschke and free safety Willie Wood were the biggest huggers on the team. Every time the Green Bay defense made a successful goal-line stand or forced a turnover, Bengston would brace himself for what he described as the "huge bearhugs" he was sure to receive as soon as Nitschke and Wood returned to the sideline.

By 1966, Nitschke had not only adopted two sons, he had adopted Green Bay as his hometown. Packer teammate Carroll Dale, who roomed with Nitschke on road trips, said that Packer team buses often sat idling curbside because Nitschke remained outside, signing autographs for children. "He never turned anyone down that wanted an autograph," Dale said, and Nitschke would take so much time signing that when he eventually did climb aboard the bus his teammates would kid him. "Ray, hey Ray, what are you doing, running for office?" someone would shout. Boyd Dowler began referring to Nitschke as "the People's Choice."

Thomas Content of the *Green Bay Press-Gazette* thought Nitschke had an "unfailing ease" with autograph seekers. One of the reasons Nitschke took so long to sign his autograph was because he made sure he signed items in a clear and legible fashion. Vern Biever, who has been the Packers' official photographer for the past half-century, said Nitschke took his time when signing to ensure his signature came across as being very neat. Unlike many in the public eye, Nitschke never scrawled his name in a hurried or haphazard fashion. Biever never saw Nitschke turn anyone down for an autograph, and the nicest thing about it, Biever said, was that a person could *read* Nitschke's signature. "It was his trademark," Biever said of Nitschke's neat signature, "and it never varied."

Nitschke owned a zest for life that extended beyond the football field. He would talk football with anyone at any time, and while he comforted children with a wide-mouth grin and some kind words, he intimidated adults with a menacing look and a voice that could stop traffic.

John Bankert, the director of the Pro Football Hall of Fame, said Nitschke scared him the first time they met. Nitschke's handshake was uncommonly strong, Bankert thought, but he didn't think Ray realized it. Bankert was intimidated by the piercing glare of Nitschke's blue eyes and his clenched jaw. Nitschke looked hard, but Bankert quickly realized that Ray didn't mean to scare him. Within a moment, Nitschke loosened his grip, his eyes twinkled, and the clenched jaw gave way to a mischievous smile. When that happened, Bankert said, "you knew that he liked you."

Tommy Nobis wasn't sure what to make of Nitschke the first time he met him. The heralded rookie linebacker from Texas was the number-one draft choice of the expansion Atlanta Falcons in 1966, and as a Maxwell

Award winner, was at a banquet with Nitschke during the off-season.

"I certainly knew of Ray when I came into the league," Nobis said. "I knew he was one of the standard-setters at middle linebacker. He had that gruff look, that voice, and he'd look at you and say, "What're ya starin' at, rookie?' He'd scare the shit out of you.

"We were at a banquet at the Washington (D.C.) Touchdown Club in 1966, and we both get into an elevator and he looks over at me and says, 'So you're that rookie who thinks he can play in this league?'

"I didn't know if he was playing with me or not. It was the first time I was ever face-to-face with him, and every time he talked it looked like the durned tie was going to burst off his neck. I'm looking at him and thinking, 'Should I swing at 'em? Should I shove 'em? Should I run?' But then I got to know him, and we would talk whenever we saw each other. Even in a sports coat and suit, if Nitschke walked into the room, you knew there was something special about him. He just radiated that feeling. That's the way Ray was."

Theresa Starkey, Ray and Jackie's niece, remembered the day during the Green Bay glory years when she brought her "Uncle Ray" to her seventh grade class for show-and-tell. The jaws of her classmates, Starkey said, dropped when Nitschke walked into the classroom.

Jack Camp, a nephew of Nitschke's, was there the day Ray was in a parade and police tried to push the fans away from him. Nitschke stopped the police and proceeded to sign autographs for the fans.

Nitschke's attitude toward signing autographs was refreshingly old-school, particularly in light of the attitudes exhibited by latter-day athletes.

"When people ask me for my autograph," he said, "I'm very thrilled that they do ask. I think it's a responsibility a ball player should have to the game. My philosophy is that it's a privilege to play."

It was even more of a privilege, he said, to play in Green Bay. He and Jackie and the kids grew to love the people, the area, and the state of Wisconsin. "There's no place like Green Bay," he said on more than one occasion, and to Nitschke, there was no NFL team like the Packers. He admired the organization and thought the story of the team's growth from a meat-packing company–sponsored town team to an NFL dynasty was special. "It's a beautiful sports story," Nitschke said, "and to be part of the tradition is just a fabulous thing."

Football was a way of life in Green Bay. Everyone, it seemed, was a fan—the middle-aged woman filling her grocery cart at the supermarket who told an interviewer, "Goodness, I haven't missed a game in 15 years;" the butcher who told a camera crew, "Our boys are really going to clobber those Bears this Sunday;" the group of small boys wearing youth-sized Packer helmets and imitating their heroes in the park.

"You can be Starr, you can be Kramer . . . "

Nitschke loved talking with them all, and to the people of Green Bay, he became a pied piper who went around doing good. Margaret Nitschke of Mayville, Wisconsin, said her husband Frank was a distant cousin of Ray's. "Frank had the Nitschke nose, the receding Nitschke hairline, the big shoulders," she said. Margaret was moved once to contact Ray by mail during the mid-sixties. Her daughter Charon was in the sixth grade at the time and, because she was big for her age, classmates at St. Margaret's school teased her by calling her "Ray." The taunts upset Charon, and her mother sent a letter to Nitschke at the Packer offices. He responded by writing a letter back to Charon and enclosed along with it one of his Green Bay jerseys and two tickets to a Packers game. When the kids at her school found out Nitschke had written her a letter and sent her a Green Bay jersey, Charon became the envy of the sixth grade.

"He made her feel a whole lot better," Margaret said. "He was very generous, a super guy. But that had to come, too. For a while, he had his ups and downs. But then he put it all together, and he became very personable."

Teammate Willie Davis, who played alongside Nitschke on the Green Bay defense, felt no individual ever made a greater transition from the football field to the community than Nitschke. Leo Waldschmidt of Howards Grove, Wisconsin, recalled how Nitschke ended conversations not with a "good-bye" or "so long" but with a "sayonara."

The man who once made the rounds at Green Bay bars now made the rounds of his community. Former Packer team president Judge Robert Parins first met Nitschke in Ray's rookie season of 1958. Nitschke was getting in trouble off the field and Parins, an attorney at the time, had occasion to help him out on a few matters. He remained friends with Nitschke through the years and came to admire the way Nitschke went from raising hell to raising a family.

"It took a great person to do that," Parins said.

Mike Horn, who played for the original Green Bay Bobcats ice hockey team, met Nitschke in 1958. They had frequented bars together during Nitschke's early years in Green Bay, and Horn was one of those outside the Packer organization who witnessed Nitschke's transformation from street fighter to family man.

"He changed after he met Jackie," Horn said. Nitschke had a fascination with ice hockey, and along with some of his Packer teammates was a regular at Bobcat games. Though Nitschke was considered by some to be a madman on the field, it was hockey players Nitschke thought were the maniacs.

"You guys are nuts," he would tell Horn. "I play once a week and I wear a helmet. You guys play twice a week and you don't even wear helmets."

Nitschke would laugh, the blue eyes would lighten, and an easy smile would crease his face. It was a look that changed dramatically once the season began. The eyes would become squints, the smile would harden into a grin, and the light countenance would revert to its craggy, hawkish features. "He had those eyes, that grin," Chicago Bears' Hall of Fame tight end Mike Ditka said. "He kept me focused out there. If you'd ever let up, he'd kill you."

Nitschke never let up, on game days or in practices. "He performed during practices," Biever said. "He put his heart into everything." Teammates called Nitschke the "Bald Eagle" because of his gleaming dome, and on occasion conspired against him to settle him down. Bill Curry, who joined the Packers as a rookie center in 1965, thought Nitschke was one of those men, like Packer boss Vince Lombardi, who harnessed and used rage. They had an aura on the field that Curry found both unique and scary. It was a feeling, he thought, that old-time hitters must have felt whenever they dug in against someone like Sal Maglie, a fearsome pitcher for the Brooklyn Dodgers in the 1950s who earned the nickname "The Barber" for the close shaves he gave to hitters leaning too far out over the plate.

Curry had first become aware of Nitschke when he watched the 1962 NFL championship game between the Packers and Giants on TV. Curry had never heard of Nitschke before that awesomely cold day in Yankee Stadium, but he soon became aware of the man in the white-and-yellow uniform with the green number 66 on his jersey. Curry was fascinated by Nitschke's play, the quick, crablike shuffle across the frozen field, the smashing hits on Giant ballcarriers. Curry's fascination increased when he saw Nitschke that same night on the TV game show *What's My Line?* He could hardly believe his eyes. There was Nitschke, appearing gentlemanly in his dark-rimmed glasses and conservative business suit. To Curry, Nitschke seemed to have a professorial demeanor.

Two years later, Curry signed with the Packers and was in awe when he met Nitschke. The sheer mass and power exuded by the Packers middle linebacker kept Curry's eyes riveted on him all day. When Curry arrived in Green Bay in the spring of 1965 for the Packers' training camp, his awe of Nitschke turned to hatred. Nitschke would show up on the practice field fully padded. "Padded to the hilt," Curry said later. "Forearms, hands, everything." The sight of Nitschke in full pads left every member on the offensive line knowing it was going to be a long, tough scrimmage. Nitschke would run around the field, yelling and shouting in a voice that to Curry sounded rough and nagging, with a streets-of-Chicago accent:

"Come on, let's have some ent'usiasm . . . "

Curry called it a constant stream of chatter that irritated everyone, but

Nitschke would just stand there grinning, then wait a play or two before he'd be running around and screaming out the plays again.

Curry said Nitschke ran through scrimmages clotheslining his teammates, crashing into them. Tired of being brutalized, the Packer offense would police the field themselves. Curry said there were times when Green Bay's linemen—Jerry Kramer and Fuzzy Thurston, Forrest Gregg and Bob Skoronski—ganged up on Nitschke. "Just to slow him up," Curry said. In September 1966, Kramer was running a dummy scrimmage drill that required him to block Nitschke. Kramer was going through the motions, and as he positioned himself in front of Nitschke, not planning to hit or block him, Nitschke brought one of his padded forearms up and smashed Kramer in the face. Stung by the blow, Kramer returned to the huddle and told backup quarterback Zeke Bratkowski to run the same play again. Bratkowski did, and Kramer went after Nitschke, pushing him down and driving him into the ground. "He got the message," said Kramer.

Nitschke was given free reign in scrimmages, Curry said, because Lombardi used him as an instrument to instill fear in his teammates. Fear in the sense that as proud professionals, they would raise their level of play to avoid being humiliated by Nitschke. Curry didn't understand Lombardi's methods at first, until one day during his rookie camp when Lombardi gathered the team together for the blitz drill. Curry had been involved in such drills during his college days at Georgia Tech, and the drill was pretty simple. The middle linebacker would rush on a mock blitz, the center would drop straight back for three yards, then hit and recoil to shield the blitzing linebacker away from the quarterback.

But when Lombardi called for the blitz drill, Curry caught starting center Ken Bowman looking at him out of the corner of his eye. The unsuspecting Curry got down in his stance against Nitschke, and at the snap was knocked off his feet. Curry was shocked; it was the hardest hit he had ever taken. He got up, thinking, "I'll hit *him* that way next time." He tried, but Nitschke decked him again. As a veteran, Nitschke had distinct advantages over the rookie. He knew the drill, had been a professional for seven years and an All-Pro, and knew the snap count. Curry was convinced Nitschke was jumping the count, was crowding the line of scrimmage and moving a split-second before the snap. Nitschke cracked Curry's helmet with the sheer force of his forearm, then snapped the rookie's chin strap with another hammer blow. With every play, Nitschke seemed to hit harder. He was literally running over Curry, scattering the backs and messing up the play. Curry couldn't get to him, and because Nitschke had bad knees and was scrimmaging without knee pads, he couldn't cut block him low either.

Every time Curry missed Nitschke, Lombardi would go into a tantrum. "Dammit, Curry! Can't you move? Can't you do anything?"

NITSCHKE

Suddenly, Curry realized what Lombardi had been talking about when he spoke of the fear of humiliation. Curry began dreading the drill, and as the Packer offense regrouped, Lombardi stuck his head in the huddle.

"Curry," he said. "I want you to cut Nitschke."

Curry was stunned. "What?"

"I want you to cut Nitschke."

Curry couldn't believe what Lombardi was saying. He looked over at Nitschke, saw the huge shoulders and arms, the bad knees. Nitschke was drilling without knee *and* thigh pads. Still, he couldn't question his coach's orders, so on the next play Curry fired out and cut Nitschke down. He half-expected Nitschke to kick him in the face, but Ray didn't say a word. Offensive players tired of watching Nitschke knocking everyone around actually cheered.

"Hey, good block," they shouted. "That-a-way to git 'em."

Curry went back to the huddle feeling rather proud of himself, until Lombardi stuck his head in the huddle again.

"Hit him *again*."

Curry went pale, then started to stammer. "Oh no, what?"

At the snap, he cut Nitschke again, and Lombardi, with that big, jack-o-lantern grin, said, "See there? You got him."

On other occasions, Curry wasn't so fortunate. Nitschke would physically punish him so much that Curry would grow frustrated and start pushing after the drill was over. Nitschke never retaliated; he wouldn't deign to fight a rookie. All he would say was, "Kid, what the hell's wrong with you?"

It was humiliating, Curry said, Nitschke brushing him off as if he was flicking away a mosquito.

Bobby Jeter shared an experience similar to Curry's. After joining the Packers in 1963, Jeter spent his first two seasons at wide receiver before becoming an All-Pro at right cornerback. The first time he attempted to block Nitschke, Jeter was jolted back into the backfield.

"Coach Lombardi told me to get my butt back in there," Jeter said. "I had all kinds of things going through my mind. And then I thought, 'Well, hell, I know the snap count and Nitschke doesn't, so I can use that to my advantage.' So the next time I drove out there, I got 'em, I moved 'em back a couple of yards. And he got up, hit me on the back, and said, 'Good block, Jeter. That's the way to attack.'"

Nitschke could, on occasion, show pity on his teammates. The Packers ran a drill called the "nutcracker" in which a defensive player positioned himself between two huge bags filled with foam rubber. The bags formed a chute, and the defender would take on an offensive blocker in order to get to the ball carrier. Many of the Packers hated the nutcracker drill, hated it for the helmet-rattling collisions that often led to the offensive and defensive players ramming each other's necks down into the chests. Kramer said the primary idea was to pave a path for the runner; the secondary idea was to draw blood.

During one nutcracker drill in 1967, Red Mack, a reserve flanker who stood 5-feet-10 and weighed 185 pounds, lined up against Nitschke. Players gathered around for the expected bloodletting. Nitschke weighed 240 pounds, and Kramer considered him to be the strongest 240-pounder in the NFL. Nitschke also used his forearm better than anyone in the game, and Kramer said that when Ray brought his forearm to the head of a lineman, it was a lethal weapon. Nitschke was not only used to beating people's heads in during the drill, Kramer said, he enjoyed it.

Looking at Mack lined up against him, however, Nitschke showed a sudden reticence.

"Oh, no," he said. "I can't go against this guy."

Mack, who may have been the toughest 185-pounder in the league, glared at Nitschke.

"Get in here you son of a bitch," Mack growled, "and let's go."

The two men lined up, Mack fired out, and Nitschke clubbed him to his knees with a forearm.

When guard Gale Gillingham joined the Packers in 1966 as a first-round draft choice out of the University of Minnesota, it didn't take him long to become acquainted with Nitschke. "He was always easy to find," remembered Gillingham, who played alongside Nitschke through the 1972 season. "He was always yelling. Ray played the consummate hard ass, but if he saw somebody needed some help, he'd give them the shirt off his back. If someone needed a pat on the back, Ray would go out of his way to find that kid and help him along. At the same time, if he thought someone was slacking off, he could be unmerciful."

Gillingham realized quickly that the Packer veterans accepted the rookies quickly if they sought to blend in. "They would be the hardest team to join if you thought you were a hot shit and something special," Gillingham said. "But if you went in there and kept your mouth shut and had some ability, they adopted you pretty quick.

"I had Bow (center Ken Bowman) on one side and (tackle) Bob Skoronski on the other, and I said, 'If I have any questions, I'm just going to ask.' And they said, 'Okay.' But people who came in there with a chip on their shoulders, there was no way they were ever going to fit in."

Like Curry had before him, Gillingham learned to scrimmage hard against Nitschke. "He was always taking shots at guys, no question,"

Gillingham said. "I just think that was Ray's way. He was a winner and he just wanted to keep guys awake. But I've seen him get his ass kicked plenty of times too, and he never squawked about it."

Gillingham recalled a scrimmage where Nitschke took a shot at guard Bill Lueck. "Lueck just beat the hell out of him," Gillingham said. "In fact, he took Ray's helmet off and hit him over the head with it. Before the helmet hit the ground, the knot on Ray's head was up about three inches."

Even in non-scrimmage situations, Nitschke couldn't resist giving a teammate a little nudge if they invaded his turf. Even if that teammate was quarterback Bart Starr.

"I can recall jogging past him after a practice session or something and he'd hit you with his elbow, hit you in the backside, and kind of push you off-stride," Starr said, laughing at the memory. "He'd say, 'Sorry, didn't mean to do it,' and you knew darn well he meant to do it."

Starr said Nitschke "energized" the practice field with his intensity, and as hard as Nitschke could be on his teammates in scrimmages, he was just as protective of them on Sundays. The first time Curry played against the Bears, in the 1965 Shrine Game in Milwaukee, Nitschke approached him during warm-ups.

"If you happen to make a play near the Bears' bench today," Nitschke said, "just get up and hurry back to the huddle."

Curry politely nodded, then asked why.

"There's a short, fat coach on this bench," Nitschke said, "who's got a real loud mouth and you shouldn't hear that kind of stuff."

Curry searched Nitschke's face for any slight tremors that might indicate he was joking. There wasn't any. Nitschke was staring him straight in the eye, and his voice was flat and calm.

"I don't want you exposed to that kind of filth," Nitschke said.

On another occasion, Nitschke was sidelined for a game against the Detroit Lions in the 1965 regular season. Lee Roy Caffey, who started at right outside linebacker, was moved to the middle in Nitschke's absence. The Lions took immediate advantage of Caffey's inexperience at his new position and scored three touchdowns to take a 21–3 lead at halftime. As players and coaches filed toward the locker rooms at the break, some of the Packers heard Lions' defensive tackle Alex Karras taunting Lombardi.

"Hey, how you like that, ya fat wop!"

In the Green Bay dressing room, while Lombardi calmly went over subtle changes in strategy for his offense, Nitschke visited a despondent Caffey. "Now Lee Roy," Nitschke said quietly, "here's what you did wrong." Nitschke proceeded to give Caffey a crash course in the art of middle linebacking. Nitschke's reassuring talk perked Caffey up; he played a solid second half, helping Green Bay shut Detroit out the rest of the way in an eventual 31–21 win.

The Lions and Bears were two teams who figured to challenge the Packers in 1966, but the biggest challenge came from the Baltimore Colts. NFL schedule-makers had indulged their sense of drama by rematching the Western Conference playoff participants from 1965 in the '66 regular season opener. The game was played Saturday night, September 10, before a crowd of 48,650 at County Stadium in Milwaukee. Because of the controversy stemming from their last meeting, the Colts–Packers game was set up to kick off the NFL season. It was also one of the most anticipated season-openers of the 1960s.

The Colts had waited all winter and summer for another shot at the Packers, and no one on the team was more ready than Unitas, who had missed the playoff game because of an injury. "This time," he said, "I was going to be able to play."

Just as Unitas was eager to take on the Green Bay defense, Nitschke was looking forward to going up against the man many still consider the greatest quarterback of all time. Like the Colts, Nitschke had been waiting all summer for the rematch. He had grown tired of Baltimore fans chirping that their team had been robbed of the conference title. To Nitschke, the '66 season opener provided an opportunity for the Packers to show that not only could they beat the Colts, they could beat them with their All-Pro quarterback on the field.

Nitschke had played against other great quarterbacks in his career—Norm Van Brocklin, Y. A. Tittle, Sonny Jurgensen—but to him, Unitas was the best. His ability to call the right plays, his poise, the way he coordinated the Colts passing attack allowed him to take control of a game. Unitas could pick a defense apart, and he could wear defenders out by consistently coming up with the right play in crucial situations. Nitschke knew that if the defense made even one mistake, Unitas would make them pay for it. Nitschke also knew that because of Unitas's poise, the game was never really over as long as he had the ball in his hand.

Nitschke thought that the coordination between Unitas and his primary receiver, Raymond Berry, was hard to believe at times. Unitas-to-Berry had been pro football's most famous pass-catch combination since 1958, and their execution of the sideline pattern was nearly perfect.

Green Bay defensive coordinator Phil Bengston game-planned the Colt offense with a design to break down the precision timing between Unitas and his receivers. The early minutes of the season opener saw Unitas having success against Nitschke and the Packers; he guided Baltimore to a 3–0 lead. But late in the second quarter, Packer planning paid off. Caffey snared a Unitas pass and returned it for a score, and moments later, Jeter picked off another pass and ran it in from 46 yards out for a touchdown and a 14–3 lead at the break.

Nitschke and the Packer defense shut Unitas down the rest of the way, and Green Bay won 24–3. The Packers ran their record to 4–0 before losing 21–20 in San Francisco, then won eight of their final nine games to finish 12–2 and clinch their second straight Western Conference title. Along the way, they had defeated Chicago twice, including a November 20 meeting made memorable by the fierce hitting on both sides. The game marked the 96th meeting between the midwest rivals, and the matchups quickened the pulse of NFL fans—Nitschke against halfback Gale Sayers; Jim Taylor against middle linebacker Dick Butkus. Sayers and Butkus were second-year stars, and they impressed Nitschke and the rest of Green Bay's veteran squad. Lombardi said Sayers might have been the best "pure" runner he had ever seen, and Nitschke looked on Sayers as the finest instinctive runner he had ever played against. Nitschke compared Sayers' running style to that of a rabbit; he had a rabbit's quickness and ability to change pace. Watching film of Sayers left Nitschke wondering at times how it was humanly possible for Gale to make a certain move. "How can the guy do those things?" Nitschke would ask himself. As great as Sayers was, Nitschke knew it was impossible for one man alone to stop him. The Packers learned that the first time they met Sayers in '65. Green Bay had taken an aggressive approach, and paid for it when Sayers gained ground on cutbacks against the pursuit. At the time, the game against the Packers was just Sayers' second start in the NFL, and he was given a quick introduction to the Green Bay defense. On a sweep to the right, Sayers saw Nitschke and left end Willie Davis shedding blockers and pounding across the Lambeau Field turf after him. The double hit lifted Sayers off the ground, and as the trio landed, Nitschke had hold of Sayers' left leg, and Davis had the right. "Okay, Ray," Sayers heard Davis say, "make a wish, baby."

Trailing 20–0 in the third quarter, Sayers scored the first of his two touchdowns that day when films show him heading off-tackle from the Green Bay 6-yard line. He saw the hole plugged, then slid wide laterally across the line, lowered his helmet, and dragged four defenders into the end zone for the score. Later, Sayers curled inside of Caffey on a pass play, took a pass from quarterback Rudy Bukich, and ran 65 yards untouched for the score. It was one of five catches Sayers made that day, and he finished with 80 yards on 17 carries in a 23–14 loss.

In the rematch at Wrigley Field, a 31–10 Bears victory, Sayers gained 62 yards on 16 carries, and scored a 10-yard touchdown. In '66, the Packers blanked the Bears 17–0 in a Week Six game in Chicago, and Sayers was limited to just 19 yards rushing. Bengston had fine-tuned his defense for the Bears star, developing what he called "a moving perimeter" in which each defender was to guard a certain area whenever Sayers had the ball. To Nitschke, the idea was to keep Sayers in the middle of that moving perimeter, keep him contained until the pursuit could arrive. Nitschke was willing to give Sayers inside yardage as long as the Packers could prevent him from getting outside.

"Keep him in a moving perimeter," Bengston told his defense the week before the Bear game, and Nitschke and the Packers had responded. The second meeting was more of the same. On a cold, gray Sunday, the Packers and Bears slugged it out in the annual renewal of pro football's oldest and longest rivalry. With Lombardi and Bears patriarch George Halas watching from opposing sidelines, the Packers and Bears engaged in a contest CBS sportscaster Ray Scott described as a "raw, mean, old-fashioned football game. . . . There were no heroes, there was no glory. It was trench warfare."

From the time he had entered the NFL in 1965, Sayers had been told by Halas that the Packers were the team to beat. Before Packers–Bears games, Halas would tell Sayers, "These are the people you measure how good you are by."

Films of the game show Nitschke and the Pack defense gang-tackling Sayers, and Butkus drawing a bead on Taylor. When it was over, Sayers had been held to 68 yards on 20 carries, and Green Bay earned a hard-fought, 14–6 win.

The penultimate game of the regular season rematched the Colts and Packers in Baltimore. A drenching rain muddied the field, and late in the game the Packers were clinging to a 14–10 lead when Unitas began the type of late-game drive Nitschke had been concerned about. Forced to scramble, Unitas was slammed from behind by Davis. Nitschke arrived a split-second later, and as Davis's hit forced the ball free, left linebacker Dave Robinson recovered the fumble for Green Bay.

The Packers' 12 victories in '66 gave them their second-highest total in the Lombardi era, and they had come within four points of a perfect season. There is a debate to this day inside the organization which team was Green Bay's greatest—the '62 squad or the '66 version. The 163 points allowed by the defense in '66 ranked behind the '62 squad's total of 148 as the best in franchise history, and Bengston's unit led the NFL for the second straight year in scoring defense and for the third straight year in pass defense. Nitschke was named all-league for the third straight season, joining Davis, Herb Adderley, and Willie Wood as all-pros on the Packer defense.

If the defense provided the Packers a team personality, as Ray Scott said at the time, then it was Nitschke whose personality loomed largest. "Ray was the backbone of that defense," Ditka said, "the glue that held it all together."

Fran Tarkenton, who quarterbacked the Vikings against the Packers in '66, always felt that Nitschke was the hub of the Green Bay defense. The other Packers were afraid of Nitschke, Tarkenton said, afraid of not playing well with him looking on. Sideline cameras caught Nitschke exhorting his teammates on, and in one particular game, calling for halfback Paul Hornung to put the ball in the end zone in a goal-line situation.

"Git it in there, Paul, git in in," he yelled, and punctuated his shouts by pumping his padded right fist into the air. "Stick it in there!"

Scott called Nitschke the one player Green Bay opponents loved to hate, and opponents hated him because he was an intimidator. "He intimidated you physically," NFL Films president Steve Sabol said, "and he intimidated you mentally."

Highlights of the '66 season show Nitschke at his ball-hawking best. In Detroit, he lifted a Lions receiver off his feet with a blind-side hit, then scooped the loose ball off the turf with his huge right hand and shook it in the face of an official to indicate a fumble recovery. Nitschke could intimidate players and officials alike. Colts tight end Jim Mutscheller compared Nitschke to Butkus and to Bears' old-time defensive end Ed Sprinkle, nicknamed "The Claw" for his clothesline hits on quarterbacks, as the most intimidating players he had ever seen.

NFL referee Jim Tunney understood Nitschke's nature. To Tunney, Nitschke was cut from the same cloth as intimidators past and future like Bill George and Jack Lambert, rock-and-sock middle linebackers who knew that football was not a contact sport, it was a collision sport. And as the spearheads of their respective defenses, it was their job to knock somebody down.

"Football is a violent sport," Nitschke said, "and you can't feel too much for the other guy. That's one of the great things about it, the basic premise of man dealing with man."

Lee Remmel, the Packers' executive director of public relations, covered Nitschke's career for the *Green Bay Press-Gazette*. To him, Nitschke was an intense, all-out performer. "That certainly endeared him to our fans, who have a great respect for that," Remmel said.

Opponents respected it but didn't always like it. Ditka once recalled the Bears' 31–10 win over the Packers in 1965, when players on both sides were content to run out the clock in the game's waning moments. It's common for even the most intense players to throttle back in the final seconds when the outcome is no longer in doubt. Merlin Olsen, the great defensive tackle for the Los Angeles Rams, would extend a hand to help the opposition up;

Pittsburgh's Joe Greene, whose nickname was "Mean," would engage opposing linemen in small talk.

"What it is, brother man," Greene would say. "How's the wife?"

Nitschke, however, refused to accept defeat and even on the last play of a losing effort against Chicago, was like a wild man, shouting at Ditka in his gravelly voice.

"Hey you, yeah you," Nitschke yelled. "I got ya! I'm gonna bite you back."

The moment impressed Ditka, who thought that everyone on the Packers was resigned to the defeat. "Everyone," he noted, "except Ray."

"I hated to play against Nitschke," wide receiver Tommy McDonald said. "You knew he was an individual who was going to give not a hundred percent but two hundred percent out there on that field. He was the number-one instigator in getting that defense to play the way that would satisfy Vince Lombardi. Ray's the type of guy that you may not want his opinion, but dad-gummit, he's going to give it to you. He talked out there, but it was a motivation-type thing, trying to get other people up, keep them up and get them going. He was a foreman on the job, and you have to have individuals like that on the field. You know, Lombardi could only go up to the little white line, so you have to have guys like Nitschke to be your focal point, you sergeant-at-arms out there on that field."

If Nitschke was the one Packer opponents hated to play against, he was also the one they game-planned the most for. Matched up against the Eastern Conference champions, the Dallas Cowboys, Nitschke became the focal point of Coach Tom Landry's offensive game plan. Led by quarterback Don Meredith, backs Don Perkins and Dan Reeves, and game-breaking split end Bob Hayes, the Cowboys featured a flashy I-formation offense that had rolled up an NFL-best 445 points in 1966. When the Dallas offense gathered to discuss the Green Bay defense, the first question they addressed was, "How do we handle Nitschke?" It was the same question offenses would ask in future years as they game-planned for a Joe Greene, a Lawrence Taylor.

"Any time we played the Packers, our number-one priority was blocking Ray Nitschke," Cowboy tackle Ralph Neely said. "We knew if we were going to be successful, we had to block Nitschke."

Because the Packers shielded blockers away from Nitschke so well, Reeves said it was difficult to find ways to reach him. "They did a great job of keeping people off of him and allowing him to get to the football," he said. "He could make tackles from one side to the other. He was a great football player in a great scheme.

"You had to account for him, you had to have someone assigned to him. They had a lot of good football players but he was the key to their defense, he was in control of everything. He was the guy that knew formations, he was the guy that got everybody in the right position, where to be, what the coverage was, and what defense they were playing. He was not only a tough guy, he was an extremely bright football player. You could see that when you were competing against him. You weren't going to be successful against Green Bay if you didn't account for Ray."

Guided by Landry and triggered by Meredith, the Cowboy offense was the most complex in the NFL. "We had 18 to 20 formations," Neely said, "and 18 to 20 plays out of each formation." This at a time when most NFL offenses used just six formations. The Cowboys also employed a variety of blocking combinations, and varied their technique on each.

The Packers' philosophy for dealing with Landry's multiple offense was to remain as basic as possible. Football is blocking and tackling, Lombardi said, and the team that blocks and tackles the best will win. In preparation for the Cowboys, Bengston kept his defensive plan simple and relied on fundamentals and execution so his players would have confidence in what they were doing. Each player was given the freedom to make small adjustments that he deemed necessary, but the basic Packer plan for the '66 title game was to hold their ground against the Cowboys' shifting formations and bracket the explosive Hayes short and long with Adderley and safety Tom Brown.

Nitschke said that by 1966 it had become harder to prepare a defense for Dallas than for any other team in the league. Landry was a fine coach, and Nitschke knew there was more to the man than the stoic image he portrayed on the sideline every Sunday. On one occasion, Landry had driven to the Cowboys' practice facility amid a morning rain only to find his parking spot occupied by rookie linebacker Steve Kiner. When Landry entered the locker room several minutes later soaking wet, he walked over to where Kiner was sitting and said, "I admire a man with courage."

Because of the high number of offensive sets Landry's Cowboys used, defenders not only had to be able to recognize each set but also be in the right place to stop them. Nitschke thought that while Landry didn't expect to beat defenses with formations alone, he did want to create a moment of doubt, a moment of confusion in the defense. Once that happened, Nitschke said, the situation would snowball.

"It was a good test," Nitschke recalled years later. "That was a well-coached Landry team. They had it all. But we were prepared for anything they did. Bengston was a real perfectionist, just like Lombardi. He ran the defense and Lombardi ran the offense, but Phil never got the credit he deserved. He kept it simple for us.

"We knew Dallas was going to have to line up somewhere eventually, and what we had to do was line up in the right place and execute. We had a lot of experience on our defense, so we weren't going to get rattled by anything."

"We emphasized the basics," Bengston recalled once. "I always emphasized that it's not the plays, it's the players."

Amid near-perfect temperatures in the Cotton Bowl in Dallas on New Year's Day 1967, the Packers and Cowboys took the field for the late-afternoon kickoff. The NFL title game was the second half of a Sunday doubleheader featuring the AFL and NFL championship games. Earlier in the day, the Kansas City Chiefs had beaten the two-time defending AFL champion Buffalo Bills, 31–7, in the frozen mud of Buffalo's War Memorial Stadium. The victory advanced the powerful Chiefs, who featured the AFL's best record, to the first AFL–NFL World Championship Game, scheduled for January 15 in the Los Angeles Coliseum.

A trip to the Super Bowl awaited the winner of the Green Bay–Dallas game, and the Packers sprinted to an early lead on a 17-yard touchdown pass from Bart Starr to halfback Elijah Pitts, and Jim Grabowski's 17-yard score on a fumble return on the ensuing kickoff.

Privately, some of the Packers thought the game was going to be a rout. Especially the members of their defensive unit, like Adderley, who said that whenever Green Bay got the lead in a championship game, they did what Lombardi asked them to do. Which, Adderley said, was to rise to the occasion and shut the opponent out.

The Cowboys, however, came back, and showed why they were one of the exciting young teams in pro football. Perkins picked up huge gains out of the Cowboys' shifting sets, and the Packer defense was suddenly on its heels. Reeves scored from three yards out, and Perkins capped the Cowboys' next drive with a 17-yard scoring burst that tied the game at 14. A review of the play shows Nitschke being faked out of position by Reeves, who ran right on a simulated sweep. Nitschke followed and was caught flat-footed when Perkins took Meredith's handoff on a counter and exploded through a wide-open gap in the Green Bay line.

To Adderley, the source of Dallas's success was simple. The Cowboys were running traps and misdirections inside, confusing Nitschke with false keys and reads. "And when you get the middle linebacker confused and going the wrong way," Adderley said, "that makes it real tough on the defensive backs to come up and make the play."

Sideline cameras show Nitschke and the defense looking stunned. They had given up 14 points in the first 15 minutes, more points than they had allowed in a championship or playoff game since the 1960 loss in Philadelphia. Landry had added formations Nitschke and the Packers hadn't seen before. Green Bay was being caught off-guard by the new plays and was trying to read and react on the run. From his middle linebacker position, Nitschke could see what the Cowboys were doing. Landry was running Perkins out of the I-formation on quick openers and cross bucks against the flow of the play.

"That was all Coach Landry," Reeves remembered. "He and Coach Lombardi had coached on the same staff in New York and they kind of knew how their defenses were constructed, how their offenses were constructed. They were playing a chess match.

"Landry's theory on beating any defense was to use a lot of mis-direction, a lot of formations so that people didn't know exactly where you were coming from. We weren't the type of team like the Packers, where they said, 'Okay, here comes the sweep. Try and stop us.' We used more formations and misdirections trying to counter those things."

On the sidelines, Lombardi sought out Bengston. "Hey, Phil," he shouted. "Shake up those linebackers!"

Nitschke and the defense were already shaken, and they came off the field in an angry, agitated state. Seeing this, offensive guard Fuzzy Thurston ran over to calm them down.

"Hey, don't worry about it," Thurston told them. "We'll get it back. Don't worry about it."

Green Bay did get it back, Starr connecting with Carroll Dale on a 51-yard TD pass. Lombardi's offensive game-planning caught the Cowboy defense off-guard. Plays that had been run from one set all season were now being run from another. Dallas's well-schooled defenders were suddenly dizzy; Green Bay's game plan left them feeling as if they were trying to watch a movie being run in reverse.

Once again the Cowboys rallied, and Dallas cut its deficit to 21–17 at halftime on an 11-yard field goal by Danny Villanueva. Nitschke knew the Packer defense had been outplayed in the first half, but he also knew they could stay in the game if they adjusted their defense to what the Cowboys were doing. All they had to do, he felt, was play the way they knew how to play, the way they had played during the regular season. The Cowboys may outcute them, Nitschke thought, but if the Packers maintained their poise, they would win.

Ironically, Green Bay's defense was aided by the Cowboys coaching staff, which decided to go away from the game plan that had been confusing the Packers—the inside traps and misdirection runs by Perkins—in favor of a passing game. Perkins had been running the ball with great success, Adderley said, but just when it seemed he was unstoppable this day, the Cowboys switched to another phase of their game plan.

The result was that after scoring 14 points in the first quarter, Dallas managed just three points in both the second and third periods. Starr, meanwhile, was having a big day passing. In the third quarter he gave Green Bay a 28–20 lead with a 16-yard scoring pass to flanker Boyd Dowler, then made it 34–20 in the fourth with a 28-yard TD pass to split end Max McGee. On a day in which the Green Bay defense and running game were not at their best, Starr proved to be the difference, decimating the Dallas secondary for 304 yards passing and four TDs.

When the Cowboys blocked Don Chandler's extra-point attempt, the Cotton Bowl came alive. Down by 14, Dallas rallied again. When Brown fell in the secondary covering tight end Frank Clarke, Meredith found the wide-open Clarke for a 68-yard score. In the game's final minutes, the Cowboys drove toward a game-tying touchdown and overtime. On the sidelines, McGee nudged a teammate and said if the Cowboys forced overtime, the Packers were in trouble. "We're dead," McGee said.

On the field, Nitschke and the Packer defense stayed patient, stayed with the game plan. Dallas drove to the 2-yard line, but just as Nitschke thought they eventually would, the Cowboy computer crossed itself up. Dallas jumped offside, a crucial penalty that cost the Cowboys five yards. It took them two plays to get back to the 2, and now it was fourth down. Since a field goal would do Dallas no good, the Packer defense dug in for the goal-line stand. As the Cotton Bowl crowd roared, Nitschke shouted to his teammates.

"We gotta hold 'em," he yelled.

In the Dallas huddle, Meredith called Fire 90, Quarterback Roll Right. It was an option roll-out by Meredith, a play the Cowboys had used with success throughout the season. At the snap, left linebacker Dave Robinson recognized the play from the films and made a hard, inside move to grab hold of Meredith. The Cowboys quarterback made an outstanding effort to get the ball away despite being draped by Robinson's 245 pounds, but he was trying to throw across his body. The result was a weak floater that hung in the night air for a few moments before settling into Tom Brown's arms in the back of the end zone.

On WTMJ Radio, Packers' announced Ted Moore called the decisive play:

> *The clock is running with 52 seconds remaining. If the Cowboys go in here and kick the extra point, we're going into overtime. They've got one play to travel two yards. . . . Meredith takes the ball, rolls out to the right, he's going to be nailed. . . . He gets a pass away and it's intercepted in the end zone by Tom Brown! And the Packers have just taken the championship!*

The Packers won the game, 34–27, and while Caffey acknowledged that Green Bay didn't played particularly well on defense, they had won because of team togetherness. "Down there, man, it was love, pure love," Caffey said of the goal-line stand. "We knew we could stop them."

To Nitschke, who finished the game with eight tackles, the Packers had stopped Dallas because they had maintained their poise, maintained their patience. Green Bay had won its second straight NFL championship, its fourth in six years. But now, for the first time, there was one more game to be played, one more challenge to be met.

A game that, for Nitschke and the Packers, represented the most important challenge they had ever faced.

TEN

IN THE LONG history of the National Football League, it's unlikely that any team has felt as much pressure to win a game as the Green Bay Packers did in preparing for that historic first meeting between the NFL and AFL.

The two leagues had been warring since August 22, 1959, when 27-year-old Texas millionaire Lamar Hunt announced the formation of the fledgling American Football League. Like millions of other Americans, Hunt had been fascinated by the drama of the 1958 NFL championship classic between the Baltimore Colts and New York Giants, and he petitioned the NFL to purchase the struggling Chicago Cardinals franchise. Unsuccessful in his attempt, Hunt joined with a group of seven other owners—the original "Foolish Club"—to form a league that would begin play in 1960. The NFL responded to Hunt's announcement by extending to the new league an iron first gloved in velvet. While NFL commissioner Bert Bell went before a Senate sub-committee and pledged to befriend the AFL, old-guard owners like George Halas recalled the bloody financial battles with the All-America Football Conference that raged from 1946–49 and recoiled at the thought of yet another new rival. AFL plans to put a franchise in Minnesota were scuttled when the NFL wooed the Minneapolis-based investing group headed by Bill Boyer and Max Winter, who had previously been rebuffed in their attempts to join the NFL, away from the AFL with a promise to field an expansion team in Minnesota in 1961. The NFL dropped another bombshell when it announced it would expand into Dallas, where Hunt had located his team, with a club that eventually became known as the Cowboys.

To stunned AFL owners, the NFL's back-door dealings had a Yalta-like deception about them. Territory became a premium, and both leagues viewed marketable outlets as spheres of influence to win over the sporting public. The war between the leagues raged from 1960–66, growing more uncivil each year as NFL and AFL owners battled for blue-chip college players, assigned "baby-sitting" scouts to sneak sought-after senior players away from the rival league, and opened their checkbooks in an all-out signing spree. The war spread to the courtrooms, where the AFL brought an antitrust suit against the NFL, and the older league responded in turn with a court case against the young rival's signing of Louisiana All-America Billy Cannon. Some members of the AFL openly campaigned for a season-ending showdown between the champions of the two leagues, a "World Series" of pro football as *Sports Illustrated* titled it in a December 1963 issue that featured the explosive San Diego Chargers, the standard-bearers of the AFL's wide-open game, as the coverpiece of a story examining the prospects of such an encounter. New York Titans' owner Harry Wismer openly campaigned for an AFL–NFL championship game, and AFL veterans like George Blanda, who had quarterbacked the Chicago Bears before taking over in Houston and leading the Oilers to the first two AFL titles in 1960 and '61 were certain the young league could hold its own against the NFL's best.

"That first year, the Houston Oilers or Los Angeles Chargers could have beaten—repeat *beaten*—the NFL champion (Philadelphia Eagles) in a Super Bowl," Blanda said later. "I just regret we didn't get the chance to prove it."

The rebels had fired the first shot over the port bow, and Halas, who had numerous personality conflicts with Blanda in Chicago, fired back for the Establishment. "The AFL can't be anything but a Mickey Mouse league," the Bears patriarch snorted. "How can it be anything else? Isn't George Blanda a first-string quarterback over there?"

Throughout the AFL's early years, Wismer became the AFL's front-man in the push for a season-ending showdown. In 1960, he claimed the Chargers–Oilers AFL title game was "far better" than the Packers–Eagles championship. From 1960 to 1962, Wismer maintained a public persistence that the AFL's best—the Oilers and Chargers—could "easily" beat the NFL's lesser teams, the Rams, Redskins, and Cowboys, and play a "representative game" against the Packers, Eagles, and Giants.

Tex Maule, who covered the NFL for *Sports Illustrated,* scoffed at Wismer's claims of equality. He denigrated the AFL in print, claiming that not a single member of the two-time league champion Oilers could start for any of the NFL's top four teams, and only one or two Houston players could start for the weaker teams in the NFL. In words that left the AFL seething, Maule compared the Oilers to a semi-pro team, one step ahead of the college boys.

"The question," Maule wrote, "is 'How good are the Oilers?' Unquestionably, they are better than Missouri or Minnesota or Mississippi. They are smarter and more versatile than these college teams; but they are not as good as the Dallas Cowboys, the newest and weakest team in the National Football League. The Cowboys, who are smarter and more versatile than the Oilers, would beat them, and easily."

Publicly, the AFL railed against Maule and what they perceived as his elitist opinions. Privately, however, AFL people like league commissioner

Joe Foss agreed with Maule, albeit reluctantly. Foss was hoping that AFL teams would have a few more years to gather strength before taking on the NFL. "If the NFL had paid attention to Harry's cries for a championship those first couple of years, we'd never have lived to see the day of the merger," Foss said. Shuddering at the thought of the Oilers or league champion Dallas Texans playing the Packers in 1961 or '62, Foss was blunt in his feelings about what an early Super Bowl against Green Bay would have yielded. "They'd have handed us our heads," he remarked.

Public opinion about an NFL–AFL championship game shifted at the end of the 1963 season, and the exact date can be traced to January 5, 1964. Amid balmy, 71-degree temperatures in sun-bleached Balboa Stadium, the San Diego Chargers stunned the football world with a 51–10 rout of the Boston Patriots. The Chargers' lightning attack, symbolized by the jagged bolts that adorned their helmets and uniforms, was electrifying. Head coach Sid Gillman had amassed an offensive armada—wide receiver Lance Alworth, quarterbacks Tobin Rote and John Hadl, backs Keith Lincoln and Paul Lowe, tackle Ron Mix, guard Walt Sweeney—and turned them loose with a state-of-the-art passing game that became the forerunner of the West Coast offense.

No one had seen anything quite like it before. San Diego's attack was based on the big play, and it emphasized explosive quickness. The running game featured quick traps and toss sweeps, the passing game was all precision routes aimed at gaining separation from befuddled defenders. Gillman's game plans were so innovative that even NFL people like former Cleveland Browns quarterback Otto Graham were impressed with "El Sid" and his high-tech offense.

"If the Chargers could play the best in the NFL," Graham said in '63, "I'd have to pick the Chargers."

San Diego became the first AFL club to invite serious comparisons with the NFL's top teams, but when Buffalo physically dominated the Chargers in the 1964 AFL championship game, Bills fans in old War Memorial Stadium held op a sign that read, "Bring on the NFL." Through the winter of '64 and '65, hot-stove debates on the merits of the two leagues intensified. Outside the Buffalo Rust Belt, the AFL was basketball on stripes, finesse football played on fast tracks amid soft sunshine. The NFL was old-fashioned football, power backs sweeping the flanks behind pulling guards under darkening, snow-filled clouds.

When the NFL–AFL war began raging out of control in 1966, cooler heads realized that the escalating cost of signing free agents threatened to bankrupt owners in both leagues. Just as the AFL launched an all-out raiding of NFL rosters to sign star quarterbacks, NFL Commissioner Pete Rozelle joined with AFL founder Lamar Hunt on June 8, 1966, to announce a merger of the two leagues. A yearly championship game would be played, and while Hunt coined the term "Super Bowl" after the "Super Ball" that his young daughter Sharon was playing with, the long-awaited first meeting between the two leagues was officially titled the "AFL–NFL World Championship Game."

Fittingly, it was Hunt's team, the Kansas City Chiefs, that would represent the rebels in this historic game. Utilizing an I-formation offense complete with multiple shifts, "moving pockets," and double tight end alignments, the Chiefs were following in the footsteps of the Chargers as practitioners of flashy, AFL-style football. Kansas City head coach Hank Stram succeeded Gillman as the league's most innovative coach. Just as Gillman had attracted attention by appearing professorial on the sidelines with his pipe, buttoned-up collar and bowtie, the short, stocky Stram was easily distinguishable in his black blazer, bright red vest and gray checked pants.

To Stram, a football team should reflect the personality of its coach. Since Stram thought of himself as a varied man, he liked to express himself through the abilities of his players. He liked the idea of seeing himself in the Chiefs' stack defense, tight-I offense, and rolling pocket. The Chiefs had 18 different offensive sets and could run 350 plays off of those sets.

"We present the same face with different makeup each play," Stram said, "and I'm a good makeup man with an excellent makeup kit."

If Stram's Chiefs were fitting representatives of the break-the-mold AFL, the Packers were perfect standard-bearers for the establishment. Green Bay was one of the old guard's original franchises and the last of the town teams that had made up the early NFL. Just as Stram's varied personality was reflected in the Chiefs' strategic variations, the Packers' tough, disciplined approach had been drilled into them by Lombardi, the inspirational leader who had built them into a hard-hitting, precision machine.

"They were pure vanilla," Stram remembered. "No nuts, no chocolate, just plain vanilla. Preparing for that game was so simple it was amazing. We saw everything in the AFL, and here we were, preparing for a team that defensively used one just one alignment and one coverage. It was unbelievable, but they were good enough to get by with it."

Nitschke recognized from the start that there was more to this game than any other he had ever played in. He had followed the Bears when they had Nagurski and Luckman; he knew the NFL's tradition. He also knew that tradition would be on the line when the Packers took the field against the upstart Chiefs. The hype surrounding the game grew, and the Packers felt it. Nitschke and his teammates were reminded daily of the Chiefs' great physical size and strength, were reminded too of the awesome responsibility they had in representing the NFL in this game. It wasn't only Packer prestige that was on the line against Kansas City, Lombardi told his team; the whole NFL was on the line as well. In the two weeks before the game, the Packers received phone calls or telegrams from every one of the NFL's owners impressing upon them the importance of beating the AFL. Lombardi trembled as he read the team telegrams from Halas and Giants owner Wellington Mara urging the Packers to victory, and the Green Bay boss grew increasingly anxious as the publicity buildup began in earnest. When a photographer from a national magazine called to ask if he could photograph him praying in church, Lombardi, the devout Catholic, ran out of patience. "No way," he shouted into the phone at the man.

To Nitschke, the game was being blown out of proportion. He knew the Chiefs must have a pretty good team. But he didn't feel they were in the Packers' class. Green Bay had already beaten Baltimore, Cleveland, and Dallas during the regular season, so why couldn't they beat the Chiefs, he wondered. Two weeks of film study did little to change Nitschke's opinion of the AFL champions. Defensive coordinator Phil Bengston broke down the Chiefs' offense, which mirrored Dallas in many ways. Like the Cowboys, the Chiefs looked to confuse defenses with shifting I-formation sets that disguised their formation until the last second. Against the Bills in the AFL championship game, the Chiefs had used 12 variations of the I-formation alone. The Packers, however, weren't overly concerned with K.C.'s pre-snap shifts and movement.

"We had an exchange of films with the Chiefs and we went about our normal preparation," Bengston recalled once. "The Chiefs had some fine personnel and they were well-prepared, but preparing for their style of offense wasn't that difficult. Dallas used more formations than the Chiefs did."

What was difficult was judging just how good the Chiefs were. Since the Packers had never played against AFL teams, they had trouble gauging the quality of Kansas City's competition. The Packers had seen Chiefs quarterback Len Dawson when he played in the NFL with Pittsburgh and Cleveland. But Otis Taylor? Mike Garrett? Buck Buchanan? Clearly they were talented enough to play in the NFL, but just how talented would remain a mystery until game time.

"It was real difficult," Nitschke said once about preparing for the Chiefs. "We didn't know how good their opponents were, so it was pretty hard to judge them. I know that was a big concern for Coach Lombardi."

The Chiefs were slick, quick, and knew how to trick, and Bengston alleviated concerns among his players by devising a defensive game plan that was not much different than what the Packers had used all year. Green Bay wasn't overly concerned with Kansas City's multiple formations or "moving pocket," which featured Dawson rolling left or right behind a wall of blockers. Bengston was concerned, however, with the Chiefs' play-action game, which if successful could freeze Nitschke and the Green Bay linebackers in place. Film study revealed that the Chiefs' play-action style was vulnerable to a linebacker blitz, but Bengston advised Lombardi he wouldn't call for a blitz during the first half. The idea was to build up in Dawson a false sense of security, and to save the surprise of the blitz until a critical moment presented itself.

While the Packers went quietly about their business, Kansas City cornerback Fred Williamson held court for reporters. Nicknamed "The Hammer," for the tremendous forearm blows he used to floor AFL receivers, Williamson was a big, physical cornerback who had knocked Buffalo receiver Glenn Bass out of a game with a high hit. Williamson padded his forearms and described his clotheslinelike hits to a *New York Times* reporter as "a karate blow having great velocity and delivered perpendicular to the earth's latitude." To teammates, he described it as "a lethal muthah," and promised to level it on the NFL champions.

"The Packers, sheeit, Taylor, sheeit, Lombardi, sheeit," Williamson said. "We're going to whip their asses, all of them, and if Boyd Dowler and Carroll Dale or any of those other guys have the nerve to catch a pass in my territory they're going to pay the price, man."

Starr said the Packers were more amused than riled up by Williamson's tough talk. "You accept people for what they are," Starr remarked. "We took it in stride."

Super Sunday dawned sunny and bright over the greater Los Angeles area. By game time, a thin layer of California smog hung over the Los Angeles Coliseum, which was only two-thirds full for the game. League allegiances were vividly on display throughout the stadium. The game was being broadcast by both CBS, which covered the NFL, and NBC, which had been broadcasting the AFL since 1964. Ray Scott and Frank Gifford were the lead announcers for CBS; Curt Gowdy and Paul Christman for NBC. Viewers found league loyalties on display in the commercial slots as well. CBS viewers were treated to a steady diet of Ford automotive commercials; NBC viewers to Chrysler ads. The Packers and Chiefs were not only represented by their own networks and corporate sponsors, they were also using their own footballs as well. When Green Bay was on offense, the Packers used the NFL ball "The Duke." When Kansas City went on offense, the Chiefs used the Spalding J5-V, which was longer and thinner than "The Duke" and was said to be easier to throw.

"Is it easier to intercept too?" Lombardi quipped to reporters before the game, and went on to compare the AFL ball's shape to "a Long Island frankfurter."

As the Chiefs massed in the tunnel before taking the painted Coliseum field, some Kansas City players suddenly realized what they were up against. The AFL had never produced a fullback with the ferocity of Jim Taylor, a middle linebacker as violent and well-schooled as Nitschke. Chiefs linebacker E. J. Holub looked around and saw some of his teammates had wet their pants and were throwing up.

Finally, after seven years of a war that had been fought in the courtrooms and newspapers, the champions of the two leagues were on the same field. It was strange for viewers to see the Packers in their green-and-gold going against the Chiefs in their road white uniforms with the bright red and yellow trim. Strange for the two teams as well, and they spent the opening minutes of the game probing one another to find strengths and weaknesses.

After Green Bay's initial series ended in a Don Chandler punt, Kansas City went on offense for the first time. With the ball resting on the Chiefs' 37-yard line, Dawson approached the line of scrimmage, and the first Packer defender he laid eyes on was Nitschke.

With his cheekbones streaked with black shoe polish to cut the sun's glare, with his craggy face covered by his half-cage facemask, Nitschke stared back at the Chief quarterback and began barking out defensive signals. Dawson saw the Packer middle linebacker shifting back and forth, saw what he believed to be foam coming out of Nitschke's mouth as he shouted signals in that loud, raucous voice, and thought to himself, "This is the meanest, ugliest man I have ever seen."

Both teams gained one first down on their initial series, and then the Packers struck. Facing a third-and-three from the Kansas City 37-yard line with 6:04 left in the first quarter, Starr beat a linebacker blitz by connecting with split end Max McGee on a quick post for the first score in Super Bowl history. McGee had entered the game for Boyd Dowler, who had reinjured his left shoulder on the third play of the game, and the 34-year-old veteran turned in a circus catch by reaching back for the ball and making a one-handed grab en route to the gold-painted end zone.

Nitschke made his presence felt on the first play of the Chiefs' next series, when he stopped a scrambling Dawson after a 7-yard gain. On NBC Radio, play-by-play sportscaster Jim Simpson made the call on Nitschke's first stop in the Super Bowl:

> *Two minutes and 55 seconds to go in this, the first quarter of the AFL–NFL championship, the Super Bowl, from the Coliseum in Los Angeles under sunny skies, little or no wind. . . . It is second down and inches to go for Kansas City. Burford goes out as a flanker to the left, I-formation now, and Garrett steps over to the right. . . . Dawson is back to pass, lots of time, now in trouble, looking gets past one man and has his own first down*

across the 40-yard line and is driven back across the 41. Dawson, looking for running room, did get enough for the first down, and Ray Nitschke, the middle linebacker, came up very quickly and threw him back across the 40.

Five plays later, Nitschke dragged Dawson down again, this time on a two-yard pickup, then dropped end Reg Carolan four yards short of a first down on a third-and-11 play at the Green Bay 33. Nitschke's tackle forced the Chiefs into a 40-yard field goal attempt, and Mike Mercer's kick sailed wide right with 34 seconds remaining in the first quarter.

The AFL champions got on the board early in the second quarter. Employing the play-action passing game that had caused Bengston concern, the Chiefs drove 66 yards in six plays. Dawson capped the march with a 7-yard scoring pass to fullback Curtis McClinton and Mercer's kick tied the game 7–7.

Nitschke grew angry on the point-after attempt when a Kansas City player gave him the elbow on Mercer's kick. Nitschke's anger wasn't with the Chiefs player but with himself. Nitschke had used his elbows on opposing players during the regular season, but since most PAT attempts are automatic, NFL players rarely went all-out during the kick. That the Chiefs player had elbowed Nitschke on the PAT indicated to the Packer veteran that the AFL champs had come to play, and it made him mad that he was the one getting hit and not doing the hitting.

The Packers responded to Kansas City's score with a drive that Bengston said later could have come straight out of a 1962 newsreel. After an illegal procedure penalty nullified Starr's 64-yard touchdown pass to Carroll Dale, the Green Bay quarterback began picking the Kansas City secondary apart with an assortment of short and medium-range passes. On third-and-five, Starr found McGee for 10 yards. On third-and-10, he hit Dale for 15. On third-and-five, he connected with tight end Marv Fleming for 11. On third-and-seven, Starr passed to halfback Elijah Pitts for 20. The play carried to the Kansas City 14, and Taylor followed by sweeping left behind pulling guards Jerry Kramer and Fuzzy Thurston and dragging two Chief defenders into the end zone for a 14–7 lead.

Surprising the Packers with their ability to counterpunch, Kansas City answered Green Bay's scoring drive with one of their own. Dawson was holding Nitschke and the linebackers in check with his play-action fakes to Garrett and McClinton, and buying time on passing downs by rolling out in the floating pocket. On second down, Nitschke hauled down tight end Fred Arbanas following a 12-yard gain, and two plays later stopped Garrett following a two-yard run up the middle. With time running out in the half, Mercer's 31-yard field goal with 54 seconds to play brought the Chiefs to within 14–10 at halftime, and brought nervous looks from both the Packers and NFL partisans during the break.

Buddy Young, an NFL man, told press box companions, "Old age and heat will get the Packers in the second half." AFL writers, who had feared a Green Bay blowout, found themselves smiling at the sight of Tex Maule fidgeting nervously at the half.

"Tex was very worried," recalled Jerry Magee, who covered the AFL for the *San Diego Tribune*. "He kept stalking up and down in the press box."

Nitschke was worried as well. He had realized early in the game that despite their great physical size, the Chiefs' offense was a finesse unit. Whether it was following the movements of Dawson's moving pocket or the darting, waterbug runs of Garrett, Nitschke could see that the Chiefs were another team like the Cowboys, a team that tried to outcute the defense rather than outhit them.

Leading by just four points at the half didn't fill the Packers with a lot of pride or confidence. In the Green Bay locker room, someone had written the words *Know Thyself* on the chalkboard. Gathering his team around him, Lombardi let loose with a few choice words.

"Hey, you guys better wake up," he snapped. "The game will be over and you'll be on the short end. What the hell's going on out there?"

Nitschke listened as Lombardi told his players that they were not only representing themselves but every player in the National Football League. Looking hard at his veteran team, Lombardi left them with one final thought.

"Are you the world champion Green Bay Packers?" he asked. "Go out on the field and give me your answer."

Reemerging into the sunshine for the second half, Nitschke knew he had played the first half uptight. The pressure of the game was thick enough to slice; he had felt it and played conservatively. If the Packers could get back to playing football the way they knew how, Nitschke was confident they could put the game away. As tight as Green Bay was, the Chiefs were wound just as tight. Garrett remembered the team being uncommonly tired at halftime. The combination of the game's emotional buildup as well as the grueling two weeks of practice were taking a toll. "We were on dead legs in the second half," Garrett remembered.

Four plays into the Chiefs' first series of the third quarter, Green Bay got the break it was looking for. With Kansas City facing a third-and-five from its own 49, Bengston signaled in the first blitz of the game. The Chiefs' tendency chart on Green Bay indicated that the Packers had blitzed only five percent of the time—three times in two years to be exact—in third-and-five situations. Bengston crossed up Kansas City with a surprise linebacker blitz, sending Dave Robinson and Lee Roy Caffey shooting in from the corners. Right tackle Henry Jordan provided an extra push up the middle, and when Jordan tipped Dawson's passing arm, the pass intended for Arbanas fluttered weakly. Free safety Willie Wood stepped in front of Arbanas at the Green Bay 45 and returned it 50 yards before Garrett dragged him down from behind at the Kansas City 5-yard line. One play later, Pitts took Starr's handoff and plunged in off the left side, and the Packers' lead was pushed to 21–10.

Wood's interception proved to be the turning point in the game. Starr launched two more time-consuming scoring drives, and the Packers scored on a 13-yard pass to McGee, who made a juggling catch in the end zone late in the third quarter, and a 1-yard run by Pitts, again off the left side behind tackle Bob Skoronski. On the sideline, Nitschke found irony in the performance by McGee, who had a game-high seven catches after finishing the entire regular season with just four receptions.

"Way to go, McGoo," Nitschke said, calling McGee by his nickname.

Leading 35–10, the Packers took care of one final bit of unfinished business. Running the power sweep to Williamson's side, Green Bay watched as the Kansas City cornerback barreled low into pulling guard Gale Gillingham and halfback Donny Anderson, caught Gillingham's knee flush on the helmet, and was knocked cold. As the Chiefs carried the prone Williamson off the field on a stretcher, the Packer sideline reverberated with calls of "The Hammer got it!" Thurston whistled the tune, "If I had a hammer . . . "

Nitschke, who had five first-half tackles, registered two more in the second, including a 7-yard sack of backup quarterback Pete Beathard on the Chiefs' final series. When the final gun sounded, Green Bay had given the NFL a convincing 35–10 win over the AFL, and a grass-stained Nitschke walked off the field with seven tackles and an appreciation for AFL-style football.

"We came away with a lot of respect for Kansas City," he remembered. "They were a quality team with a lot of talent."

Amid the joyous Green Bay locker room, Lombardi stood holding a game ball in his hard hands. "An NFL ball," he joked to reporters. At first, he refused to be drawn into comparing the Chiefs to NFL teams. "I have nothing to say about it," he said. Finally, he relented.

"That's a good football team," he said of Kansas City. "But it is not as good as the top teams in our league." He paused. "That's what you wanted me to say, and now I've said it. It took me a long time to get that out."

Later, Lombardi deeply regretted the remark. "I came off as an ungracious winner," he told a friend, "and it was lousy."

Not far from where Lombardi was holding court for the media, Starr stood at his locker talking with reporters. He had been named the game's Most Valuable Player after completing 16 of 23 passes for 250 yards and two touchdowns. Starr had picked apart the AFL's best defense with his heady play-calling and precise passing. He converted 11 of 15 third-down plays and six of seven third-down passes, lending weight to his reputation as the best clutch quarterback of his era. He had come a long way from the unheralded, 17th-round draft pick who had joined the Packers in 1956, two seasons before Nitschke. Starr was entering his third season when Nitschke joined the team in 1958, but the Alabama native was so quiet and unassuming that Nitschke soon realized that no one on the team was paying any attention to Starr. It didn't seem likely, Nitschke thought at the time, that Starr had much of a future in the NFL.

It was an opinion shared by Lombardi, who took over the Packers in 1959. He immediately identified the quarterback position as one of Green Bay's glaring weaknesses, and even after Starr had helped guide the Packers to the 1960 Western Conference championship and title game appearance against Philadelphia, Lombardi spent the off-season trying to engineer a trade for Dallas rookie quarterback Don Meredith.

"Some guys see them and some don't," Lombardi grumbled after Starr missed a wide-open receiver in the Packers' 17–13 loss to the Eagles. "I'd like to get that guy, Meredith."

Lombardi offered Dallas head coach Tom Landry any two players on the Packers' roster for Meredith. Landry refused, and beginning in 1961, Starr's emergence as the leader of Lombardi's offense paralleled Nitschke's rise as the leader of Bengston's defense.

As different as they were in background and personality—Starr, the soft-spoken Southern gentleman; Nitschke, the volcanic and violent Chicago street tough—they shared similarities that linked them together, on and off the field. Both had preceded Lombardi to Green Bay, and both spent the early years of their pro careers as frustrated bench-warmers. Starr wore a Green Bay uniform for 16 years, from 1956 to 1971; Nitschke's career with the Packers lasted 15 years, from 1958 to 1972. They're just two of four Packer players who have had their jersey numbers permanently retired by the club. In Packer history, Starr and Nitschke rank first and second, respectively, in years played with the team. Both were honored with special days at Lambeau Field, and Starr and Nitschke were once voted the two most recognizable faces in Wisconsin. Starr was named to the Pro Football Hall of Fame in 1977; Nitschke followed one year later. Both also had an interest in coaching. Starr was an assistant coach with the Packers in 1972 and coached the team from 1975 to 1983. Nitschke would have liked to have coached, but as he said once, "nobody ever asked."

To Packers' trainer Domenic Gentile, Starr and Nitschke symbolized the

NITSCHKE

Packers of that era. Both in their own way became extensions of Lombardi. Starr epitomized Lombardi's calculating perfectionism; Nitschke embodied his coach's fierce, competitive fire.

Like Nitschke, Starr became a student of the game, endlessly studying films for the smallest advantage. Gary Knafelc, a tight end with Green Bay from 1954 to 1962, roomed with Starr for six years on Green Bay road trips. The two spent hours reviewing different plays. Lombardi had installed an advanced passing system based on breakoff patterns and optional reads. When Starr called a play in the huddle, he wasn't calling it for one receiver; he was going to throw to the open man based on the coverage. Starr would read the defense and knew who would be open regardless of whether he was facing a blitz, man coverage, or a zone rotation. Lombardi's system required intelligence and instant recognition of defenses, not only by Starr but by Green Bay's backs and receivers as well. The Packers' passing game appeared to fans and opponents to involve basic routes, but as Dowler said, it was made to look easy by the hours of practice the players put in every June and July. In games, Green Bay's seemingly uncomplicated passing game carved up coverages, and on more than one occasion frustrated defenders would tell Dowler, "I don't know what you guys are doing. Doesn't look like you're doing anything but the ball keeps moving down the field."

"That's the way it's supposed to look," Dowler would respond. "That's the way it's planned."

It worked because the Packers were students of the game. Center Ken Bowman said that Starr's greatest asset wasn't his throwing arm, it was his brain. Halfback Paul Hornung said Starr never made mental mistakes, and the reason for that, Knafelc said, was thorough preparation. Knafelc would quiz Starr on game situations, giving him the down, the distance, the field position, and asking "What would you call?" Starr would consistently come up with the right play, and the two men repeated the process constantly. By game time, Starr was so confident in his ability to call the right play that he never got rattled, regardless of what the defense was showing him.

Like Nitschke, Starr wasn't as publicized as other players at his position, and just as Nitschke was often overlooked in favor of Joe Schmidt, Bill George, and Dick Butkus, Starr was often overshadowed by John Unitas, Sonny Jurgensen, and Y. A. Tittle. From 1960 to 1965, the Green Bay offense was geared to the twin thrusts of power backs Jim Taylor and Paul Hornung operating behind a smoothly meshing line. Critics overlooked his league passing titles in 1962 and '64 and labeled Starr a robot whose sole responsibility was to implement Lombardi's basic game plan. When the Green Bay ground attack began to slow in 1966, Starr proved his critics wrong. Throwing an NFL record-low three interceptions in 251 attempts, he led the league by completing 62 percent of his passes and averaged 9 yards per pass. In the post-season, Starr ravaged the Dallas and Kansas City pass defenses, completing 35 of 51 passes for 554 yards and six scores. He had gone from a man who had leaned on his teammates to one who could lead them. Over the course of the 1964–1965 seasons, Starr set an NFL record by throwing 294 consecutive passes without an interception, a mark that stood for two decades. He was named league MVP in 1966, and led the NFL four times in percentage of passes completed.

As with Nitschke, Starr's chance at playing regularly stemmed in part from a teammate's falling out with Lombardi. In Nitschke's case, it was starting middle linebacker Tom Bettis. For Starr, it was quarterback Lamar McHan. The turning point in Starr's career can be traced in part to Sunday, October 30, 1960. The Packers were trailing the Steelers in Pittsburgh, and Lombardi made the decision at halftime to bench McHan in favor of Starr. The Steelers had been playing an overshifted zone to the strong side, and McHan had struggled against it throughout the first half. Starr went in during the third quarter and began picking the Steelers apart. He hit Knafelc on two turn-in patterns of 15 yards each to put the Packers in scoring position. Realizing the safety was responsible for the tight end, Starr pump-faked another turn-in pattern to Knafelc to draw the safety up, then threw deep to Dowler for a 20-yard score. Green Bay won 19–13, but on the plane ride home Knafelc heard McHan say he was going to tell Lombardi off for benching him. McHan was later traded, and Starr began playing regularly.

Kramer said that while Starr was rarely the best quarterback in the league from a statistical standpoint, for three hours each Sunday Starr was almost always the best quarterback in the game he was playing.

Unitas, the quarterback to whom Starr was most often compared in the sixties, expressed his admiration for Starr's abilities. To Unitas, Starr was arguably the best short passer in the NFL. To his Packer teammates, Starr was not only a great passer, but a great leader as well. Thurston said that every time Starr stepped into the huddle, the Packer offense assumed something good was going to happen. "That's just the way he was," Thurston said, "the feeling he inspired in everybody."

Like Nitschke, Starr played hurt. During the 1961 season he played despite a painful torn stomach muscle. In 1965, he took the field against the Browns in the NFL title game with his ribs broken and corseted in tape. In 1967, a rigorous preseason schedule left Starr battered and bruised. A sprained thumb prevented him from gripping the ball properly, and a pulled thigh muscle hampered his movement dropping back. With Hornung having retired because of a pinched nerve in his neck and Taylor having played out his option and joined the expansion New Orleans Saints, the success of the Packer offense rested squarely on Starr's shoulders. Green Bay struggled to a 17–17 tie in the season opener, then beat Chicago 13–10 in Week Two. Against Atlanta the following week, Starr took a blow to his right armpit by blitzing linebacker Tommy Nobis and was sidelined. With Starr out, Green Bay's drive to the newly formed Central Division title now came down to the success or failure of its great defense.

In Week Four, Nitschke keyed a 27–17 Green Bay victory over the Lions in Detroit by returning a tipped pass 20 yards for a score. It was Nitschke's first touchdown since 1960 and came courtesy of a double blitz by Nitschke and Robinson. When Lions quarterback Milt Plum tried to beat the blitz with a short pass, Robinson jumped and tipped the ball. Nitschke hauled it on the run, and with his left leg aching, limped his way into the end zone for the game-breaking touchdown.

Nitschke's all-out effort against the Lions summed up his 1967 season. Whether it was running down Colts halfback Lenny Moore on a sweep, dropping Rams back Dick Bass in the backfield, or hitting a Browns receiver so hard he dropped a Frank Ryan pass, Nitschke was a leader who carried the rest of the defense with him.

Of all the members of Green Bay's walking wounded, Starr thought Nitschke played through more injuries than anyone. Defensive captain Willie Davis saw Nitschke's atrophied leg, saw the mass of deep purple bruises covering his lower body from hip to knee, and drew inspiration from his teammate.

"Ray was a guy who was almost oblivious to pain," Davis remembered. "I saw the guy play with almost every injury imaginable. As a middle linebacker that's almost a prerequisite, to play with some pain, because they're after you all day. Every guy along that offensive line, and the tight end, is after that middle linebacker at one time or another by assignment. And Ray paid some prices for that. He was in the hot tub probably more than the rest of us."

With Nitschke as its hobbling ringleader, Green Bay limited Chicago to just six first downs and held superstar halfback Gale Sayers to 68 yards on 20 carries in Week Two in Lambeau Field. Sayers was frustrated by a sore knee and by a defensive alignments that lined up ends Davis and Lionel Aldridge across from the Bears' tackles and slanted them inside. Green Bay tackles Henry Jordan and Ron Kostelnik also pinched in, and the result was that the scheme knocked off the Bears' pulling guards, leaving Sayers alone against Nitschke and the Packer pursuit.

Nitschke and the Packers limited the Falcons to 58 yards on 50 plays en route to a 23–0 shutout in Week Three, then earned their second shutout of the season in Week 10 with a 13–0 win over San Francisco. One week later, Sayers galloped through the Green Bay defense for a 43-yard touchdown run and 117 yards rushing, but the Packers held the Bears to 13 points, and won 17–13 to clinch the Central Division title.

Lombardi was relentless in his drive for a third straight NFL championship, and he drove himself and his team through a grueling campaign. He pounced on sloppy plays, and sideline cameras caught him in mid-rant.

"What the hell's goin' on out here?" he shouted, shoving his clenched fists deep into the pockets of his beige, camel-hair overcoat. "Everybody grabbin', nobody tacklin'. Grab. Grab. Grab. Nobody tacklin'. Put your shoulders into it out there!"

Starr's return from injury in Week Six had spurred the Packers to a 48–21 win over the Giants in New York, but plagued by injuries that wiped out their first- and second-string backfields, Green Bay limped through the final weeks of the regular season and finished 9–4–1. The Packers had won largely on the strength of their defense, a unit that saw eight of its 11 members named to various All-Pro teams in their careers.

In time, a record five members of the Green Bay defense would be voted into the Pro Football Hall of Fame, but both Bengston and his players are often overlooked when talk turns to the great defenses of all time. When the Baltimore Ravens were drawing comparisons to the great defensive units of all time during their record-breaking run to the Super Bowl in 2000, the Packers of the sixties were rarely mentioned. Unlike the "Fearsome Foursome," "Doomsday," the "Purple People Eaters," or the "Steel Curtain," Green Bay's defense was never glamorized by a gimmick nickname. But Cowboys All-Pro offensive tackle Ralph Neely, who played against the best defenses of the sixties and seventies, believes the Packers of the sixties were the best unit he ever faced. Pittsburgh and Miami had great defenses in the seventies, Neely said, but for a complete defense, from front line to linebackers to defensive backs, he ranked the Packers ahead of everyone.

Neely's point is well-taken. Some of the NFL's legendary defenses—the Rams' "Fearsome Foursome" and the Vikings' "Purple Gang"—offered great front fours but not necessarily great defenses overall. Pittsburgh featured Hall of Famers on each of the three lines of defense in tackle Joe Greene, linebackers Jack Lambert and Jack Ham, and cornerback Mel Blount. To date, the '85 Bears list two Hall of Famers on their famous unit, middle linebacker Mike Singletary and end Dan Hampton.

Of all the great years the Packers' defense put together, the '62 season was arguably their best. And in a comparison of seven of the greatest defensive seasons in NFL history, the '62 Packers ranked higher in more categories than the '48 Eagles, the '56 Giants, the '75 Steelers, the '85 Bears, the '90 Giants, and the '00 Ravens.

By 1967, Green Bay's defense was aging. Four of their starters were age 31 or older, and the media began writing them off as "old men." Battered and bloodied, the Packers fought off challengers to their throne with the grim defiance of the defenders of Bastogne. The '67 season was the year of "the big push," as Lombardi called it, and the Packers entered the Western Conference championship game heavy underdogs to the Los Angeles Rams. L.A. had rallied to beat Green Bay 27–24 in a Week 13 game in the Coliseum, and the Rams boasted afterward that they had broken the Packers' magic. The week of the playoff game, Lombardi spurred his team with bulletin-board remarks made by the Rams, and on the Tuesday before the game, gave his team a speech and a slogan.

"Everything you do this week, you run to win," Lombardi said. "On or off the field, run to win."

The words, borrowed from St. Paul, burned into Nitschke's brain, and as he ran through practice that week, he kept reminding himself, "I'm running to win." On Saturday, December 23, Nitschke and the Packers took the field in Milwaukee's County Stadium under cold, overcast skies. The Rams scored first, quarterback Roman Gabriel throwing a 29-yard touchdown pass to flanker Bernie Casey in the first quarter. L.A. threatened again, but when Robinson blocked Bruce Gossett's 24-yard field goal attempt, Green Bay grabbed the momentum.

Tom Brown's 39-yard punt return in the second quarter set up the Packers' first score, a 47-yard sprint off right tackle by halfback Travis Williams. On WTMJ Radio in Milwaukee, Packers' announcer Ted Moore provided the call on a play that ignited Green Bay's comeback:

> *Starr checks the defense, the handoff goes to Travis Williams, slant over the right side, goes to the outside, he's at the 40, 35, 30, 25, 20, and he's gonna go in! Travis Williams slanted over the right tackle spot and goes 47 yards for the touchdown! And there's the 'Roadrunner' really turning on that speed. . . . The daylight was there, as Jerry Kramer, Forrest Gregg, and Marv Fleming opened the way.*

Starr followed shortly thereafter with a 17-yard touchdown pass to flanker Carroll Dale. Leading 14–7 at halftime, the Packers' punishing defense took physical control of the game. Gabriel was sacked five times by Jordan, and Nitschke played a particularly reckless game. "But it was all right," he said later, "because I was running to win."

In the Packers' defensive huddles, Jordan was popping Nitschke on the shoulder pads and shouting, "Come on, let's get 'em." Nitschke was hitting the Rams so hard he was hoping to see them bounce off the thick, winter-brown turf with each hit. He hated to leave the field that day, hated to see the Green Bay offense coming off the sideline.

In the press box, Red Smith of the *New York Times* described Nitschke as "a living flame." Nitschke's competitive fire had been fanned into a burning incandescence, and even Rams head coach George Allen was impressed. Allen thought so much of Nitschke that when he was defensive coach of the Bears, he named one of his defenses the "47 Nitschke" after the way Ray played a certain situation. Allen said once that when Nitschke got wound up "he could take apart an offense all by himself." Nitschke, Allen said, seemed to go a little crazy at times; he was a wild man who was almost impossible to contain.

Wood used to tell Davis that while he could hear Nitschke hollering during the game, he couldn't understand half the time what Nitschke was hollering about. Jeter recalled Nitschke's yelling too, and remembered when the other members of the defense would have to calm him down.

"He was a very aggressive player who liked to win," Jeter said. "Once he was out there on that field, he was something else. He did a lot of talking, and sometimes we'd have to talk to him to settle him down."

The Rams had entered the game with the number-one ranked offense in the NFL, but Nitschke and the Packer defense held them to one touchdown and 75 yards rushing. When Green Bay had the ball, Nitschke crowded the sideline, hollering encouragement. He watched as Gregg and tight end Marv Fleming carried out Lombardi's game plan to neutralize Ram defensive end Deacon Jones.

"Coach Lombardi has a theory that if you beat a team at its strength you win the game," Nitschke said at the time. "So we set out to whip Deacon Jones."

The Packers had opened the game by running right at Jones, double-teaming him with blocks by Fleming and Gregg. In time, Nitschke said, Jones became so conscious of the double-team he began looking for it. The result was that he was hesitating rather than rushing into the backfield, and Gregg was beating him on his blocks. With the source of their strength taken away, the "Fearsome Foursome" was filled with confusion. The rest of the Ram defense, Nitschke thought, was wondering what had happened to Jones and why wasn't he getting to Starr? "They began to hesitate and wait," Nitschke said, "and then they were getting whipped as bad as Jones was."

Fullback Chuck Mercein's six-yard plunge on a draw play gave Green Bay a 21–7 lead in the third quarter. Starr, who completed 74 percent of his passes and threw for 222 yards, burned the Rams one final time in the fourth quarter when he found Dale for a 48-yard completion that carried to the L.A. 2-yard line. Williams blasted the final two yards for the touchdown, and Green Bay stunned the Rams with a 28–7 win.

"That was a big game," Nitschke recalled once. "The Rams had a great defense, the 'Fearsome Foursome,' and they had beaten us in the next-to-last game of the season. Before the game Lombardi quoted the Bible and told us to 'Run to win.' That was our motivation. 'Run to win.' And we ran away with the game."

Kramer said later that the Packer defense had played a fantastic game, and that Nitschke and Jordan, in particular, were incredible. Both had been left off the NFL's All-Pro defensive team, and since both Nitschke and Jordan have tremendous pride, Kramer thought they set out to prove that they were still the best in the league at their respective positions. Nitschke stopped Ram runners at the line of scrimmage, Kramer said, stopped them whether they tried to run left, right, or through the middle.

In the locker room, the team knelt to say the Lord's Prayer, and Nitschke followed by walking around, hugging and kissing his teammates. "Thank you, Jerry," he told Kramer, then turned to Gregg and remarked, "Thank you, Forrest." To no one in particular, Nitschke muttered, "I just wish the game hadn't ended."

On Christmas Eve day, the Packers settled back to watch the Cowboys beat the Browns, 52–14, in the Eastern Conference championship. That night, members of the team gathered in Nitschke's house. Jackie had invited them to stop by, and as his living room filled up Nitschke couldn't figure out why everyone was still hanging around. In time, he ran out of chairs, and teammates and their wives took to sitting on the floor. Around 9 P.M., Jackie told Ray to look out the front window. She had heard a noise, she said, and wanted Ray to see if anyone was there. When he looked out, Nitschke saw a new 1968 Lincoln Continental sitting on his front lawn. It was Jackie's Christmas present to him, and Ray was so thrilled that tears came to his eyes.

"He was like a little boy," Kramer said later. "He had to take the car out for a spin right away."

When he returned, Nitschke told Kramer that when he was small, someone had once given him a ride in a Lincoln. "Ever since then, I've dreamed of owning one," Nitschke said. "I never thought I would."

Kramer looked at Nitschke and thought he was ready to bawl. He also thought that there wasn't a running back in the NFL who would have believed that Ray Nitschke was capable of crying.

One week to the day later, Nitschke and the Packers took the field for the 1967 NFL championship game against Dallas. An overnight cold spell carried in on Canadian winds had plummeted temperatures in Green Bay from 20 degrees Fahrenheit late Saturday afternoon to minus-13 at kickoff. Winds clocked at 15 miles per hours dropped the wind-chill temperature to minus-38. The mass of arctic air caused Lambeau Field to flash-freeze, turning the stadium turf as hard and slick as glazed pavement.

Years later, Nitschke recalled the Packers' intensity on that New Year's Eve afternoon, at that time the coldest day in the long, cold history of Green Bay.

"The elements? That's all part of the mental toughness that Lombardi always talked about," he said, "When you go out there, you go out there with the idea of winning. We knew we were kind of at the end. We were getting older, and some of the guys, like Taylor and Hornung, weren't around anymore.

"But that particular team and that particular year, we committed ourselves to winning that third championship in a row. That's something no one else has ever done. We knew we were playing against a young, strong Cowboys team, but when we went out there, we went out there with that idea that we were going to win. We believed that."

Running onto the field, Nitschke was struck less by the frozen field than by the frozen fans, a standing room only crowd of 50,861 who ignored the sub-zero temperatures and rocked the historic stadium with their cheers. Squinting through the bright sun, Nitschke scanned the stands and realized he could barely see any faces. Thousands of fans, seeking protecting from the dangerous cold, had covered every inch of exposed skin, layering themselves with hats, coats, jackets, and blankets. As Bengston gathered his defensive team around him for last-minute instructions, he was struck by the red halo surrounding the field. In September, the coloration of the stands at Lambeau was usually white and light, reflecting the late summer clothing of the fans. By October, Lambeau took on the look of late autumn, muted browns and oranges of men's jackets and hats and women's coats and scarves. On the day of the Ice Bowl, the stands took on a bright reddish-orange tinge thanks to the thousands of hunting jackets, lap robes, and helmet-masks worn by fans.

When the Cowboys scanned the stands, they were struck by a large sign that read "Cold enough for you?" A few Dallas players silently cursed Lombardi, whom they thought had deliberately turned off his famous underground heating unit that was supposed to keep Lambeau field soft and playable in wintry conditions. The underground blanket of heating coils had been working all morning, but when stadium workers removed the tarpaulin covering the field, the moisture generated by the heat froze instantly when exposed to the intense cold. As the Cowboys grimly searched for some semblance of footing in the pregame "warm-ups," they became aware of an overwhelming smell of peppermint schnapps. Looking up, Ralph Neely saw fans swigging from small metal flasks. "Wish I had some," he thought.

Across the ice-slick field, Nitschke looked up in the stands, saw the clouds of condensed air pouring forth from thousands of faces, and thought the least the Packers could do was win the game for them and send them off to the pneumonia ward happy.

More acclimated to cold-weather games than the Cowboys, Green Bay jumped to a 14–0 lead in the second quarter. The first time the Packers had the ball, Starr engineered a 16-play, 82-yard drive that ended with an 8-yard touchdown pass to Dowler. In the second quarter, Starr outfoxed the Doomsday defense by drawing them in on a play-action fake and lofting a 46-yard scoring strike to Dowler.

Blaring horns trumpeted the Packers' 14–0 lead, but the Cowboys came back late in the half to score 10 points on two Green Bay turnovers. Defensive end George Andrie's recovery of a Starr fumble and 7-yard return for a score halved the Dallas deficit, and Willie Wood's fumble of a Cowboy punt led to Danny Villanueva's 21-yard field goal. As the halftime gun sounded, the brittle air over Lambeau Field was filled less with the cheers of Packer fans than the rumble of hollow-throated gas heaters that were blowing into the tarpaulins that formed makeshift shelters on both sidelines.

The game had settled into a grim defensive struggle, and Nitschke, who had five tackles in the first half, felt that on this day, the Packers' four-point lead might be enough to pull out the win.

Green Bay maintained its slim lead through a scoreless third quarter, and by the start of the fourth the game had settled into what pro football historians David Neft and Richard Cohen described as "a titanic struggle under nightmarish conditions." No professional football game had ever been played in conditions to match what has become known in NFL lore as the "Ice Bowl." Players on both sides breathed steam and spit ice, and officials were forced to call the game without whistles because the small wooden peas inside their whistles had frozen. When umpire Joe Connell attempted to use his whistle at the start of the game, he pulled half of his lower lip off. He had forgotten to cover the whistle with a rubber mouthpiece, and the metal had frozen fast to his lips. When Connell pulled the whistle from his mouth, his lips tore and blood flowed out; within seconds the blood froze fast on his chin. For the rest of the game, referee Norm Schachter's crew regulated the action by shouting at players, "Stay away!" and "Keep off him!"

As the sun began to set behind the scoreboard, taking with it the last remaining remnants of heat, fans built small fires in the stands and huddled around them. One spectator died from the intense cold, and players on both sides were feeling the effects of frostbite.

The Cowboys stunned Nitschke and the Packer defense on the first play of the fourth quarter. Halfback Dan Reeves ran left on an apparent sweep, then pulled up and lofted a long pass to flanker Lance Rentzel. The Dallas flanker had slipped behind the surprised Green Bay defense and was all alone downfield, and the 50-yard scoring pass put the Cowboys up, 17–14, eight seconds into the final quarter.

As the clock wound down, neither team could mount much of a sustained offense. The icy conditions and skill levels of two of the greatest defenses of their era were proving dominant. Tempers began to flare on both sides, and Reeves angrily accused Nitschke of kicking at Dallas fullback Don Perkins.

"He went wild after we had gone ahead," Reeves said after the game. "He actually kicked at Don Perkins after Don had gained five yards. He's an animal. It made all of us mad when he took a kick at Don like that, right in front of everyone, and no one called it."

Nitschke resented Reeves' statement, resented being called a dirty player. Perkins had run wild on Nitschke and the Packer defense in the 1966 championship game in Dallas, and the fact that he became the first and only back to run for more than 100 yards against Bengston's defense in a post-season game insulted the Packers' middle linebacker. Nitschke made up his mind before the '67 title game that Perkins, as good a back as Nitschke knew he was, wasn't going to get anywhere near 100 yards in the rematch at Lambeau Field. On the play in question, a short pickup by Perkins in the fourth quarter, the film shows Nitschke wrapping Perkins up, driving him back toward the line of scrimmage, and after releasing him with a shove, kicking at the frozen ground close to where Perkins was.

"I kicked the ground because I was disgusted with myself," Nitschke said. "I didn't have anything against Perkins."

Nitschke insisted through the years that he wasn't mad at Perkins for picking up the yardage, he was mad at himself for failing to make a tackle that would have stopped the play for no gain.

Years later, Reeves couldn't recall the incident. "All I know is Ray was one of the all-time great competitors," he said. "He was one of those unique people who loved to hit, and did it often."

With 4:50 left in the game, the Packers took the ball for perhaps the final time of the '67 title game. Starr had been dumped by the Dallas defense eight times for a loss of 76 yards, and the Green Bay offense, which looked so strong in the first half, had ground to a halt. On the Packer sideline, Nitschke stood shivering, trying to ignore the frostbite that would afflict six of his toes. "We're losing," he thought, "but we have the ball. And we have Starr."

In the Packers' huddle, Starr stared into the frozen faces of his teammates and said, "Let's get it done."

Over the next three minutes, Starr pried apart the Doomsday defense with short passes. On the sidelines, Nitschke thrust his padded right fist into the gray, icy air and shouted, "Don't let me down! Don't let me down!" At the 11, Starr crossed up the Cowboys with "65-Give," an influence play aimed at All-Pro tackle Bob Lilly. As Lilly chased a simulated Green Bay sweep, Mercein galloped through the gaping hole for an eight-yard pickup. Nitschke knew about the "give" play, knew Starr had it in his game plan. He had wondered when Starr would call it, and smiled as he saw the play develop, saw Lilly, whom Nitschke regarded as a great defensive player, chase the sweep, saw Mercein running right up the gut. It was beautiful, Nitschke thought, the best play he had ever seen Starr call.

"It was a great call, man," Nitschke recalled. "Bart saved it for the right moment, the right time."

From the three, halfback Donny Anderson plunged to the one to give Green Bay a first-and-goal with 30 seconds remaining. "We're close," Nitschke thought. "How are they going to stop us?"

Starr sent Anderson driving into the Dallas line two more times, but the slick field and the stubborn Dallas defense stopped him shy of the gold-painted goal line each time. With 16 seconds remaining, Starr called his final timeout and headed to the sideline.

The wind-chill factor had dropped to an estimated minus-70 degrees. Nitschke's feet were so numb they felt detached from his body. He had never been so cold in his life, but as he stared at the stadium clock, he shoved the weather conditions from his mind. "Who cares about that?" he thought.

What Nitschke cared about was Lombardi's decision during the timeout to ignore the potential game-tying field goal and gamble everything by going for the win. To Nitschke, Lombardi's decision to go for broke and settle the game one way or the other was based on the coach's love and respect for his veterans. Eleven members of the team that day—Nitschke, Starr, Kramer, Thurston, Gregg, Skoronski, Dowler, McGee, Davis, Jordan, and Wood—had been there in 1960 when the Packers had played in their first championship under Lombardi. Through the years they had endured the torturous grass drills in the summer, endured the bitter wind of the '62 title game against the Giants in Yankee Stadium, the icy mud against the Browns in '65. They had played with pride and won, they'd made mistakes and lost. They'd put in peak performances, they'd played hurt, and through it all, they had become Lombardi's extended family, his adopted sons.

"When you get that close, if you can't make a foot you shouldn't be out there," Nitschke said. "The field was getting worse, but we had it right there, in our hands. That's what it's all about."

As Lombardi and Starr conferred on the sidelines, Nitschke felt that if placekicker Don Chandler was sent out there, it would have meant that his coach no longer had the confidence in his veterans to take that last step, to win a game that would decide not only a berth in Super Bowl II, but also Green Bay's drive to an historic third straight NFL championship.

As Starr returned to the field, some Packers heard Lombardi mutter, "If we can't score from the 1, we don't deserve to be champions."

In the huddle, Starr called "Brown Right, 31-Wedge," a drive play between Kramer and Bowman, then amid a cloud of frost, told his team, "We're going in from here."

As fans in Lambeau Field held their collective breath, Moore made the call in clipped tones WTMJ Radio:

> *Here are the Packers. . . . Third down, inches to go to paydirt . . . 17-to-14, Cowboys out in front. Packers trying for the go-ahead score. Starr begins the count, takes the snap, he's got the quarterback sneak and he's in for the touchdown and the Packers are out in front! There's 13 seconds showing on the clock and the Green Bay Packers are going to be world champions, NFL champions, for the third straight year. . . .*

Moments later, as Nitschke ran off the field amid the post-game celebration, he experienced feelings he had never felt before. The Ice Bowl was an instant classic, and the drama and circumstances surrounding the game left Nitschke shook emotionally. When he reached the Packers' crowded locker room, he saw that many of his teammates were in tears. As he made the rounds crying and embracing his teammates in his trademark bearhugs, Nitschke savored the moments as among the greatest in his life.

Amid the celebrations in the Green Bay locker room, CBS sportscaster Tom Brookshier was conducting interviews with various Packers. When he saw Nitschke approaching, Brookshier announced, "Here's Green Bay's madman, Ray Nitschke."

Brookshier was smiling when he said it, but the smile faded when he saw Nitschke fixing him with a glare usually reserved for opposing ballcarriers.

"I'm not a madman," Nitschke snapped. "I just enjoy football."

In his earplug, Brookshier heard director Bob Dailey say, "If Nitschke hits Brookshier, let's cut to a commercial."

A former Philadelphia cornerback, Brookshier had played against Nitschke in the 1960 NFL title game. As a CBS sportscaster, he had seen Nitschke play on several occasions, but even Brookshier was surprised to see Nitschke kicking the air viciously after the Perkins gain. "I thought, 'Wow, this guy's wild,' " Brookshier said.

When he introduced Nitschke to the national television audience of more than 50 million people as "Green Bay's madman," Brookshier said he thought he was being cute. He soon realized his mistake when he looked over and saw Nitschke standing there, red-faced.

"He was a behemoth," Brookshier said. "And he was furious."

Nitschke was angry, he said later, because all he could think of was that he was being insulted in front of his family, in front of his friends. He was concerned how they would take it to hear Nitschke being called a dirty football player. He was no madman, he told Brookshier, he was just trying to play the game as hard and as well as he could.

Chicago Bears' middle linebacker Dick Butkus defended Nitschke's play against the Cowboys in the Ice Bowl, defended his icy response to Brookshier. "Nitschke is just rough and tough," Butkus said. "I nearly fell over when Brookshier said that to him."

Bears guard Mike Pyle watched Nitschke's ferocious play against the Rams in the Western Conference playoff, against the Cowboys in the NFL championship game, and said he had never seen Nitschke play so aggressively.

"He must have been seeing nothing but dollar signs," Pyle said.

For Nitschke and the Packers, there was one big payday remaining. For the second straight year, Green Bay would represent the NFL in the Super Bowl against the champions of the AFL. Oakland had supplanted Kansas City as the league's dominant team, winning the Western Conference with a 13–1 record that ranked as the best in AFL history, and the Raiders had overrun Houston 40–7 in the title game.

Nitschke wasn't worried. Leaving the warmth of the locker room, he limped through the minus-20 degree darkness and climbed into his new Lincoln Continental. He had frost-bite in his toes and was fighting a cold, and when he returned to his home in Oneida for New Year's Eve he put his feet up and thought about what Kramer had told a TV reporter after the game.

Glancing around at his teammates hugging and weeping together, Kramer remarked that there was a great deal of love amongst the Packers. "Maybe," he mused, "we're living in Camelot."

Nitschke thought about that, thought too about the man whose career with the Packers was so closely paralleling his own. The man whom no one, including Nitschke, thought would make it in the NFL. The man who had just scored the winning touchdown in arguably the most memorable game ever played.

"Bart Starr utilized everything God gave him," Nitschke said. "He rose to the challenge. His best games were in the big games."

For the Packers, there was one more big game to play. Having already played 22 games that season, Green Bay's "big push" was finally nearing its end.

ELEVEN

THREE DAYS after Green Bay's 21–17 win over Dallas in the epic Ice Bowl game, Ray Nitschke sat on a trainer's table in the Packers' locker room having the big toes on both feet bandaged by trainers. The daytime temperature in Green Bay on Wednesday, January 3, 1968, had warmed up to five degrees above zero, and as he sat on the trainer's table getting treatment for frostbite, a team trainer advised him that the only way to keep the condition from worsening was to avoid going out in the cold again.

"How the hell do you do that," Nitschke asked, "and go out and practice in five degrees?"

At that moment, head coach Vince Lombardi walked in. Hearing Nitschke's complaint, Lombardi offered some advice to his middle linebacker. "Just go out," he said, "and get up a good sweat."

Green Bay guard Jerry Kramer, who was nearby weighing himself, saw Nitschke begin to ask his coach how he could work up a sweat in five degree cold, then watched as Ray resigned himself to the fact that he was in an argument he couldn't win.

"Aw, forget it, man," Nitschke said.

Nitschke and the Packers went out and practiced, and when the temperature the next day was six degrees below zero with 15-mile per hour winds whipping across the practice field, Nitschke remarked in the locker room that he wasn't going outside. The Packers seemed close to revolt, particularly when defensive end Willie Davis asked Lombardi what the temperature was in Miami that Thursday.

"About 78 degrees," Lombardi answered. "Why?"

Davis just shook his head. "Oh, nothing," he answered. "Just wondering."

All the Packers were wondering why they were still in Green Bay, why they hadn't headed to Florida to prepare for the Oakland Raiders and Super Bowl II. The Packers were suffering; Nitschke had frostbite on his feet, Starr on his fingers. Nitschke was also suffering a debilitating head cold; so too, was Kramer, whose cold reached down into his bronchial tubes and stomach. Nitschke limped noticeably; Kramer wondered if his lungs had frostbite.

The Packers practiced for 45 minutes amid the subzero cold and bitter winds before even Lombardi had enough. With a half dozen of his players exhibiting flu symptoms, he cut practice short by 15 minutes. "The hell with it," he suddenly announced. "Let's go in."

Three days later, on January 7, Nitschke and the Packers whisked themselves through minus-seven degree temperatures as they boarded a 727 for the trip to Florida. When they arrived, the temperature was 75 degrees. As he settled into his room amid the Packers' headquarters at the Galt Ocean Mile Hotel in Fort Lauderdale, Nitschke realized he wasn't physically ready to play in the Super Bowl. The intense cold from the Ice Bowl game had caused his toes to turn purple and his toenails to fall off. "I damn near froze my toes off," he said. He had dropped eight pounds due to the flu, and he was still limping with frostbite. Limping everywhere, that is, except in the presence of Lombardi.

Amid an interview session with reporters at the hotel, Lombardi was answering questions when a reporter asked about the physical effects of the Ice Bowl on his team. Nitschke's ears, toes, and fingers were whitened by frostbite, and Packers' publicist Chuck Lane said the skin was falling off Green Bay players by the yards. Fixing reporters with a glare, Lombardi remarked that only the Dallas players had been hobbled by the cold.

"The Dallas Cowboys got frostbite," he said. "Ray Nitschke just had a blister. Only a blister. That's all it was. A blister."

Nitschke, who was limping by at that precise moment, immediately stopped limping when he heard his coach's remark. Writer Mickey Herskowitz saw Nitschke's sudden recovery and attributed it to what he described as Lombardi's "Throw-Away-Your-Crutch-And-Walk School of Coaching." When reporters pressed him for a response on going from playing in subfreezing temperatures in Green Bay to playing in the Miami heat, Lombardi brushed off their questions.

"Weather," he said emphatically, "is a state of mind."

The Packers were headquartered at the same Fort Lauderdale training complex the New York Yankees had used every spring during their glory years. When a reporter pointed out that Nitschke was now dressing where Mantle and DiMaggio had dressed before him, the big linebacker shrugged. "It might have meant something a few years ago," he said.

The Raiders rode into Super Bowl II with a reputation for intimidation. Oakland had overrun AFL defenses by scoring a league-high 468 points during the regular season. Quarterback Daryle Lamonica led both leagues by throwing for 30 touchdowns, and thick-legged Raider backs rushed for an AFL-best 19 touchdowns. Coached by John Rauch, Oakland popularized the use of the fullback as a deep pass receiver, and 220-pound fullback Hewritt Dixon, a converted tight end, led the team with 59 receptions.

Game films reveal the Raiders' offensive firepower—halfback Clem Daniels sweeping left for a long gain against defending AFL champion Kansas City in Oakland; Dixon breaking five tackles on a flare pass against Buffalo in old War Memorial Stadium; Fred Biletnikoff outfighting Chiefs cornerback Fred Williamson to gather in a Lamonica bomb on Thanksgiving Day in Kansas City; a massive, 17-play drive in the rain against the Oilers in Houston's Rice Stadium; halfback Pete Banaszak bowling over New York Jets cornerback Randy Beverly on an off-tackle run in the penultimate game of the regular season.

The Raiders ravaged the AFL with a 13–1 record that ranked as the best in AFL history, and matched Green Bay's 13–1 finish in 1962 as the best of the decade to that point. As Nitschke and the Green Bay defense watched the three game tapes provided by Raiders—victories over Kansas City, Buffalo, and the Jets—they made notes on each of Oakland's key offensive players:

Lamonica: "Likes to work from play-action . . . rollouts, bootlegs; can drop back and throw;"

Dixon: "Strong runner, big and powerful. Heavier than press book indicates;"

Banaszak: "Not impressive in size or moves, but churns out yards. Watch him if he gets an opening;"

Biletnikoff: "One of the best in his league. Other ends, (Bill) Miller and (Billy) Cannon, are hot, too. All are heavy guys;"

Gene Upshaw, offensive lineman: "A rookie, but he sure doesn't look like it. Treat him like a veteran;"

Jim Otto, All-Star lineman: "One of the great ones."

As Green Bay's chief scout, Wally Cruice, ran down the rest of the Raider offense, including speedy end Warren Wells and the Oakland offensive line, he again emphasized that the AFL champions were big, strong, physical players. Comparing the listed size of the Raiders' players to what he was seeing on film, Cruice told Packers' defensive coordinator Phil Bengston, "The last time they weighed these guys was in high school."

Cruice reminded Nitschke and the Packer defense that the Raiders had ties to the Green Bay and greater Wisconsin area. Lamonica had been the Packers' 12th round draft pick in 1963, and Raider defenders Ben Davidson and Howie Williams were members of Green Bay's 1961 and '62 NFL championship teams, respectively. Placekicker George Blanda had played against the Packers while with the Chicago Bears in the 1950s; Banaszak was from Crivitz, Wisconsin, and Otto, in whom Lombardi had shown interest during the NFL–AFL wars, was from Wausau. While Cruice remarked that the great many ties several Raiders had to the Packers and Wisconsin would undoubtedly provide emotional fuel, Nitschke was unimpressed.

"I don't care if they come blowing Chinese bugles, riding horses, and waving sabers," he said.

Nitschke's attitude toward the AFL champions reflected the Packers' approach to the game. This was their second straight Super Bowl, and they weren't as excited for the game as they had been the year before. They weren't taking the Raiders lightly, but when it came to big games, losing was not in the Packers' lexicon. They had played together so long that individually they were able to pick up very quickly on what the opposition was trying to do. They would spend the first half deciphering the opponent's game plan, then spend the second half prying them apart.

Over the course of their second championship run of the sixties, the Packers had become a second-half team. The reason for that, Nitschke said, was that the team they played on Sundays was invariably not the same team they had studied in movies the week before. Lombardi had warned his team on several occasions that they were marked men. Opponents, he said, had read the papers and seen the stories asking, "Who can beat the Packers? Can anyone beat them?" The response, he said, was that teams were now saying "We can do it, we can beat the Packers." This was the price of winning, Lombardi said. It was the price that came with being five-time champions, and the Packers were paying it because everyone in the NFL wanted to beat them.

"They're giving it their maximum supreme effort," Lombardi said. "There's no loafing, no halfway, against the Green Bay Packers."

Nitschke saw the worth of Lombardi's words firsthand on the field. Even the NFL's worst teams were bringing a special effort and dedication to bear against Green Bay. They would give their all in the first half, play the Packers to a standstill, but then, realizing that they couldn't dominate Green Bay even with a peak performance, endured a letdown in the second half. Nitschke watched as opponents slowly but steadily lost their poise and character. Since the Packers played hard the whole game, they almost always took advantage of the opponent's second half meltdown and gradually pulled away.

That's what Green Bay had done to Kansas City the year before, and of the three game films the Raiders provided, Nitschke and the Packers gleaned the most from Oakland's victory over the Chiefs. Since the Packers were familiar with the Chiefs' personnel, the Oakland–Kansas City reel provided a point of reference from which Green Bay could work. To Nitschke, the Raiders provided a vastly different challenge than Kansas City had in Super Bowl I. With their shifting alignments and multiple offense, the Chiefs were a flashy team that played fancy football, the kind of team, Nitschke said, that the Packers liked to enlighten in the ways of fundamental football.

Oakland, on the other hand, was a team that resembled Green Bay in its approach to the game. Unlike Kansas City cornerback Fred Williamson, who had belittled Green Bay before Super Bowl I, the Raiders spoke highly of the NFL champions. Their tone was set by their general managing partner, Al Davis.

"Imagine," Davis said with a syrupy smile, "the li'l' ol' Raiders on the same field with the Green Bay Packers. *Imagine* . . . "

Rauch called the Packers "the very best team in all of football," and Lamonica's locker contained a 1966 hardcover book titled *Quarterbacking*, written by Bart Starr. "I admire Starr," Lamonica said. "I consider it a real privilege to play against the man who is rated tops in the business." One of the Raiders compared playing against the Packers to "playing against our fathers," and massive defensive end Ben Davidson told AFL reporters, "I hope we don't get run off the field."

As the Raiders watched the three Packer game films supplied by Lombardi, Otto studied Nitschke's play at middle linebacker. "Nitschke was someone you had to handle," Otto remembered. "This was the first time I was going to be playing against him, and I liked his style of play. I liked his toughness because that was basically my game too. The Green Bay Packers had a tremendous defense, there's no doubt about it, and Nitschke was the leader of that group. He was always aggressive, always where the play was."

Otto could see from the films that the Packers pinched and slanted their tackles, Henry Jordan and Ron Kostelnik, to shield Nitschke from the center's blocks. "If you were quick enough you could get to Nitschke," Otto said, "but that was a formidable threesome they had inside, with Jordan, Kostelnik, and Nitschke."

Oakland would look to counter with an offense that Nitschke felt was similar to the Packers in that it could nickel-and-dime defenses to death all day. Nitschke studied Lamonica, studied how the All-AFL QB liked to throw to his backs. Nitschke also studied Dixon, and saw that he was a strong, aggressive runner, and since he had led the Raiders in receptions, Nitschke prepared himself to slow Dixon down from the start.

At the same time the Packers were preparing for Super Bowl II, they were also preparing to play what many of them believed would be their final game for Lombardi. Nitschke could see the strain the long season was having on his head coach. Lombardi didn't appear to be the same man he had been just a few years earlier; to Nitschke, he didn't look as healthy as he should have. Lombardi had always demanded that his teams win, and to win as consistently as Green Bay did in the 1960s, a price had to be paid. The Packers paid that price, and their bruised bodies were testament to that. But to Nitschke, Lombardi had paid the heaviest price of all. Kramer once figured out that on an average, the Green Bay coaching staff headed by Lombardi made less money at the time than a Green Bay garbageman. Nitschke wanted to see Lombardi on the sidelines for the '68 season, wanted to be driven through the summer drills toward yet another title. But when he saw his head coach's condition, saw his hands shaking and the toll nine years of demanding perfection had taken on him, Nitschke knew Lombardi was ready to step down.

Nitschke's beliefs were confirmed the Thursday before Super Sunday. Standing up to address his team, Lombardi began rubbing his hands together.

"Okay, boys," he began. "This may be the last time we'll be together, so . . . uh . . . "

Players could see their coach's lips quivering, his body trembling. Nitschke thought Lombardi was ready to start crying. With that, the man *Newark Star-Ledger* sports writer Jerry Izenberg referred to as "Invincible Vince" turned his back to his team and sat down in a chair. "Let's break up," he said.

On the morning of Super Sunday, the Packers gathered at 10:45 A.M. for a pregame meal, then boarded chartered buses for their ride to the Orange Bowl and the 3 P.M. kickoff. The stadium was sold out, and the crowd of 75,546 guaranteed that this would be the first football game to gross more than $3 million dollars. Combined with the $2.5 million CBS paid for the rights to broadcast the game to a record viewing audience of 70 million people—more than one-third of the entire population of the U.S.—Super Bowl II became the richest single athletic event to that time.

Taking the field amid sunny, 68-degree temperatures, Nitschke saw the palm trees swaying beyond the open end of the Orange Bowl, saw that the decorated field had been dyed green to look good on color TV. Testing the footing, Nitschke found that the closed end of the stadium was sandy, and that the yard stripes up and down the field were gullies. The Orange Bowl had become an AFL stadium in 1966 to accommodate the arrival of the expansion Miami Dolphins, but Nitschke and the Packers had played there before. In 1963 and '64, the Orange Bowl had hosted the NFL Playoff Bowl, the post-season game between the runners-up in the Eastern and Western Conferences. Green Bay had finished second in the West in both 1963 and '64, and was familiar with the nuances of the stadium, the sudden wind shifts and the grass sod that covered the sandy turf underneath. Nitschke watched the pregame festivities, saw the two giant, 30-foot high figures on floats—one trimmed in Packer white and yellow-gold, the other in Raider silver and black—square off at midfield and puff smoke at one another through three-foot wide nostrils.

In the Green Bay locker room before the game, Nitschke dressed in his road white jersey with the green-and-gold trim, streaked shiny black shoe polish on his cheekbones to cut the sun's glare, then listened as the pregame speeches began.

Offensive captain Bob Skoronski stood up first and said that if the Packer lost this game, they would lose everything they worked for all season. "I don't have any damn intention of losing this ballgame," he said, "and I don't think anybody else here does."

Defensive captain Willie Davis followed and said the next 60 minutes would determine what would be said about the Packers the next day. Offensive tackle Forrest Gregg implored his teammates to go out and take the game to the Raiders right away. Oakland, Gregg said, is a little bit afraid of Green Bay, and the Packers could gain the early edge by putting it to the AFL champions from the first play on.

Max McGee followed, said it would be a tough thing to live the rest of their lives having lost this game, then he yielded the floor to Nitschke. Nitschke's message mirrored his style of play—no-frills and direct.

"Let's play with our hearts," he said.

Nitschke set the tone for Super Bowl II on the game's first play from scrimmage. Reading a Raiders' sweep at the Oakland 28-yard line, he shot through a gap in the line, lowered his left shoulder into Dixon's right knee, and flipped him. Flipped him, in the words of a *Time* magazine reporter, "cleats over clavicle."

In the press box, *Detroit News* columnist Jerry Green saw the hulking Dixon, a player he knew was a home-bred AFL star, take Lamonica's handoff and start left. "Nitschke, fangs flashing, met Dixon at the line of scrimmage," Green wrote. "The collision was terrifying. Dixon was bowled over, bounced backwards, and set down in a heap."

In what he later acknowledged as smart-aleck fashion, Green turned to his NFL colleagues and in a voice loud enough for AFL writers to hear, remarked, "Well, this game's over."

Nitschke's hit on Dixon remains most vivid in the mind of Lee Remmel, who covered the Packers for the *Green Bay Press-Gazette* for more than 29 years. To Remmel, Nitschke's hit on Dixon remains one of the signature plays of Ray's long career.

On CBS Radio, play-by-play announcer Jack Drees made the call on a play that set the tone for the entire afternoon:

> *First-and-10 for Oakland, Banaszak, and Dixon the running backs . . . Lamonica is snug under center. He gives the ball to Dixon and . . . Dixon is stopped! Coming in there was Nitschke as Dixon tried the left side of the line, was upended at the line of scrimmage by Nitschke, and dropped down on the 28.*

Lamonica had called "69 Boom Man"—a fullback sweep to the weak side that had been the Raiders' number one running play all season. Banaszak, who was starting at halfback in place of the injured Clem Daniels, recalled coming out of the huddle on that first play, looking across the line and seeing Nitschke, Jordan, Davis, and Adderley, all of whom were players he had once collected bubble-gum cards of when he was younger. Banaszak's responsibility on the play was to block left linebacker Dave Robinson, but he never touched him. Films show Nitschke flying past the fallen Banaszak to drop Dixon.

"Nitschke came over me to get Dixon for no gain," Banaszak said. "I had his cleat marks all over my back."

Seeing Nitschke and the rest of the Packers up close and in person left Lamonica as impressed as his counterpart on the Chiefs, Lenny Dawson, had been the year before.

"We were a very young ballclub," Lamonica remembered, "and we were facing some old warhorses who could really put the leather to you. Nitschke, Dave Robinson . . . those guys were solid. We weren't in awe of the Packers, but they had that mystique."

Throughout the game, Nitschke battled Otto, nicknamed "Double-Zero" for the silver uniform number he wore on his black jersey. Otto had been an All-AFL center from 1960 to 1967, and would become the last of the pro football linemen to wear a double-bar facemask instead of the half- or fullcage masks that were coming into favor. Like Nitschke, Otto's rough features, usually accompanied by a trickle of blood running down his face, unsettled opposing players.

Nitschke was unmoved. He had given Oakland what he later called, "a pretty good introduction to the NFL brand of defensive football," and proved instrumental in upending the wide running game. Oakland had overwhelmed the AFL's best defensive team, the Oilers, in the league championship game two weeks earlier with sweeps. In that game, Dixon gave the Raiders their first touchdown when he swept left and thundered 69 yards behind Banaszak and Upshaw on the first play of the second quarter. Throughout the game, Dixon and Banaszak continued to pound away at the Oilers behind a fired-up offensive line, and by day's end, Dixon had 144 yards rushing and a 6.9 yards per carry average, and Banaszak had 116 yards on the ground and averaged 7.7 yards per attempt. As a team, the Raiders ran 48 times for an AFL championship game record 263 yards. Oakland's power sweeps battered Houston's right side, and in the film of the game, Banaszak and Dixon can be seen dancing through the Oilers defense to set up four Blanda field goals.

Bengston knew all about the AFL title game, about Blanda's shrinking the field with kicks that ranged from 36 to 42 yards, and knew the Raiders' ageless kicker represented a serious threat any time Oakland penetrated Packer territory. Nitschke knew it too, and helped shut down the Raiders' ground-eating sweeps by firing through the gaps left by Oakland's pulling guards and hauling Dixon and Banaszak down from behind.

Nitschke's success against the Raiders stemmed in part from Oakland's difficulties in dealing with the quickness of right defensive tackle Henry Jordan. Otto said that one reason the Raiders' wide running game failed was because they could only pull one guard rather than two. Upshaw had to stay back and take care of Jordan, Otto said, because the Packer tackle was so quick off the ball.

"Maybe," Otto mused, "we should've run right at 'em."

With Nitschke heading a mobile linebacking corps that prevented Raider backs from turning upfield, the Packers took physical control of the game. Lombardi told his defense that anytime they can take away an opponent's number one play, they could force them into trying something they're not as effective in doing. With the Oakland offense providing no pressure, Green Bay engineered time-consuming drives. Playing with what one wire-service reporter described as "the effervescence of overworked morticians," the Packers drove 34 yards in 11 plays on their first possession and took a 3–0 lead on Don Chandler's 39-yard field goal.

The next time Green Bay had the ball, Bart Starr pried apart Oakland's unconventional three-four defense with a 17-play, 84-yard drive that consumed almost nine minutes off the white-on-green scoreboard clock. Chandler's 20-yard field goal gave the Packers a 6–0 lead, and as Izenberg watched Chandler, not Blanda, provide the early points, the thought occurred to him that no team in football had ever been more cruel than the Packers. They delighted, he wrote later, in beating teams at their own game.

Having lulled the Raiders to sleep with two long drives, Starr struck quickly on the Packers' next possession, when he found flanker Boyd Dowler for a 62-yard touchdown and a 13–0 lead.

The Raiders finally responded with a scoring drive of their own, Lamonica hitting end Bill Miller for a 23-yard touchdown. But Chandler's third field goal of the first half, a 43-yarder, gave Green Bay a 16–7 lead at the break.

Nitschke had played an active first half, and sideline cameras showed him taking deep inhalations from an oxygen mask on the sideline. "I had lost 10, 15 pounds from the flu," he recalled. "But I was going to be there if I had to be there on a stretcher. We played every game for 60 minutes; we let it all hang out. There was no tomorrow for us. We got the adrenaline flowing, and we let it go, man."

At halftime, Nitschke joined with some of the team's aging veterans—Starr, Kramer, Gregg, Skoronski, Davis, Jordan, Fuzzy Thurston, and Max McGee—and pledged to play the last 30 minutes for Lombardi.

"Knowing that Lombardi was going to retire gave us an edge," Nitschke said. "That was extra motivation for us. We weren't going to get beaten by anybody that day."

Starr's mastery of the Raiders' shifting defense continued throughout the second half. On Green Bay's second series of the third quarter, he beat an Oakland blitz by sending fullback Ben Wilson up the middle on a draw play that gained 13 yards, then drew the Raiders in with a play-fake to Wilson on a third-and-1 from his own 40 and lofted a 35-yard completion to McGee. Starr followed with an 11-yard pass to split end Carroll Dale, a 12-yard comeback pass to halfback Donny Anderson, and then handed off to Anderson for a two-yard run over the right side for a 23–7 lead.

Lamonica had enjoyed some success in the first half by rolling out and throwing, but Nitschke and the defense adjusted by widening the splits in their line to shorten the room on Lamonica's rollouts and blitzing more. As the Packers widened their lead and the gloaming settled over the Orange Bowl, Nitschke could see the Raiders suffering the same kind of second-half letdown the Chiefs had the year before.

Lamonica was stunned at the deep drops taken by Green Bay's linebackers—Nitschke, Robinson, and Lee Roy Caffey. "They closed up my passing lane," he said. "On my first touchdown I had to throw the ball over Robinson's head. Here's a guy who's 6–4 and 250 pounds and he's 30 yards downfield with the receivers.

"On our sweeps, the linebackers ran 45 degrees and they really got out there. I found out too late that the sweeps weren't working."

A 31-yard field goal by Chandler on Green Bay's next series made it 26–7 and marked the sixth time in their first nine possessions that the Packers had put points on the board against the AFL's most feared defense. Chandler's field goal was his fourth of the game, and Nitschke remarked later that while Blanda was the kicker getting all the pregame attention, it was Chandler who was piling up the points.

As the final seconds ticked off on Green Bay's 33–14 win, Nitschke's legs were covered with welts. Dried blood stained his knee bandages. But he was still out on the spongy Orange Bowl field, still smashing into any Raider who violated his turf. He finished the game with nine tackles and impressed the Orange Bowl audience with his play. One writer noted that Nitschke played with "joyous abandon," and San Francisco quarterback George Mira remarked in a column he was writing for the *Miami Herald* that the Raiders had made a mistake trying to run sweeps against Nitschke.

"You don't run outside on Ray Nitschke," Mira said. "He's tough and reads plays a lot."

When Steve Sabol of NFL Films recalls Super Bowl II, the thing he remembers most about Nitschke is how many times the Packers middle man stopped the powerful Dixon on short-yardage plays. "Nitschke played to win," Sabol said. "He didn't need the media or television, he didn't need the billboards and all the publicity. He would've played the game in a parking lot."

Afterward, reporters crowded around Nitschke's locker. He was kind in his comments. The Raiders, he said, were "a real sound football team" that compared favorably with the previous AFL champion, Kansas City. But when *Green Bay Press-Gazette* sportswriter Lee Remmel asked if he was concerned when Oakland had halved the Packers' lead in the second quarter, Nitschke shook his head.

"No," he said. "There was no way they were going to beat us. Phil had us well prepared. It was just a matter of executing."

The Raider running game that ravaged the AFL was limited to a total of 107 yards. Dixon and Banaszak, who had combined for 260 yards rushing in the AFL title game, were held to a combined 70 yards by the Packers.

"We knew going into those games that those teams may have scored a lot of points in their league," cornerback Bob Jeter recalled, "but they weren't going to score a lot of points against us."

The Packer defense had done its job but paid a heavy price. The backs of Nitschke's legs were completely black-and-blue, and Jackie noticed that it took her husband longer to recover from the bruises than it had in earlier years. Asked how much longer he might play before retiring, Jackie said that the way her husband looked at the end of the '67 season, he would likely stay in the NFL "only more year."

That was good news for NFL ball carriers, who had engaged in brutal man-to-man warfare with Nitschke during the season. Though he was left off the NFL's All-Pro team, Nitschke's status among his peers continued to grow. In a *Sport* magazine article, five former All-Pro linebackers were asked to name the best middle linebacker in the game. Bill George voted for Chicago's Dick Butkus, and Chuck Bednarik picked Atlanta's Tommy Nobis, but Nitschke was the choice of Bill Pellington, Joe Schmidt, and Pat Richter. Pellington and Richter cited Nitschke's leadership ability, and Schmidt spoke of Nitschke's amazing lateral mobility and quickness. The magazine also asked Colts quarterback John Unitas his opinion on who the best middle linebacker was, and Unitas didn't hedge. They had all hit him hard, he said, and all were close in ability. But what set Nitschke apart in Unitas's eyes was his experience.

"He just seems to get the job done more consistently," Unitas said. "Nitschke was the toughest one I played against last year."

The toughest the Raiders had played against too. Even in defeat, Otto and Lamonica considered it an honor to have played in Super Bowl II against Nitschke and the Packers. "I had grown up in the Wisconsin area," Otto said, "and going up against a team from the great Vince Lombardi era was very exciting for me."

Exciting too, for a 30-year-old Oakland assistant coach named John Madden. Several times during the game, Madden had stolen quick glances across the field at the Packers' sideline, and at the man who had become his coaching idol. Madden stared at Lombardi and took it all in: the black blazer, white shirt and red-and-blue striped tie; the gray slacks and the black football shoes with the white laces. As linebackers coach for the Raiders, Madden's responsibility was to try and stop Lombardi's offense.

"I'm on this sideline and Vince Lombardi's on the other sideline," Madden said to himself. "I'm telling my linebackers how to stop Lombardi's plays." To Madden, who had followed Lombardi around the coaching lecture circuit since 1963, that was like trying to stop God's plays.

Madden wasn't alone in his assessment of Lombardi. A joke making the rounds at the time focused on a football player who had died and gone to heaven. When he arrives he sees a team of angels scrimmaging while a short man screams at them from the sidelines. When the player asks St. Peter who that fellow on the sideline is, St. Peter replies, "Oh, that's God. He thinks he's Vince Lombardi."

Nitschke thought Green Bay's second straight Super Bowl victory had elevated the Packers' head coach to folk hero status. *Sports Illustrated*'s cover story on Super Bowl II carried a picture of Lombardi being carried off the field on the shoulders of Kramer and Gregg and a headline titled, "The Super Champion—Lombardi of Green Bay."

Like his coach and many of his teammates, Nitschke was alarmed at what was going on in the country around him—the protests and riots in Watts and Newark, the political assassinations, the clash between the establishment and the counterculture. The Packers themselves were well-ordered and disciplined; big band music in the age of Aquarius. Younger, hipper AFL fans at the Orange Bowl had booed every time Starr led his team out of the huddle in the fourth quarter. The two generations, Nitschke thought, had discovered a big gap between them.

The old ways were changing, and Nitschke felt that a lot of Americans were worried and uptight about what their future would hold. Already, the American public had lost a popular president, and would lose a civil rights leader and a future presidential candidate to assassin's bullets. Cities were being set on fire, streets and campuses were filled with protesters. The times, they were a-changin', and not just for Bob Dylan. Nitschke thought that many Americans had lost track of what was going on, had lost track of whether they were winning or losing in their everyday lives. Football helped clarify matters, he thought, if only for three hours on a Sunday afternoon. Fans could see what was happening down on the field and knew whether their side was winning or losing.

Because the Packers were winners, because they had become the dominant team in professional sports, people outside of the NFL seeking clarity amid the social confusion suddenly wanted Lombardi's opinion on more than just the power sweep; they wanted his views on the changes sweeping the country. People may have been changing, Nitschke thought, but one thing still remained the same. The American public still respected a winner.

On February 1, 1968, Lombardi officially announced his retirement as head coach of the Packers. He would remain as Green Bay's general manager, but would turn the day-to-day coaching activities over to Bengston. Nitschke knew the difficulties Bengston would be facing. If the Packers repeated in 1968, it would be because it was Lombardi's team. If the Packers failed to repeat, it would be because it was Bengston's team. Still, Nitschke thought Green Bay was good enough to win without Lombardi. In a *Sports Illustrated* cover story headlined "Green Bay's Greatest Team," Nitschke, who had been named the team's MVP by Green Bay fans in a radio poll taken by WNFL, said the '68 Packers should be the best Green Bay team of all time.

"With Starr healthy for a full season, Grabowski and Pitts back in the lineup, Marv Fleming at full speed, and with Anderson and Williams carrying another year's experience, we should be more explosive offensively," he told *SI*'s Tex Maule. "I don't anticipate much change in the defense, although we do have some fine young players."

There were reasons for the Packers to play with passion in 1968. Some members of the team had grown tired of the publicity paid to their head coach and were anxious to prove they could win without him. It was a situation similar to the 49ers of 1989, when members of that team were resentful of the praise being heaped upon their head coach, Bill Walsh, and were determined to prove they were as much a reason for San Francisco's great success as the man writers dubbed "the Genius." Just as the Packers replaced an offense-minded head coach in Lombardi with his chief lieutenant and defensive coordinator, the 49ers replaced Walsh with their assistant head coach and defensive coordinator, George Seifert.

The difference between the '68 Packers and '89 49ers, however, was that while San Francisco returned its star cast intact under Seifert, the Packers were forced to deal with the dual retirements of Chandler and McGee. The loss of McGee hurt because he was a big-game player whose laid-back attitude kept the locker room loose. Chandler's departure hurt even more because Lombardi, as GM, never found a suitable replacement. In 1967, Chandler had made 19 of 26 field goal attempts, and had personally provided the difference between victory and defeat in three games. Without Chandler, the Packers might well have finished 7–5–2 rather than 9–4–1. In '68, the Packers started fast, beating Philadelphia 30–13 in the regular season opener. But kicking problems led to Bengston scrambling for reliable field goal kickers during the season. By season's end, he had tried four different kickers, including fullback Chuck Mercein, to no avail. The Packers as a team made just 13 of 29 field goal attempts, and lost or tied four games that could have been wins. Instead of a 10–4 finish that would have allowed the Packers to repeat as Central Division champions, Green Bay finished 6–7–1 and in third place behind Minnesota, which won the division with a mediocre 8–6 mark.

Halfback Paul Hornung said once that Lombardi alone accounted for at least three victories a season for the Packers. In 1968, three victories would have given Green Bay a berth in the NFL playoffs.

"That's an interesting thought," Kramer said. "We missed Vince's fire, his strength, motivation, and presence. In some of the games we lost, you'd have to believe he would have made the difference. Whether or not we could have dug deep once again when the playoffs started is another question."

In the end, the Packers were doomed by the lack of a reliable placekicker, by Starr missing almost half the season with a bad arm, by a defense stripped of its depth due to injuries that crippled tackles Jordan, Ron Kostelnik, and Jim Weatherwax and hampered ends Davis, Lionel Aldridge, and Bob Brown. Playing without the protection of his front line forced Nitschke to fight his way through waves of blockers in every game. He suffered severe pain in both shoulders and a chronic neck injury, and would sit in the trainer's room getting taped and bandaged before taking the field. Nitschke played hurt throughout the '68 season, playing against the Vikings with pinched nerves in *both* shoulders, and getting ejected from a game against New Orleans in Week 10 for forearming tight end Monty Stickles after the play had ended. Nitschke and Stickles had been feuding for years; Nitschke thought Stickles was a dirty player who blocked in the back and hit opponents in the back of the head. Stickles thought Nitschke approached football not as a game but as a gung-ho marine storming the beach.

"Ray and I would have one or two fights every time we played," Stickles said. "To me, it was a game. To him, it was war and destruction."

"That was a classic matchup of two guys not liking one another," said Tommy Nobis, who as a middle linebacker for the Atlanta Falcons watched films of Packers–49ers games every season. "We used to laugh, it was such a show to watch those two. Ray would line up over him on extra points and they would get after it. What would happen is, Stickles would take a shot at Ray's knees and try to cut him. If it was a sweep to his side of the field and Ray was in pursuit, Stickles would do something that would tick Nitschke off. And you can just bet that the next time Stickles came running over the middle on a pass route, Nitschke would clothesline him. We watched the 49ers on film because we played them twice a year, and there was one game that was just absolutely brutal for both of them, because they were both getting leveled by the other."

Nitschke's temper finally boiled over in '68 when Stickles was with the Saints, and though he admitted he could have gone after Stickles' head, he forearmed him in the chest instead. It was enough to get him ejected from the game, and to enhance his reputation as an intimidator. "There were probably some offensive guys who didn't like Nitschke," Nobis said, "because he was going to do whatever to get a guy down and maybe they didn't appreciate his techniques." Indeed, at season's end, Nitschke joined Butkus, Deacon Jones of the Rams, Alex Karras of the Lions, and Dave Wilcox of the 49ers on *The Sporting News'* list of the five meanest men in football.

Nitschke's hard play inspired his teammates, inspired Bengston, and at season's end, he was named team MVP for the second straight year.

Nitschke was disappointed in the Packers' season, and his disappointment deepened as he watched Super Bowl III and saw Joe Namath and the New York Jets defeat the favored Baltimore Colts to give the AFL its first championship game win over the NFL. The Jets' victory came on the same Orange Bowl field that the Packers had established NFL superiority on the year before against the Raiders, and Nitschke thought the Colts had let the league down. What made it worse for Nitschke was that the AFL's first victory had been engineered by Namath. As a quarterback, Nitschke thought Namath was outstanding, but he didn't appreciate the way the flamboyant Jets star carried himself off the field. Just as Namath had guaranteed a win over the Colts, Nitschke guaranteed that if it had been the Packers playing the Jets in Super Bowl III, Green Bay would have given the NFL three wins in a row over the AFL.

Having endured his first losing season since 1958, Nitschke looked to rebound in 1969. Lombardi, missing what he called "the fire on Sundays," left the Packers' organization on February 5 to become head coach and general manager of the Washington Redskins. His departure saddened Nitschke, whose sometimes volatile relationship with his head coach had softened in recent years. In a surprising display of emotion, Lombardi had kissed Nitschke on the cheek following a big win in the difficult 1967 season, and had gone out of his way to express his thanks to Nitschke for his play during the championship years. Lombardi told Nitschke he had always liked and admired him, but had realized that he was a player who didn't constantly need a pat on the back. To Lombardi, Nitschke was a player who always had to be ridden, always had to be critiqued.

"There were times when I didn't want to do it," Lombardi told him, "but it was for your own good."

In time, Nitschke came to accept Lombardi's coaching methods. Nitschke thought Lombardi had handled him just right, had gotten the most out of him. And his coach's constant demand for excellence—"There's a right way to do things and a wrong way," Lombardi would say. "Which way are going to do it, *mister*?"—impressed Nitschke.

"He helped to turn me around as a person," Nitschke said. "He inspired me by his determination in what he did."

Marie Lombardi said once that her husband had turned some men into football players and some football players into men. Of the two, she said, her husband had always been most proud of the latter. Nitschke, the ex-rowdy, was one of those football players that Lombardi had helped turn into a man.

"He set a standard," Nitschke said, "that I chose to follow."

Later, Nitschke would tell Vince Jr. how much his father had meant to him.

"He was most appreciative about what my father had done for him," he said.

At the start of the 1969 season, Lombardi was gone, Kramer and Skoronski retired, and age was creeping up on the team's heroes of the past—Nitschke, Starr, Davis, and Jordan. Once again, placekicking was a problem. Green Bay kickers converted a league-low 6 of 22 attempts, costing the team at least two wins. The Packers again finished in third place in the Central Division, albeit with a winning record at 8–6. They were still a tough team, but their greatness was fading. They had been replaced by the Vikings as the most physical team in the NFL, and Minnesota had ridden the hard-edged performances of Joe Kapp, Bill Brown, Alan Page, and Carl Eller to a second consecutive Central Division championship, this time with a 12–2 record that was the best in the league.

As the luster of Green Bay's glory years gradually wore thin, so too did the cool veneer that had always polished their performances in the Lombardi years. Opposing players like Alex Karras of Detroit could hear Packer linebackers cursing out other members of the defense when games started going bad. It was sweet, Karras said, because he had never heard anything like that before when playing Green Bay. Under Lombardi, the Packers had always played with what Karras called "a superior aloofness." To Karras, the

Packers had carried themselves during their title days as if they had all been born in some great palace somewhere and that losing wasn't worth considering. "They were elite," Karras said.

Even in defeat, Nitschke maintained that elite status, and in 1969 was named the greatest linebacker of the NFL's first 50 years. In choosing Nitschke as the best ever at his position, the editors of the book *The First 50 Years: The Story of the National Football League* wrote that as the field leader of one of football's greatest defensive units, Nitschke suffered the problems of recognition that sometimes plague teams blessed with numerous All-Pro players. In an age of Packer dominance, it was impossible to give credit to every Green Bay player, so Nitschke was frequently passed over when it came time to choose players for the Pro Bowl.

But in an era ruled by great middle linebackers, the editors wrote, Nitschke deserved his reputation as the best ever. "In the emotional cauldron of professional football," the editors wrote, "the big linebacker from Green Bay brings the game down to its most elemental form—man against man. In the final analysis, this is football's criterion of excellence."

The honor was one of the highest of Nitschke's career to that point, and he joined 12 of his Packer teammates in being named to the NFL's All-1960s team. For Nitschke, it was an appropriate climax to a decade that saw him go from second-string in 1960 to second-to-none in NFL history. The 1970 season, however, saw the realignment of the two leagues under the NFL umbrella, and also saw the final breakup of the Lombardi Packers. Davis, Jordan, and Dowler retired, and Adderley, Pitts, Caffey, and Fleming were traded. Of the starters that remained, Starr suffered through another sore-armed season and Robinson was sidelined by a torn Achilles tendon. In the realigned National Football Conference, the Packers finished 6–8 and in last place in the Central Division.

Bengston resigned at the end of the 1970 season, victimized by both injuries and the success of his famous predecessor. For Nitschke, the dawning of a new decade brought changes in both his personal and professional lives. In 1972, Ray and Jackie added to their family by adopting a baby girl, Amy. Around the house in Oneida, Nitschke was a much different person than he was on autumn Sundays. Jackie told a reporter once that her husband was very tenderhearted, never used any harsh or mean words toward the family, and was always willing to help around the house, be it cleaning up, doing the dishes, baby-sitting, or changing diapers. When it came to disciplining the children, Jackie said, she was the one who had to administer an occasional spanking.

"It just breaks Raymond's heart," she said, acknowledging that her husband would much rather get down on the floor and roll around with the kids than be stern with them. John said later that while many words had been used to describe his father—a player, leader, winner, a champion—to his children he was simply "Dad." And, he added, they could not have asked for a better father.

As a child, Richard was impressed by his father's dedication to his football career, even as he entered the twilight years of his playing career. On game days in Lambeau Field, Richard would watch as his father would remain behind late into the day, lifting weights after the locker room had emptied. Then, he and his father would help team trainer Domenic Gentile and equipment manager Dad Braisher clean up. "We would fold towels, do whatever," Richard remembered.

Being adopted by his parents, John said, was the most significant, most blessed day of his life. Amy, who never knew her father as a football player, said the legacy he provided for her was of a giving, loving man, a man of compassion and respect for others.

To his teammates, Nitschke's transformation from wild man to family man never ceased to amazed them. Kramer kiddingly remarked once that Nitschke had turned into a monk—"no drinking, no carousing, no nothing," Kramer said. When Nitschke's teammate, linebacker Dan Currie, asked him once what it was like not drinking anymore, Nitschke looked at him and smiled.

"Quiet, man," he said. "Real quiet."

Nitschke lived for his children; Kramer called him the most devoted father he had ever seen. In an era when NFL players were still modestly paid in relation to today's salaries, Nitschke was one of the few Packers who didn't take an off-season job. He was approached once in the mid-sixties by representatives of the Everseal Industrial Glue Company, who were looking for a salesman in the Wisconsin area. Nitschke didn't want the job and turned it down, so the company reps approached backup offensive tackle Steve Wright. After Wright took the job, he laughed when he heard that Nitschke had been the company's first choice.

"If you can imagine the least likely salesman in the world," Wright said later, "it would be Ray Nitschke." To Wright, Nitschke was the kind of guy who would walk into an executive's office, throw down a hunk of glue in front of him, and say, "You want some glue? Here. Buy it."

Nitschke turned down dozens of other job offers during his playing career, preferring instead to stay home and spend time with his family. He had a treehouse built in the family's backyard, and teammates thought it was so elaborate the only thing it lacked was a color television. When John saw a fishing program on television one day in 1966, he approached his father and asked why he had never taken him fishing. The following off-season, Nitschke took John to Florida on a month-long fishing trip.

The addition of Amy to the family followed the Packers' hiring of Dan Devine as Green Bay's new head coach and general manager. For the first time since his rookie season in 1958, Nitschke would be playing for someone other than Lombardi or Bengston. Nitschke had played the first seven games of the 1970 season hampered by a sore back, and like many of his teammates, he was preoccupied with thoughts of Lombardi, who had passed away from cancer on September 3. Bald and battered at age 33, Nitschke rebounded to play a strong second half. When Devine took over as head coach, he studied films of the Packers' 1970 season and saw the aging, hurting Nitschke moving slower than usual. Convinced Green Bay had to go with a youth movement, Devine played Jim Carter, a third-round pick from the 1970 draft out of the University of Minnesota, ahead of Nitschke throughout the exhibition season.

Nitschke started the regular season opener against the Giants, a 42–40 loss in Green Bay, and when the Packers hosted the Denver Broncos in Milwaukee's County Stadium the following week, he rode the bench for the first time since 1960. Leading 34–13 in the fourth quarter, Green Bay coaches motioned for Nitschke to go into the game. The great linebacker balked; hurt and angry, his pride stung, he felt for the first time in his life that he didn't want to get into a game. The feeling passed, and Nitschke pulled his helmet on. As he ran onto the field with those short, mincing steps, Packer fans rose and applauded. Hearing the ovation, Nitschke wiped his face, wiped away the tears streaming down behind his full-cage facemask. In a matter of an instant, Nitschke had gone from being angry with Devine to feeling tremendous love for Packer fans.

"It was unbelievable how I felt at that moment," Nitschke told Gentile. "It was one of the great moments of my career."

The relationship between Carter and Nitschke became strained. Carter had grown up in St. Paul, Minnesota, a six-hour drive west of Green Bay, and the thought of playing alongside legends like Nitschke and Starr was glamorous to him. Yet Packer fans turned on Carter when he was given Nitschke's starting role in 1971. The two regarded each other warily. In a biting comment, Nitschke said once that if he was going to be replaced at middle linebacker, it should only be by someone who had more talent than he did. Carter went around telling teammates he *was* better than Nitschke. The rivalry escalated in 1972, when Carter hurt his knee in a Week Six game against Atlanta in Milwaukee and had to leave the County Stadium field. The fans who had previously booed him now cheered, and Carter took it as a derisive cheer for his leaving the game. Nitschke, however, saw it as cheers not for Carter being injured, but for his entering the game.

Carter made the Pro Bowl in 1973, but he forever felt distanced from Packer fans. When a woman asked him once during a live call-in show from

Fuzzy Thurston's Left Guard restaurant if he would ever fill Nitschke's shoes, Carter cussed her out. "Go to hell," he said.

On December 12, in the 100th Bears–Packers game, Green Bay honored Nitschke with his own special day. The only Packer player who had been so honored previously was Starr. Bill King, a retired Green Bay police sergeant and civic leader, had contacted Nitschke to tell him that the Packers and their fans wanted to organize a Ray Nitschke Day. Nitschke agreed, and for weeks before the game the town was filled with bumper stickers and buttons that read "We Love Ray." Some 50,000 stickers and buttons were sold, and became so well-received that Nitschke's young nephew, Frank, wouldn't go to bed at night unless he had a Nitschke button pinned to his pajamas. King asked Nitschke what gifts he'd like to be presented with and suggested a new car. Nitschke declined. He had a car, a house, everything he really needed. Declining any expensive gifts, Nitschke asked King to take money raised for Ray Nitschke Day and establish a college scholarship fund. Nitschke knew that if it hadn't been for his own athletic scholarship, he would never have even gone to college, never become a pro football player. To Nitschke, establishing a college fund in his name would prove more satisfying than having another car in his garage. Nitschke insisted too, that the fund be open to all needy students, not just athletes.

Devine told Nitschke he would start against the Bears. Carter was moved to outside linebacker for the game, and as Nitschke printed the words "Beat the Bears" inside his knee pads, he thought of all the previous games he had played against the team that had been his boyhood favorite. Thought of his first game against Chicago, when as a member of the Chicago All-Stars he had traveled to Rensselaer, Indiana, to scrimmage the Bears. As he warmed up he caught sight of 6-foot-8 defensive end Doug Atkins. To the 21-year-old Nitschke, Atkins was huge and built like a Greek god. Once the game started, Nitschke grew comfortable after the first couple of plays, and after barreling into the Bears' big fullback, Rick Casares, along the Chicago sideline, was stunned to hear Bears' coach George Halas screaming at him.

"Here was my boyhood idol, cussing me out," Nitschke said later. From that point on, Nitschke developed an intense rivalry with Halas and the Bears. The intensity grew with Nitschke's first visit to Wrigley Field as a member of the Packers. Since he was from Chicago, Nitschke thought he'd get a few cheers from the fans when his name was announced. Instead, all he heard was Bear fans cursing him.

Through the 1960s, Nitschke saved some of his best games for the Bears. Lombardi stoked his club's competitive fire by declaring the week before each game with Chicago "Bear Week." Willie Davis said that while Nitschke got up for every game, the Packers' middle linebacker would psyche himself to another level for the Bears. Nitschke had interceptions against the Bears in 1962 and '66, and in '68 he preserved a 28–27 Packer victory by picking off a Jack Concannon pass with 1:07 left. The loss kept Chicago from clinching the Central Division title, and the Bears finished the season one game behind Minnesota and out of the NFL playoffs.

Nitschke punished the Bears at every opportunity. In 1964, he slammed tight end Mike Ditka so hard following a reception over the middle he could see Ditka's eyes roll over white before he spun to the ground. For a moment, Nitschke was scared. He thought he had killed Ditka. Knocked cold, Ditka was carried off the field by Chicago team trainers.

Chicago center Mike Pyle recalled Nitschke's interception that cost the Bears a shot at the Central Division title, but said once that the memory that lingered longest and strongest in his memory was of teammate George Seals going down with a blown knee. Seals was a power lineman, a 6-foot-2, 260-pound guard who ran the field like a marauder. Opposing defenses feared and hated Seals, and when he went down against the Packers, Pyle saw Nitschke standing over Seals, yelling at him, taunting him.

The Bears respected Nitschke, respected his hard hits, his approach to the game. Halas called Nitschke "a hard hitter but never a cheap-shot artist."

When Butkus joined the Bears in 1965, pro football writers at the time began comparing him to Nitschke. Butkus was probably a better defender in the short pass zone, Nitschke in the medium-range zone. The big difference was in how they played off their blocks. Nitschke broke up blocking schemes with his huge, punishing forearms; Butkus shed offensive linemen with his quickness and balance. Even the Lombardi Packers, drilled in precision angle blocking and owning the best offensive line of the 1960s, found it difficult to get a clear shot at Butkus. Forrest Gregg said when the Packers tried to cut Butkus, he'd jump over them. If they went too far upfield in their blocks, he'd slip inside them. If they waited too long trying to negate his inside move, Butkus would go over the top of them. Kramer recalled Butkus's great strength, his great hustle.

Nitschke and Butkus had a warrior's respect for one another. What Nitschke liked about Butkus was his tenacity as a player. To Nitschke, Butkus played every down with everything he had. "That's the way you're supposed to play the game," Nitschke said.

Butkus was incensed when the Bears lost to the Packers in '68. He argued with teammate Lloyd Phillips and nearly shoved him off the field for not taking the game seriously enough. When the Bears lost on Nitschke's interception, Butkus was enraged. "I was so damn mad," he said later, "I could have bit the goal posts."

Sunday, December 12, found Butkus standing in the tunnel waiting to take the field on Ray Nitschke Day. Game programs featured a three-page tribute to Nitschke. Under a heading that read "The Packers' 66" the tribute began with the words "Ray Nitschke is an internal contradiction, the kind of split personality that can be found only in a sport like professional football." The words were accompanied by a 12-photo collage of Nitschke's career, along with an insert from Marie Lombardi, Vince's widow:

> *Dear Ray and Jackie, Congratulations! There is a very happy coach in Heaven today who is very proud of you and all the Packers and the City of Green Bay for honoring one of its finest. You are a credit to the game, the Packers and Green Bay. God bless.*

Amid frozen sunshine, Lambeau Filled was filled with 56,263 fans. It was cold and muddy, and Butkus noticed that everyone on the Packers was wearing warmup jackets; everyone that is, except Number 66. As Butkus watched Nitschke, he thought first how fortunate Nitschke was to have played for Lombardi.

Like Butkus, Nitschke was a graduate of the University of Illinois, and Butkus had always admired him more than any other player. They had first met in November 1962 when Butkus was a sophomore at Illinois. Nitschke had arrived at the university for a visit, and the two men were introduced by Dick's older brother Ronnie, who played defensive tackle and was a teammate of Ray's for a brief time. They made small talk, and Butkus struggled years later to recall what Nitschke had told him. Keep your head up? Wash behind your ears at night? Butkus couldn't remember, but it hardly mattered. He was quiet and self-conscious at the time, and what mattered most to him was that Nitschke, a man who was doing what he wanted to do with his life, had taken the time to talk with him.

A month later, Butkus sat in front of television and watched Nitschke dominate the 1962 NFL championship game against the Giants in Yankee Stadium. As he watched the game, Butkus felt he was out there helping Nitschke make every tackle. When Nitschke was named the game's MVP, Butkus was thrilled. If Nitschke had asked him, Butkus said, he would have gladly chauffeured Ray around in the new sports car Nitschke received as the MVP.

Seven years had passed, and Butkus and Nitschke hadn't spoken much since. They had become on-field rivals for the role of the best middle linebacker in the game in the late 1960s, and as Butkus watched Nitschke moving around out on the field he knew that the comparisons would continue this day as well. Nitschke headed toward the microphones positioned at midfield. He was accompanied by Jackie and his two sons, all bundled against the cold. John, the older of the two boys, carried his father's huge helmet by the facemask with both hands. Nitschke cut a familiar figure as he stood before the mikes—the bald head, the heavily padded forearms, the green-and-gold Packer uniform—but he had left off the black shoe polish beneath the eyes, and left in the partial plate he'd worn since his front teeth had been knocked into the dirt against Ohio State.

Three of Nitschke's former coaches—Elmer Johnson, Andy Puplis, and Ray Eliot—were introduced, and King announced the establishment of the college fund established in Nitschke's name. A token, he said, of the respect, admiration, and esteem the Packers and their fans held for Nitschke.

"You are more than a football player," King announced. "You are more than a professional athlete. You are a symbol of how all of God's children should live."

Stepping to the microphone, Nitschke told the cheering throng, "This is finest day of my life." He had been gifted by God, he said, to be an athlete, and he thanked all the people who had helped make his life something his children could respect. With his eyes misting up, Nitschke told the crowd, "Words can't express how I feel." With that, the aging warrior turned and joined his family as they walked toward the tunnel.

Seeing Nitschke in the tunnel, Butkus had an urge to walk up to him, stick out his hand and say, "Congratulations, Ray. You deserve it." He didn't, the moment passed, and Butkus regretted it for years. Moments later, they were both running out into the bright sunshine, playing on the same field together for the final time.

Willie Wood said later that the Packers were trying to win that day as much for Nitschke as for the team, and Green Bay set the tone on the game's first play from scrimmage when quarterback Scott Hunter threw a 77-yard touchdown to Carroll Dale. By game's end, Green Bay had gained a 31–10 win, and as Nitschke walked off the field, he was approached by Chicago defensive end Ed O'Bradovich, who gripped him in a friendly bearhug.

Asked later how he had played on Ray Nitschke Day, Nitschke shrugged.

"I could've played better," he said.

From Proviso High to the University of Illinois to the Green Bay Packers, the man voted the best linebacker in the NFL's first 50 years never left a football field believing he couldn't have played a better game.

TWELVE

OFFICIALLY, Ray Nitschke pulled his Green Bay Packers uniform off for the final time in the gathering dusk of Christmas Eve, 1972, following a 16–3 loss to the Washington Redskins in an NFC Divisional playoff game. He helped lead the team out of the tunnel onto the spongy RFK Stadium turf, and though he didn't start the game, Nitschke represented the Packers at midfield for the ceremonial coin toss prior to the game. He had been named a team co-captain prior to the season, and though he spent much of the year blocking for field goals and extra points on special teams and donning a headset on the sidelines to help with defensive signals, he remained an intimidating presence. Prior to an exhibition game against Houston, Nitschke's intensity frightened Oilers quarterback Dan Pastorini when they met at midfield.

"All right, dammit! C'mon ref, toss the damn coin," Nitschke said, jawing at the referee in his loud, nagging voice. "Let's get it over with . . . I want the hell out of here! Let's get this game going!"

Under Vince Lombardi, the Packers had learned to always call "heads" at the coin flip and always take the ball if heads came up. Someone told Lombardi once that heads was a better percentage call because the eagle side of the coin weighed more. Lombardi believed the idea, believed too that when the Packers won the toss, they should take the ball. "Vince always wanted to drive the ball down somebody's throat before they drove it down ours," offensive captain Bob Skoronski said.

Skoronski and defensive captain Willie Davis would gauge the other team's strength by the strength of their captain's handshake. Skoronski figured that if a captain on the other team had a handshake like a dead fish, then he had to be a pushover and so did his team. Skoronski and Davis always gave out the most brutal handshakes they could. They would grab the opposing captain's hand and submerge it in their own. "Then we'd squeeze like hell," Skoronski said. Skoronski and Davis believed if they could intimidate a player at the coin flip, it was one less guy Lombardi had to worry about during the game.

As a team captain, Nitschke picked up where Skoronski and Davis left off. He intimidated Pastorini at the coin flip, to the point that the Oilers quarterback later told a teammate that he was frightened by Nitschke's intensity. Though he spent much of the 1972 season on the sidelines, Nitschke was pleased that Green Bay was back on top in the Central Division, pleased that with a 10–4 record, the Pack was indeed back, as bumper stickers throughout Wisconsin proclaimed. He was not pleased with his lack of playing time, however, telling former teammate Bill Curry before a 1973 exhibition game, "I can play, man, I can go. I can still do it."

In the final days of his playing career, Nitschke would sit in hotels on game day, and to observers like Curry, who ran into him at the Pfister Hotel in Milwaukee, Nitschke's presence created an impression of being caught in a time warp. To Curry, it was almost eerie, seeing the Packer legend sitting there in a lobby chair, his bald head gleaming in the lights. The old warrior had a regal presence about him; Curry thought Nitschke could have passed for a sultan or a potentate of ancient times, surveying all that had once been his. Prior to one of his last games, Nitschke was in the lobby of the Pfister Hotel when he spotted Curry.

"If I do play," Nitschke told him, "you better buckle it up."

When Curry remarked that he always had to buckle it up against him, Nitschke remarked, "Yeah, but I'm fighting for my life this time."

Nitschke never got in the game. With five minutes left and the Packers leading by some 20 points, fans in County Stadium began chanting "We want Nitschke!" Nitschke didn't move, and as he stood there, straight as a statue, it struck Curry that Packer coach Dan Devine was trying to turn Nitschke into a monument before Ray was ready to become one. Curry was reminded of his former teammate in Baltimore, John Unitas, and how he had been treated at the end of his career. Colt lineman Dan Sullivan once said, only half-jokingly, that Unitas was the only guy whose number they tried to retire while he was still in uniform.

Curry thought Nitschke's situation was just as sad, and as the final minutes ticked off the stadium clock, Curry was drawn closer to the Packer bench, which in County Stadium was on the same sideline as the visiting team's. At the final gun, Curry ran over to thank Nitschke for all he had done for him, and as he watched the big Number 66 shuffle off the field in that familiar gait, Curry realized he had just touched a living legend. As Nitschke left the County Stadium field for the final time, it appeared to Curry that the Packer great had, like so many others, been brought down in the end by the very sport he had helped so much to build.

Packers trainer Domenic Gentile watched Nitschke struggle, physically and emotionally, in his final days. In the 1972 season, Nitschke tore his right hamstring prior to a game against Detroit, and the back of his leg from his groin to his knee turned black from the hemorrhaged muscle.

Since he was already playing with a left leg that had atrophied early in his career, Nitschke by Gentile's account played against the Lions on one-half of one good leg.

Though his body was wearing down, Nitschke remained an intimidating figure, a physical enforcer from the old days. On Sunday, September 24, he stood on the sidelines as the Packers struggled against the Oakland Raiders at Lambeau Field. As Green Bay fell behind 20–14 in the fourth quarter, Oakland center Jim Otto could hear Nitschke yelling at middle linebacker Jim Carter from the sideline.

"I was having a very good game against Carter and the interior linemen," Otto recalled. "It was a tough day, but we were moving the ball and doing the things we had to do. And Ray was on the sidelines, screaming and yelling at Carter not to let Otto block him.

"Finally, Ray came into the game, and he came in with the intent of not doing anything but destroying me physically. And he darn near did. He was screaming and hollering; he'd scream out the signals and directions for his linemen and then scream out the player's name that he was going after, you know, 'I'm gonna git you, Otto.'

"He hit me with his fists, forearms, and everything, broke my helmet, broke my cheekbone, broke my nose, and detached the retina in my left eye. It was a very brutal attack. But I kept right on playing, kept right on hitting, and eventually my face swelled up. I couldn't see out of my left eye and wouldn't see out of it for the next six months.

"I looked the worse for wear after that game, I'll guarantee it. My folks were over from Wassau and they went to the airport with us and they couldn't believe it. The whole left side of my face was swelled up, my eye was closed. And I said, 'Well, Mr. Nitschke did that, mom.' "

Unlike other athletes of his era—Jim Brown, Sandy Koufax, Bill Russell—Nitschke hung on to the game he loved despite the slow but steady erosion of his skills from age and injury. Hung on, he said, to prove he could survive 15 years in a sport that challenged him not just physically but mentally and emotionally as well.

Nitschke survived, and when it finally came time for him to make his retirement official, he at last seemed at peace with his decision.

"I guess the time has arrived," he said. "It comes for everybody. It has happened before and will happen again. . . . For the benefit of myself and the Green Bay Packers, I feel it's the right thing to retire. Every good thing must come to an end someday and so must my football playing days."

For close to 15 years, Nitschke had starred in Packer game films. Starting in 1975, he would go on a 13-year run as a prominent part of a series of 128 national television commercials. He had done some acting before. In 1968 he appeared in *Head,* an unusual motion picture starring the TV rock group

The Monkees. The picture proves a satire of several movie genres, and Nitschke's role occurs in a vignette on war movies. Nitschke plays the part of "Private One," a shell-shocked soldier who is wearing a blue-and-gold Notre Dame-style football uniform with the number one on it. When Monkee Peter Tork is sent out during a battle to get extra ammunition, he takes momentary cover from the exploding shells in a bunker, where he meets up with Private One. Nitschke repeats the mantra, "We're number one!" to a wary Tork, then slams helmet first into the side of the bunker. Interpretation of the scene is left to the viewer, but at a time when Lombardi's "Winning isn't everything, it's the only thing" slogan was being chiseled into stone, it was ironic that The Monkees chose one of the more famous Packers to play the role of Private One. The movie was written and produced by Jack Nicholson, and featured appearances by Terri Garr and Frank Zappa, along with another famous sports personality, former heavyweight champion Sonny Liston.

Nitschke appeared in his second movie in 1974, playing the part of Bogdanski, a hard-edged prison guard and member of the prison's semi-pro football squad in *The Longest Yard*. The film starred Burt Reynolds as Paul "Wrecking" Crewe, a former All-Pro player who leads the prison's team of inmates. Crewe is at odds with the warden, played by Eddie Albert, and just before the climactic game at film's end, Bogdanski appears in the prisoner's locker room. Looking to intimidate the inmates, Bogdanski punches a hole in the locker room wall, then takes up his role as the warden's enforcer during the game. Bogdanski inflicts physical pain on the prisoners before the inmates get even at the end and win the game.

Nitschke always negotiated his own business deals, and shrugged off advice that he could get rich if he hired a business agent. "I'd rather handle that stuff myself," he said, and proceeded to do so. He became a spokesman for Oldsmobile and joined Dick Butkus in a series of Midwest regional TV commercials. One commercial found Nitschke dressed as a woman and appearing as his fictionalized sister. He did good-will work for a major Wisconsin dairy and public relations work for Clairmont, a trucking firm.

His most remembered part, however, was as one of the ex-athletes on the Miller Lite beer commercials. His first Miller Lite commercial teamed him with Rosey Grier and Ben Davidson and showed the three big men doing needlepoint. Another spot had the balding Nitschke surrounded by chrome-domed look-alikes.

Nitschke took his TV appearances seriously and was proud of the fact that the Miller Lite series had become the most successful advertising campaign in the history of commercial television. To a generation of younger viewers, Nitschke was recognized not for his Hall of Fame career with Lombardi's legendary Packers, but for his appearances in beer commercials. He was comfortable with that, comfortable with the fact that people saw him as more than just a frightening specter on the football field but as someone they could approach and talk to.

"I think I'm a pretty nice guy," he said. Nitschke enjoyed people, enjoyed meeting them and getting along with them. He told Warren Gerds of the *Green Bay Press-Gazette* in a 1987 interview that people related to him because they knew he was trying to be a good guy and was striving to improve himself as a human being.

"I treat everybody like I want to be treated," Nitschke said. "That's kind of been my philosophy."

Nitschke's business trips sometimes took him away from home for as much as two weeks at a time. "He traveled a lot, and did a lot of speeches for different companies, a lot of motivational speeches," his daughter Amy remembered. "He did a lot of autograph shows too, but when he was home, he was really there for us. He was always very loving, very caring, but he was kind of comedic too. He could be a real jokester."

Once he retired, Nitschke didn't speak to his children much of his NFL career. But there were times when his memory was prodded, and he would open up to them about what it was like to have played in such a special era.

"We'd go to the games together and that would trigger some memories," Amy said. "He would compare life then to what it was later. But there were other times I would say something to him and I would have to prod him, you know. There were times when he didn't seem comfortable talking about it."

Amy's earliest memories of her father date back to 1975, when he was already three years out of football. The stories she's heard since of his playing days, the video clips she's seen, she said, are hard to relate to the man she knew as her father growing up.

"I didn't really see that part of him," she said, "and I'm sure it was probably very different for my brothers because they're older than I am. They were around when he was still playing, when he was getting ready for the game, getting his mindset ready to play. But he was so out of football when I was young, I can't relate him to that at all."

On July 29, 1978, Nitschke took his place among the game's immortals when he was inducted into the Pro Football Hall of Fame. Other inductees that day in Canton, Ohio, included Lance Alworth, Weeb Ewbank, Alphonse "Tuffy" Leemans, and Larry Wilson. When Nitschke's bust was unveiled, the words inscribed on it provide a terse description of his career:

> *First Green Bay defender from 1960s to be enshrined . . . Exceptional team leader, tough, strong, fast . . . Savage defender on rushes, cat-like quick against passes . . . Named NFL's all-time top linebacker, 1969 . . . All-NFL*

three years . . . Intercepted pass for TD in 1964 Pro Bowl . . . Had 25 career interceptions . . . MVP in 1962 NFL title game.

Dressed in the beige sports jacket that all new inductees wear, with a white shirt and brown-and-tan patterned tie, Nitschke stepped to the podium to address the sun-splashed audience. He spoke with passion and feeling, pausing at times only to check his notes and adjust his dark-rimmed glasses.

"Football gave me a chance to express myself, to get recognition, and to do something well," he told his audience. "I was committed to the game of football, and I'll never forget the great game that it is. It's given Ray Nitschke the chance for an education, to better himself, to be a better human being."

He had been enshrined the previous February in the Packer Hall of Fame, and in 1981 was inducted along with Bart Starr into the Wisconsin Hall of Fame. His number 66 was retired by the Packers in 1983, and in 1997 one of the team's practice fields was named after him. In 1994, Nitschke was named by writers and historians to the NFL's 75th Anniversary Team and to the Team of the Sixties.

Surprisingly, he is not listed among the distinguished graduates of Proviso, a list that includes NASA astronaut Eugene Cernan, a 1952 graduate; actor Dennis Franz ('62) and actress Carol Lawrence ('50); Olympians Gerald Holan ('49) and Blanche Kloss ('55); and 13 pro athletes, including major league pitcher Lee Stange ('54), NBA players Glen "Doc" Rivers ('80) and Michael Finley ('91); and NFL defensive back Ray Buchanon ('87). Nitschke's glaring omission rankles some of his former teammates at Proviso, but the school has at times honored him with a display of various Nitschke mementos, including the plaque he received on Ray Nitschke Day at Lambeau Field.

Nitschke accepted each honor with a humble grace, because he knew, as Paul Hornung said, how much the game had given him.

"I've always said that pro football did more for Ray Nitschke than anyone else," Hornung remarked. "There was a time when he was headed out of the league and down, until he stopped and turned it around."

As he aged, Nitschke cut back on his traveling, and when at home would settle in and watch sporting events on his big-screen TV. The TV fronted the north wall of his family room, which also housed a large oil painting of him in uniform at Lambeau Field. He watched a variety of sports, but had the greatest interest in football and baseball, the two sports he had starred in at Proviso and had received pro offers for. In his later years, his interest in football other than the Packers was confined largely to the college game. He could see the passion in the college players, and as

Amy heard him say, many of the kids who were playing college football were still playing for the love of the game.

When he wasn't watching sports, he tuned in The History Channel or took in an occasional war movie if he happened to catch one while channel-surfing. He enjoyed movies about World War II, but not about Vietnam. One of his favorite war movies was Patton, starring George C. Scott. Scott's portrayal of the all-conquering general was such that several members of the Lombardi Packers said they're always reminded of their former coach when watching the film.

Though he was a fan of the old movies, Nitschke rarely rented them on his own. He would sit down and watch a movie with his children if one of them brought a video to his house, but he rarely went out of his way to visit the video store.

His taste in reading materials was just as selective. He read newspapers every day, and enjoyed *Golf Digest* and *Time*. After Jackie passed away, he made it a point to read an AA daily devotional. "He liked motivational books," Amy said, "something where he could read a page every day."

He continued to do various commercial and charitable causes. His name adorned the weekly *Ray Nitschke's Packer Report*, which began in 1970. For nine years, Al Pahl was a ghost-writer for Nitschke's column. Pahl would call Nitschke after every Packer game, interview him, then write Nitschke's column, which appeared on the inside cover of the publication.

"Ray couldn't write a lick," Pahl said, "so some time Sunday night I would get a hold of Ray, wherever he was. Might be Orlando, Anaheim, or Chicago. If Ray hadn't seen the game, I actually had to tell him the highlights. Then he would give me his thoughts. Then we'd get off the phone and I would go back and dress it up. But Ray took this very seriously, so he always made sure I could contact him."

Nitschke was a spokesman for Norwegian Cruise Lines, and he and Jackie liked the cruise ships and would take one or two trips a year. On one occasion, when Ray and Jackie were on a cruise during a Packer game, Pahl had to set up a ship-to-shore connection to conduct the interview.

Pahl was impressed by Nitschke's dedication to his publication, and impressed too by the sheer physicality of the man. Nitschke, Pahl said, had huge hands and shoulders, but Pahl was more taken with what he described as Nitschke's "huge heart." The two men became friends, and in their nine years working together, Pahl said Nitschke never refused to sign an autograph with a smile, never refused to stop and talk to strangers. At the request of a friend, Nitschke once telephoned a man who was dying of cancer to offer words of encouragement; on another occasion, he helped smooth a difficult relationship between a father and his stepchildren by talking the man up in front of the kids during a chance meeting at the mall.

Nitschke made friends far and wide. Terry Ainsworth, who lives in Birmingham, England, telephoned Nitschke regularly and even opened his own Packers Hall of Fame overseas. Nitschke was close to many of the Packers of the mid-1990s, and Reggie White, for one, was always appreciative of his support. "Ray was always there for us," White said.

White said many of the Packers from that era were awed by Nitschke and the other legends of the Lombardi years. As the years went by, Nitschke became a source of inspiration for many of the people he came in contact with. Whether it was signing an autograph for 4-year-old Steven Golla—"To Steve, always try hard, do well in school, and never give up. . . . Ray Nitschke"—or handing over a perspiration-soaked Packer hat to Wisconsin governor Tommy Thompson at a game in Dallas, he seemed to loom larger than life.

"His indomitable spirit embodied the Packers," the governor said. "I had great respect for the man. Just being with him was a thrill."

Nitschke could startle people with his cement-mixer voice, as he did Carla Dionne of Marinette, Wisconsin. She was in the pet supply aisle at the Wal-Mart in Green Bay, struggling to lift a 50-pound bag of dog food from the bottom shelf when she heard a graveled voice behind her:

"Either you need to stop feeding your dog so much or you need to get smaller dogs."

She spun around and was greeted by the sight of the massive Nitschke, grinning at her. He bent over, picked up the 50-pound bag and with what she described as the ease of a man tossing a pillow, tossed the heavy bag into her cart.

He routinely took off his 1967 Super Bowl ring to allow others to try it on for size—"It was so big I could fit three of my fingers in it," longtime friend Tony Fiovani said—and delighted showing it to children. "Hey, kid," he'd say, pulling the diamond-encrusted ring off his finger. "How'd you like to see something special?"

He never turned anyone down for an autograph or a posed photo, and he didn't just sign autographs, he personalized them:

"Congratulations to my good friend, Cliff Kinabrew, from old #66";

"To Gabe Yandoli, a big-time Packer fan, Best wishes always, keep happy and well";

"To my friend Billy Toogood . . . You're a real fine young man. . . . Hit 'em hard";

"To Karen, a beautiful football fan . . . Love ya and God bless."

Anticipating autograph requests, Nitschke carried extra copies of his 8x10-inch black-and-white glossies and Hall of Fame pictures with him. When Jim Kardoskee of Oconto Falls, Wisconsin, asked him once for autographs for himself and his uncle, Nitschke willingly obliged. When

Kardoskee asked for a third autograph, Nitschke winked at the boy's mother.

"Kind of pushing a good thing, aren't you?" he asked. "Who's it for?"

When Kardoskee told him it was for his brother—"He'd kill me if I got one for my uncle and not him," he said—Nitschke signed it without delay. He would muss the hair of little ones with his bearlike paw, then lean over and in a stage whisper, say, "Take care of your parents."

When friends asked how he could always be so accommodating, Nitschke would issue a quick smile.

"I'm a has-been football player," he would say. "This is good for my ego."

He talked to strangers about commitment, about giving all they had to give in work and in life. He touched people with his grace and dignity, a gentle giant with a fondness for overpowering hugs and oversized cigars.

He was standing in the lobby of a Chicago hotel, smoking his cigar when he was mistaken by a couple as a part of the staff. He had been hired as a greeter for a local business, and was wearing a dark tuxedo and red bow tie. As the couple approached with their bags, he tried to hide the cigar by placing it behind his back. When the couple dropped their bags at his feet, he brought the huge cigar slowly around from his back, took a long draw, and told them, "Nitschke don't do bags."

What he did do was charitable causes. Ray and Jackie spent 22 years as co-chairpersons of the Cerebral Palsy Telethon, and Ray supported his wife's involvement in The Bridge, Inc., an organization dedicated to helping recovering alcoholics and their families. Nitschke also served on the board of the Green Bay Boys Club and as chairman of the Kinney Kidney Foundation of Minneapolis.

Marianne Oates, a communications coordinator for Schreiber Foods in Green Bay, worked with Ray and Jackie on the Cerebral Palsy Telethon from 1977 to 1985. She remembered Nitschke personally signing hundreds of donor letters every year, and recalled the couple making numerous appearances at fund-raising events, visiting the centers to chat with clients and participating in countless photo sessions.

Nitschke's involvement with his wife's causes impressed those who knew the couple. Jackie was a recovering alcoholic, and when the Jackie Nitschke Center was dedicated in April of 1997 to honor her for having spent the last 16 years of her life helping others battle the addiction, Nitschke stood in a stairwell at the center introducing himself to those who had come to the dedication.

"Hi," he told each person. "I'm Jackie Nitschke's husband."

Al Guldan, Nitschke's accountant, watched Ray that day and had seen the gruff man's sincerity.

"He was so proud of her," Guldan said.

Jim Temp, a former teammate of Nitschke's on the Packers and now a member of the Packers Executive Committee, remembered once how Jackie always called her husband by his full name, "Raymond," and how her voice seemed to brighten his face.

Guldan once related to Ray and Jackie the story of their first meeting with Nitschke in the summer of 1972. The Packers training camp had opened and Guldan, then 11 years old, and his nine-year-old brother Buzz biked from their house in Ashwaubenon to Green Bay. Knowing that Packer team trainers sometimes threw away rolls of tape with a few feet left on them, the brothers began rummaging through garbage cans at the camp for tape to use on their hockey sticks. When Buzz, who was wearing sandals, cut his foot and began crying, Al bent down to inspect the damage. At that moment, the brothers heard a raspy voice behind them.

"Hey! What're you guys doin' there?"

Turning around, they were startled to see Nitschke towering over them. He took the two boys into the locker room, where a team trainer took care of Buzz's bloodied foot. A call was placed to Al's older brother, and Nitschke waited with the boys until they were picked up.

When Guldan finished his story, Jackie smiled. "That's my husband," she said.

As the couple's accountant, Guldan saw how much money Ray turned down in endorsements, and the amount of non-profit work he and Jackie did.

Jackie's influence on Ray extended to one of his favorite hobbies, golf. He played at the Oneida Golf & Riding Club, which was located just five miles from his home, and despite an unorthodox swing, eventually got his game down to a 1-handicap. Art Daley, a member of the Oneida Club and the former sports editor of the *Press-Gazette*, said Nitschke's swing was strictly homemade, but he made up for it with physical strength.

"He really crushed the ball," Daley said.

Still highly competitive, Nitschke enjoyed playing golf with friends at Oneida. The game served as an outlet for his aggression. As he grew older, tightness in his back limited him to a three-quarters swing and deprived him of remaining a consistent long-ball hitter, but he loved the game too much to stop playing. He played for personal pride and played for money—small side-bets with his golfing partners. There was one Saturday morning, however, when Nitschke's golf game was unexpectedly cut short. Nitschke had already played 18 holes that morning and had joined playing partner

Jock Seals and two others for another round. The foursome was on the first tee when they saw Jackie coming down from the ninth hole.

"Raymond, are you playing 18?"

"Yeah."

"Oh no, you're not."

Nitschke left the group after the ninth hole. "She really ran the roost," Seals said of Jackie.

On another occasion, Guldan was on the course with his young stepson when they saw Nitschke on a nearby practice green. Guldan wanted to take the boy over to meet the Packer great but was reluctant to interrupt his practice. Jackie, however, didn't think it would be an intrusion at all.

"Raymond," she called.

"Yeah?"

Moments later, Nitschke went over to Guldan and his stepson, visited with them, and signed an autograph for the boy.

The Nitschke children watched the dynamics of their parents' relationship with a sense of fascination. "It was very interesting," Amy said. "They had fun together, they loved doing things together. They loved playing golf and they had their interests, but they both had their tempers too; neither one minded voicing their opinion. There was a point where they just couldn't take each other and they needed a break. So that was a nice thing about my dad traveling a little bit. They really appreciated each other when they were together."

Richard recalled days when his parents, like all parents, would argue. "Mother was in AA," he said, "and there were times before she quit drinking that they would have fights. But it was never anything serious. They were together, and that was it."

Ray and Jackie were friendly with quite a few couples, and would go on golfing outings locally or to Florida or Arizona. The children went along at times too, and were always subject more to their mother's words than their father's.

"She was more of a disciplinarian, as far as us kids go," Amy said. "She could really put her foot down with my dad."

When she did, and called him "Raymond," the kids knew their dad had done something wrong. "He was in trouble," Amy laughed.

Temp thought Jackie was Ray's entire life, and when she passed away from cancer in the summer of 1996, the loss hit him particularly hard. She had struggled with cancer for years. In May 1995, she had a cancerous lung removed; in April 1996, a cancerous brain tumor was taken out. When she passed, Rev. Arni Jacobson, the pastor of the Bayside Christian Fellowship Church in Green Bay that Ray and Jackie attended, said Jackie's illness had profoundly impacted Ray's life. He replaced Sunday morning golf with church and began living a Christ-centered life.

Jacobson observed Nitschke's conversion to religion first-hand. He first met Nitschke in 1992, when Jackie invited the Reverend and his wife to attend a Packers preseason game. Jackie had been a church-going member of the congregation for years, and when Ray and the Reverend met for the first time at the game, Nitschke let his feelings on church be known immediately.

"The first thing he said to me was, 'My wife likes you, I'm going to like you, just don't talk to me about church,'" Jacobson recalled. "His mom died and his dad had been killed by a street car, and he kind of felt God had dealt him (a harsh blow). We saw each other at quite a few social functions, and then his wife became quite ill."

Jacobson said that during the time of Jackie's illness Nitschke really embraced a close relationship with the Lord. When friends called to inquire about Jackie's health, Nitschke would tell them, "It's in God's hands."

Amy said that her father's conversion was many years in the making. The death of his parents, she said, had left him bitter and angry. "It was very hard for him to cope with that," she said.

Jackie had been raised Catholic, and while she observed her religion, Amy remembered her going through stages where she would alternately lose and then regain interest. Because Jackie had to get an annulment from her first marriage, she found it difficult to go to Mass with her parents when they visited. "That left a bad taste in her mouth," Amy remembered. "There was a period of eight years or so where she wasn't very religious."

Jackie would go to church on occasion, but her involvement in it wasn't very strong. "She went mostly for the kids," Amy said. "Dad would go sometimes. If he didn't go, we would ask mom, 'If Dad's not going, why do I have to?' And then here would come Dad, in his suit."

Friends invited Jackie to non-denominational services, and she soon began attending Bayside Christian Fellowship.

"It took some time, but Dad started coming around too," Amy said. "When my mom got sick, he started looking around for answers, trying to understand. And his faith in God became a very big thing for him."

Kay San Miguel remembered seeing Nitschke in church when Jackie was ill, and seeing him weeping so that tears were dripping off his nose. Jackie was dying, he told San Miguel, and he was taking care of her. She had always taken of him, Nitschke said, and now he was taking care of her. He gave San Miguel a hug, and as he walked away, San Miguel said she saw in this giant of a man a hero.

When Jackie passed, a part of her husband went with her. When friends visited him Nitschke after Jackie's death, they got the impression that the spark that once ignited Ray's life had been reduced to a flicker. Nitschke began thinking more about heaven and the after-life, and talked with his children about his own eventual funeral arrangements.

He filled the void left by Jackie's passing by spending more time with his children and grandchildren. Nitschke would take Amy and his one-year-old granddaughter, Jacqueline Rae, to the Oneida Club and show the baby off to his friends. "He was really proud of that granddaughter," Temp said.

He walked three miles a day, rousing the Siberian husky he named Butkus from his plastic, igloolike home in the yard to accompany him. He spent increased time at Skip's Place, a coffee shop located on Holmgren Way near Lambeau Field. Skip's became an automatic stop for Nitschke, and he indulged in blueberry pancakes and trading small talk and good-natured insults with the hired help and customers. Nitschke always sat on the same stool—second from the end at the counter. Rob Heinz, co-owner of Skip's, remembered Nitschke's gruff bantering with the customers, remembered too the time Ray stood to have his picture taken with some women, only to find out later his zipper had been down for the photograph.

"There were a couple of places he would hit," Richard remembered. "Skip's Place, a little Greek restaurant called the Golden Basket. He used to go in and give the waitresses some shit once in a while. He didn't mean anything by it, he just liked picking on some of them, just for the hell of it. He would get a kick out of it when some of them would argue with him. He was funny that way."

Nitschke's personality could be overpowering, and he drew a crowd wherever he went. When the Packers returned to the Super Bowl in January 1997 for the first time since the Lombardi era, Nitschke spent part of the week in New Orleans, the host city. Despite the number of celebrities and football greats in town, Nitschke was surrounded by fans every time he visited Bourbon Street.

"I'm bigger now than when I was playing," Nitschke would tell his family, and Amy knew why. Her father loved being with fans, she said, and fans loved being with him. When people would stop and tell him he was their favorite player in the 1960s, Nitschke would grin. "Aw, you're kidding," he would say, then shake their hand and make small talk. Hardly a day went by when someone wasn't bringing up his playing days under Lombardi. "I think I'll always be 'Number 66,'" Nitschke said. And he continued to add to his legend by becoming a spokesman for America's Pack Fan Club, making appearances at hardware shows for "Easy Painter" products and endorsing clothing for NFL Throwbacks and Champion sportswear.

Nitschke saw his dealings with the public as a way of repaying the debt he felt he owed to football. He saw himself as someone who had been lucky enough to make a living doing exactly what he wanted to do, and felt the game of football had been so good to him that he wanted to give back to the game by treating people in the same manner he wanted to be treated.

At times, the attitudes of modern athletes disturbed him. Dick Butkus remembered being with Nitschke at an NFL Properties luncheon prior to one of the Super Bowl games. Butkus had arrived first, and was sitting in a chair by himself when Nitschke arrived. Butkus watched as the Packer great went around the room, renewing acquaintances with players from his own era and introducing himself to others. There were two current NFL stars slouched on a couch, and when Nitschke introduced himself to them, their response was indifferent. From his chair, Butkus saw Nitschke turn and approach him.

"I'm watching him, and he comes up to me," Butkus said. "He'd always hit you on your shoulder, and he comes up and says, 'When someone older than you comes up and introduces himself, you get your ass up.'"

Every summer, Nitschke would attend the Pro Football Hall of Fame induction ceremonies in Canton, Ohio, and he made it a point to impress upon the new inductees at the formal luncheon how special it was to be a part of the Hall. Joe Horrigan, the Hall of Fame's historian, recalled Nitschke's passion during the luncheon that has since been renamed in his honor.

"He would read the new guys the riot act," Horrigan said. Gale Sayers said the luncheon was Nitschke's time to shine, and Frank Gifford recalled once how Nitschke would rant and rave, in a style that seemed Lombardi-like, and remind each Hall of Famer how much it means to be part of such a select group. St. Louis Cardinals Hall of Fame safety Larry Wilson said the intensity from one of Nitschke's speeches stayed with him for three or four years. "It pumped you up," Wilson said.

Nitschke's circle of friends wasn't limited to football players. Vern Biever recalled a day when he and Nitschke were walking around the grounds at Canton when they spotted former Speaker of the House Tip O'Neill.

"Hi, Ray," O'Neill said.

"Hi, Tip," Nitschke answered.

Biever laughed at the memory of the exchange. "Ray knew everybody," he said, "and everybody knew Ray."

Don Smith, who served as the Hall's vice president of public relations from 1968 to 1997, thought Nitschke epitomized what Canton was all about. Smith first met him in 1978, when Nitschke was inducted into the Hall. To Smith, Nitschke felt more strongly about his induction in Canton than any other Hall of Famer he had ever known. So strongly in fact, that in 1996, when Jackie was dying of cancer, she insisted her husband attend the induction ceremonies without her. Nitschke did, and he delivered a passionate speech about the honor the Hall of Famers share, and that it was important enough that his dying wife had insisted he make the trip. Three days later, Jackie died, and not long after, his health began to suffer as well.

The flame that had brightened Ray's life for so long had been extinguished, and Richard could see that his father was no longer the same man, physically or mentally. "We were at the (1998) Super Bowl and he was complaining about stomach problems," Richard said. "And without my mom to drag his ass to the hospital or to the doctor . . . And that's what it would have taken for him to go."

In early March 1998, just before he left for a trip to Naples, Florida, to visit Amy and his granddaughter, Nitschke's favorite stool at Skip's Place collapsed suddenly and fell apart. Just days later, on Sunday, March 8, Nitschke was traveling with his daughter and granddaughter to visit friends in Venice, Florida, when he began experiencing chest pains at around 12:30 P.M. Amy pulled in to a Venice convenience store to get water, and when she returned to the car, she realized her father had suffered a heart attack. She performed CPR, and he was rushed to Venice Hospital. At 1:30 P.M., Ray Nitschke was pronounced dead. He was 61 years old.

Nitschke's memorial service was held at Bayside Christian Fellowship at 2 P.M. on Saturday, March 14. It was the first public event at the new facility, a fact that struck Rev. Jacobson. "Ray was so excited to see it finished," he said, "and to be part of it."

Nitschke's Hall of Fame bust, his 75th Anniversary All-NFL team trophy, a portrait and several photos were displayed at the service. In attendance were numerous former teammates—Bart Starr, Willie Davis, Carroll Dale, Jim Taylor. The ceremony drew in excess of the church's capacity of 1,250, and was carried live on WBAY-TV Channel 12. A videotape shows Mary Smits and Bill Jartz guiding viewers through the service with a minimum amount of conversation and commentary. The setting outside seemed reminiscent of so many of those big games Nitschke had played in during the Green Bay glory years—the air was clear and cold, the winter-brown grass covered with patches of ice and snow. Some Packer fans attended the ceremony wearing a replica of Nitschke's forest green jersey with the gold and white piping on the sleeves and the big number 66 in white on the front and back. One of those wearing the green-and-gold was John McMahon, who traveled from Milwaukee to attend the ceremony. His Nitschke jersey had been signed by Ray in 1997, and he said the funeral would mark the last time McMahon would wear the jersey. He was going home to have it framed for hanging on his wall.

Nitschke's remains were cremated, and he was buried in Green Bay. A Ray Nitschke Memorial Fund was established at Northwest Bank in Green Bay, with funds being distributed to several charities. Just as he had in life, Nitschke was continuing to give to others even in death.

Praise for Nitschke as a person and a player poured forth from numerous sources.

Amy thanked God for bringing her into his life 26 years ago. "He is the best father I could have ever had," she said. "I will miss him deeply."

"You could never ask for a better father," John said. "Richard, Amy, and I are going to miss our father. We are going to miss those big hugs."

Rev. Jacobson thought Nitschke squeezed more out of life in his 61 years than some of the oldest people that have ever lived. "I haven't seen Ray for the last time," he said. "In my spirit, I can hear him say, 'Pastor, I am having a wonderful time, wish you were here. Jackie sends her love.' "

The list of those offering their memories of Nitschke as a player and a person was long and impressive.

Vern Biever: "He came to play . . . you could tell by the expression on his face, even on the sidelines. . . . Off the field, Ray was a very kind gentleman, a very quiet man."

Carroll Dale: "Ray was a man that in my memory always loved people genuinely."

Lee Remmel: "He was loved by thousands and thousands of Packers fans, because he always had time for them. I remember sitting in the hotel lobbies when we were on the road and he obligingly posed for many photos and signed hundreds of autographs."

Former Bears tight end and head coach Mike Ditka: "There's no one I went against who I respected more than Ray. There was no love lost between us, but that's the way he wanted it. He left everything he had on that field. . . . There aren't many like him anymore."

Willie Davis stood and spoke of Nitschke's life as a journey, a journey that began in Chicago and ended in Green Bay. Along the way, Davis said, Nitschke created a love affair with Packer fans, and with the city itself.

"There will be a lot of people that will play middle linebacker for Green Bay and in the National Football League," Davis concluded. "In my opinion, there will never be another Ray Nitschke."

EPILOGUE

FRIDAY, OCTOBER 2, 1998, dawned cool and partly cloudy over greater Green Bay. Downtown, a crowd of some 500 people gathered to dedicate the new Main Street Bridge that spans the Fox River. The $22 million steel-and-concrete structure was built to stand as a link between east and west Green Bay, to serve the needs of not only those who travel by car but walkers and bicyclists as well.

In short, the sturdy bridge symbolizes the name of the man who served the needs of the people of Green Bay for so many years, the man to whom the bridge was dedicated that cool autumn day.

"Not only now is my father part of the Green Bay Packers history, now he's part of the Green Bay city history," Amy Klaas told the gathering at the dedication of the Ray Nitschke Memorial Bridge. She choked back tears as she saw a dozen or so people wearing Packer jerseys with uniform number 66 on them. Three city workers were also wearing Nitschke replica jerseys as well.

Wisconsin Governor Tommy Thompson told the crowd that the sturdy bridge was a fitting tribute to a sturdy man. "To me," Thompson said, "there was no greater Packer than Ray. I tell you, we've all got Ray in our hearts and minds today."

Amy and her brother Richard tossed a bright green memorial wreath with their father's name on it from the side of the bridge into the Fox River, and 66 white doves were released into the air. Toward the end of the ceremony, a bronze plaque bearing a sculpture of Nitschke was unveiled, and as people stood in line waiting to have their picture taken with Nitschke's likeness, some wondered if the plaque looked mean enough. Sue Wilde, who together with her husband Bob Antolec own the De Pere Foundry where the plaque was cast, wasn't worried.

"He looks plenty mean enough," she said.

Shirley Knaus, whose family was acquainted with Nitschke, told *Green Bay Press-Gazette* writer Tom Cioni she just had to be at the dedication. "I wouldn't miss this for the world," she said.

LaVerne Webster, who lived near Nitschke in Oneida and talked with him at times, was glad the day had finally arrived when the people of Green Bay could give something back to the man they admired. "He is so deserving," she said at the ceremony. "It's a wonderful day, a long-awaited day."

Today, the Ray Nitschke Memorial Bridge supports traffic of all kinds—business men and women in cars, mothers pushing strollers, cyclists, walkers. That a bridge bearing Nitschke's name and likeness serves the needs of his community and links east and west Green Bay is fitting, since Nitschke himself gave so much to the people of his area during his lifetime and served as a bridge between Green Bay's past and present.

"We all loved Ray Nitschke," Willie Davis said. "In Wisconsin, there was no player more revered than Ray."

Nitschke not only linked Packer history, he bridged the history of two generations of great middle linebackers. He was drafted by the Packers in 1958, at a time when the position was being pioneered by Bill George, Joe Schmidt, and Sam Huff, a time when NFL announcers like Ray Scott and Jack Drees were still referring to middle linebackers as middle guards. Nitschke learned from the greats, learned the angles they took, the drops, the way they played the pass. He would study them up close or on film to see how they played sweeps and attacked blockers, then incorporated their finer points into his play.

"I took parts from every one of them," he said once. "You pick out each player's things they did well."

By 1969, Nitschke was widely regarded as the greatest middle linebacker in the NFL's first 50 years. He was the centerpiece of a championship defense that featured nine all-pros and five future Hall of Famers, and served as a link between those who had pioneered his position in the late fifties—Huff, Schmidt, and George—and a generation of middle men who were rising stars by the mid- to late sixties—Dick Butkus and Nick Buoniconti, Tommy Nobis, Willie Lanier, and Mike Curtis.

"Nitschke was a serious run-stuffer, as they all were in those days," said Paul Zimmerman, a pro football historian and senior writer for *Sports Illustrated*. "He could cover sideline-to-sideline and get in a frenzy and play dynamically as far as his range goes. It didn't seem like he played in a system sometimes because I saw him in some sort of crazy pursuits."

Offenses struggled to find ways to cope with Nitschke's ferocious play. "He'd run through a stone wall to get you," remembered former Chicago fullback Ronnie Bull. "He wouldn't let anything stop him. And he tried to intimidate you. He'd let you hit him, and then just shed you. It was like he was saying, 'I'm not going to let you block me.' "

Chicago assistant coach Jim Dooley spent hours breaking down Green Bay's defense down on film, and what he discovered was what the Bears had believed for years—the entire Packer defense was coordinated to the movements of two men, Nitschke and free safety Willie Wood. Bull compared it to pulling strings—where Nitschke and Wood lined up and where they moved at the snap of the ball dictated the movements of the other Packer defenders.

"They were the guys their defense was built around," Bull said. "Those were your two keys. Where they lined up told you exactly where they were going."

NFL offenses countered in a variety of ways. In Dallas, Tom Landry tried to get Nitschke to take himself out of the play by giving him false keys—misdirections and counters that got him moving in one direction while Cowboy backs Don Perkins and Dan Reeves flowed against the grain. In Los Angeles, George Allen took a more basic approach. Recognizing Nitschke as the focal point of the Packer defense, Allen instructed quarterback Roman Gabriel to occupy Nitschke early by running Les Josephson and Dick Bass right up the middle. It wasn't the easiest way to make yards, Gabriel said at the time, but it was worth it.

"If he has to think about the middle," Gabriel said of Nitschke, "he can't go flying all over the place and mess up everything else."

Allen always thought of Nitschke as one of those special players who could do things others couldn't. "He was big and strong," Allen said once, "yet quick and agile." To Allen, Nitschke was smart and alert, as good in pass coverage as he was against the run. Impressed as he was with Nitschke's hard hits, Allen was just as impressed with his clutch play. "He always seemed to make a big play or two in a big game," Allen said. "He was a money player on a team that always had the stakes piled high on the table."

Nitschke built a reputation as a savage run-stopper, but his mobility and lateral quickness for a man his size—6-foot-3, 235 pounds—made him one of the great middle linebackers of all time. Where he ranks among the all-time greats is a debate for NFL historians.

"How would he rate against Butkus? Not as good," Zimmerman said. "How would he rate against Tommy Nobis? Better. Mike Curtis? Better. Willie Lanier? Not as good. Joe Schmidt? Tough to say. Schmidt was underrated, a very precise player, not quite the fire and dynamite of Nitschke but very effective. Probably a tie.

"How would he rate against Jack Lambert? Difficult to say because Lambert had so many good people around him. Of course, Nitschke did too. Probably just a shade below Lambert because of speed. Mike Singletary? It's a wash. Nitschke was probably a little bit better because Singletary in that ("46") scheme had a lot of things helping him.

"How would he rate against Ray Lewis? Not as good. Ray Lewis moved his game to another dimension at the end of the (2000–2001) season. His coverage was just knock 'em dead."

Zimmerman, who has studied on film or covered in person all of the great players in NFL history, graded Nitschke higher than two of his Hall of Fame predecessors—Bill George and Sam Huff—and overall rated him as one of the top five all-time at his position.

Nitschke was a classic, straight-up style middle linebacker, and the images of him that are frozen in Zimmerman's memory stem from his performance in the brutal 1962 NFL championship game against the Giants in Yankee Stadium.

"I was young and sitting in the stands and it was so cold that day, the coldest I've ever been at a football game," he said. "I remember him going from sideline to sideline making tackles. Shit, the guy was in another dimension. What a game. But that was when the position meant something. It wasn't a guy who played just one or two downs out of the three."

Fritz Shurmur, who was the Packers defensive coordinator for their Super Bowl teams of the nineties, said once that the guy who stood in the middle of your defense back in the sixties was a symbol of what you were as a defensive team. If a team had a Nitschke or a Butkus, Shurmur said, they were a good defense. If not, they were just another team.

"I don't think you find guys like that anymore, with that kind of persona," Shurmur said then. "Those guys had a special temperament. Ray brought a special, competitive temperament to the game."

Joe Horrigan, the Pro Football Hall of Fame's historian, rated the all-time middle men and said perhaps the only difference between Nitschke and Butkus was that the Bears great called his own signals. But Horrigan felt that Nitschke probably hit harder than Butkus. "He threw more people than Butkus," Horrigan said. "Ray truly enjoyed hitting people. He had a personality trait that made him that much more aggressive. He clobbered people."

Dave Manders, a center for the Dallas Cowboys from 1964 to 1974, remembered being impressed most by Nitschke's quickness and intelligence. "Nitschke seemed liked a combination of Butkus and Huff," Manders said. "He was strong like Butkus and quick like Huff."

Steve Sabol ranks Butkus as one of the game's elite players—along with Jim Brown and Jerry Rice. "Butkus to me is the greatest linebacker," the president of NFL Films said, "but he didn't have the effect on his teammates that Nitschke did. Nitschke lifted the play of his teammates, and he left an impression on offenses that they were going to have to play a superhuman game to win.

"When you're comparing middle linebackers like that, sometimes it's like comparing saints. Is Saint Mark better than Saint Matthew? The thing about Nitschke is that he was always in position, and he never missed a tackle. They keep a stat now, Yards After Contact, that measures how many yards a runner gets after he's hit. If they had kept that stat back when Nitschke played, I bet Ray's number would be lower than anyone's. He was a deadly tackler. He would wrap his arms around the runner's back, the hands would lock. . . . He was very sound technically."

Red Cochran, who served as an assistant coach with the Lombardi Packers and has been an NFL scout since the fifties, said Nitschke was such a good all-around athlete he would have excelled in today's more specialized game. "Nitschke with his speed would have still been a three-down player," Cochran said.

Pro football came of age in the sixties, and the game's rise paralleled that of television. This was the electronic generation, and TV ratings at the time showed that pro football was becoming a major part of America's leisure time. For those who watched the game intently on TV, the images that remain from the sixties are lasting; they are, as The Supremes sang in their Motown classic, reflections of the way life used to be.

The game then was John Unitas, in his bristlebrush haircut and hightop cleats, and Joe Namath, with his long, black mane and white leather shoes. It was the passion of Vince Lombardi; the professorial approach of Sid Gillman. It was the NFL versus the AFL, CBS versus NBC; Ray Scott and Pat Summerall, Curt Gowdy and Al DeRogatis. It was "31-Wedge" in the Ice Bowl and "65 Toss Power Trap" in Super Bowl IV. It was Jim Brown following his blockers in the November mud and it was Lance Alworth soaring to snare a pass in the soft San Diego sunshine.

And it was Nitschke, hunched over center, breathing steam in some icy December classic, covered in Packer green and gold; covered in pads and tape stained with blood and mud.

"You'd see him," Oakland center Jim Otto remembered, "and any wraps on his hands were coming apart. There was no care for the wear. He just kept right on going."

"I can close my eyes," Zimmerman said, "and see him going sideline to sideline. He could get outside, and he always took great angles. Some of them don't know how to play the angles, but he was always on the money with those angles, gauging them right."

Nitschke played his position with a warrior spirit, and Packer photographer Vern Biever loved his intensity. To him, Nitschke's hawkish features and emotional style made him a picture-perfect subject. "He gave you that feeling of intenseness," Biever said.

Nitschke's rise to prominence in the sixties paralleled that of NFL Films, and whenever the fledgling company needed an expressive closeup, they would focus in on Number 66.

"I was a young cameraman at that time," remembered Sabol, "and anytime we wanted a compelling shot we went to Nitschke. The way he looked, that voice of his—he personified that era of great middle linebackers."

In his own way, Nitschke symbolized the NFL of the sixties, and for that, he remains a beloved figure. Long into his retirement years, fans would look him up in the Green Bay White Pages, would travel to 410 Peppermint Court in Oneida, where his two-story brick home with its four white pillars out front sat in a cul de sac. The west side of Nitschke's home was flanked by a wooded area; the south side by a two-car attached garage and two large, leafy trees.

For Al Pahl, the driveway that led to the garage provided the setting for one of his lasting memories of Ray. Pahl had made his way through a deep snow to visit Nitschke, and he had pulled his SUV into Ray's driveway. When he tried to back out of the driveway, Pahl's tires began spinning in the snow. Nitschke came out to lend a hand, and began pushing on the front of Pahl's truck. From his seat behind the wheel Pahl could see Nitschke's huge hands bending the plastic shield that rose above the hood of his truck as protection against stones and debris from the highway. Rolling down his driver's side window, Pahl leaned over, stuck his head out and began yelling at Nitschke to stop pushing.

Later, Pahl considered the course of his actions.

"I was probably the only guy," he said, "who ever yelled at Ray Nitschke and got away with it."

Be it Pahl or any fan who was interested in spending time with a living legend, the harsh Green Bay winters did not deter them from traveling to Nitschke's house. Near the end of a phone conversation in the winter of 1997, Nitschke excused himself for a moment to answer the doorbell. He returned several minutes later, and apologized for the interruption.

"Sorry, man," he said. "We're havin' a blizzard here and some guy drives out to have a helmet autographed for his kid."

Nitschke laughed, a short, raspy bark.

"Packer fans are nuts, man," he said.

Ray and Jackie's house was always open to friends and fans, and visitors were greeted by the strong stench of Ray's oversized cigars. To Pahl, the smell of cigar is the overwhelming memory he has of the house. Once, Ray and Jackie gave an oversized, two-foot stuffed koala bear to Pahl's youngest daughter. The bear smelled so strongly of cigar that Pahl had to keep him on the patio by day and in the garage by night. "He lived outside for about two months," Pahl said.

For Pahl, for all of the people who came in contact with Ray Nitschke during his lifetime, the impact he left on their lives is still strongly felt. People related to his life struggles, his fight to make himself worthy, and drew inspiration from the sudden and dramatic conversion he underwent.

"It was like a curtain had been drawn," Vince Lombardi Jr. said. "You read and you hear about those kinds of things, but you rarely see them."

People saw it in Nitschke, and were impressed. Dave Robinson said that as great a player as Nitschke was, he was an even better person. To Ray Scott, Nitschke's real talent—brightening the lives of everyone around him—was most evident once his playing career ended. When Willie Davis thinks of his old teammate, he thinks of the special bond between them, a bond that surpassed all racial and social barriers, a bond strong enough to link a white man from urban Chicago with a black man from rural Arkansas.

"Everyone talks about the love those old Lombardi teams had," Davis said. "Well, I can tell you, I loved Ray Nitschke. I loved the man."

Wisconsin governor Tommy Thompson said at the time of Nitschke's passing that to live in the hearts of those left behind is not to die. "Ray Nitschke," he said, "certainly lives in the hearts of millions of people in Wisconsin and across America."

Perhaps it is less an impact than an imprint that Nitschke left behind, and it can be felt not only by those who knew him, but by those who wished they had.

When Ronnie Lott was inducted into the Pro Football Hall of Fame in 2000, he listened to Joe Greene tell him how emotional Nitschke would get every year at the luncheon. "He was always the guy who was enthusiastically welcoming the new group in," Greene told Lott. Later, Lott looked for Nitschke's bust in the Hall, and lingered before it for awhile.

"You know what? He spoke to me," Lott said later. "He spoke to me about the game. He represented what football is all about. He was a true warrior, a true man."

And because he was, Nitschke left his mark off the field as well as on, and his passing left a void in the lives of those he came in contact with.

"That's why so many people were affected by his death," Sabol said. "His heart was as warm as it was strong. When you'd see him he'd talk to you in that voice of his—'Hey, how ya doin'?' He was the last warrior, and there was a certain grandeur about him.

"When he left that field for the last time, something left with him that will never return."

INDEX

ACKNOWLEDGMENTS

AS WITH ANY PROJECT OF THIS SIZE, there are many people involved who helped bring the final work to completion.

First, I would like to thank my family for their continued support and encouragement. Without their patience and understanding of the time demands involved in writing a book, I would not have undertaken such a project. So thanks to Michelle, Patty, and Katie, as well as my mother, Roberta, and my sisters, Kathie and Patrice, and their children.

Thanks also to Ross Plotkin, Ginger Strader. and Barbara Werden, for their work in the editorial process; to Packers photographer Vernon Biever, for the excellent photos that comprise the book's insert; to Burt Wilson, for his help in the editing process; and to Deb Grove, for taking the time to take the author's photo.

Of course, this book could not have been completed without the contributions of the Nitschke family. Years ago, Ray Nitschke took time to speak with me on the phone for extended, long-distance interviews. His warmth and strength of character were evident during those interviews, and I will forever be grateful for the kindness he showed me. Two of his children, Richard and Amy, were also very gracious in passing along to me memories of their famous father. Unfortunately, Ray's wife Jackie had already passed from cancer before this project had even began, and Ray's son John was not available for interviews at the time for personal reasons.

The list of those whose personal interviews past and present contributed to this book is a lengthy one, more than seventy-five names in all, and chief among those are many of Ray's contemporaries from the NFL: Bart Starr, Paul Hornung, Jerry Kramer, Boyd Dowler, Gale Gillingham, Willie Davis, Herb Adderley, Bob Jeter, Dan Currie, Bobby Dillon, Phil Bengston, Dick Butkus, Frank Ryan, John Morrow, Dan Reeves, Ralph Neely, Bob Lilly, Ronnie Bull, Mick Tingelhoff, Sam Huff, Tommy Nobis, Chuck Bednarik, Tommy McDonald, Bobby Mitchell, Jim Otto, Daryle Lamonica, Len Dawson, Mike Garrett, Otis Taylor, Bobby Bell, Jerry Mays, Hank Stram, former Green Bay sportswriters Lee Remmel and Art Daley, Packers former play-by-play announcer Ted Moore, Sports Illustrated senior writer Paul Zimmerman, NFL Films historian Steve Sabol, and Pro Football Hall of Fame historian Joe Horrigan. To all of the above, and to all the friends and relatives who took the time to recall their personal memories of Ray Nitschke, thank you.

ED GRUVER, *April 2002*